Tourism and Politics

To the wandering islands
and one of the best ones

Tourism and Politics

Policy, Power and Place

Colin Michael Hall
University of Canberra, Australia

JOHN WILEY & SONS
Chichester • New York • Brisbane • Toronto • Singapore

Copyright © 1994 Colin Michael Hall

Published by John Wiley & Sons Ltd,
Baffins Lane, Chichester,
West Sussex PO19 1UD, England
Telephone National Chichester (01243) 779777
International +44 1243 779777

Other Wiley Editorial Offices

John Wiley & Sons, Inc., 605 Third Avenue,
New York, NY 10158-0012, USA

Jacaranda Wiley Ltd, 33 Park Road, Milton,
Queensland 4064, Australia

John Wiley & Sons (Canada) Ltd, 22 Worcester Road,
Rexdale, Ontario M9W 1L1, Canada

John Wiley & Sons (SEA) Pte Ltd, 37 Jalan Pemimpin #05-04,
Block B, Union Industrial Building, Singapore 2057

Library of Congress Cataloging-in-Publication data
Hall, C. M. (C. Michael)
    Tourism and politics: policy, power, and place/Colin Michael
Hall.
        p. cm.
    Includes bibliographical references and indexes.
    ISBN 0-471-94919-1
    1. Tourist trade and state.   I. Title.
G155.A1H347   1994
338.4'791—dc20   94-18156
                                                       CIP

British Library Cataloguing in Publication Data

A catalogue record for this book is available from the British Library

ISBN 0-471-94919-1

Typeset in 10/12pt Palatino from author's disks by
Mayhew Typesetting, Rhayader, Powys
Printed and bound in Great Britain by
Bookcraft (Bath) Ltd

Contents

Preface

Politics is a fundamental yet much ignored component of tourism development and tourism studies. Research into the political dimensions of tourism—a social and economic phenomenon which has substantial implications for the allocation of power within host communities, cultural representation, socialisation and international relations—is in a relatively poor state. Therefore, it is hoped that this book will help make some readers aware of the potentially rich vein of research that is available in the politics of tourism and, perhaps, also ask some fundamental questions regarding the political economy of tourism development in contemporary society.

This book finds my writing and concerns going full circle. My honours degree was undertaken in political science and public policy, and after a number of years wandering in the wilderness of environmental history, heritage, visitor management and tourism studies, I keep returning to critical issues of power, values, interests and control within the decision-making process. Given the complexity of this area, my attempts to understand and, hopefully, convey whatever impressions I can of this political minefield to the reader are likely to last for a considerable time yet!

Many people have helped to provide the stimulus for researching and writing in the area of politics and tourism. Steve Britton, Dick Butler, Jenny Craik, Malcolm Crick, Bruce Davis, Keith Hollinshead, John Jenkins, Richard Le Heron, Neil Leiper, Geoff McBoyle, Dave Mercer, Bruce Mitchell, Stephen Page, Doug Pearce, Ralph Pervan, Maurice Roche, Dennis Rumley, John Warhurst and

Michael Wood have all contributed to the writing of this book, either through assistance, discussion or through the provision of material, although the interpretation of their thoughts and research is, of course, my own. The case study of the politics of ecotourism development in the Solomon Islands in Chapter 5 is based on a paper by Brenda Rudkin and myself (Hall and Rudkin, 1993); a more detailed version of the case study is to be found in Rudkin and Hall (1994a). I would like to thank Brenda for the opportunity to share her insights and our discussions on the politics of ecotourism development in this book and, although they unfortunately cannot be named, we would also like to thank the people of the Weather Coast who assisted us in developing the case study. I would also like to acknowledge the contribution of Maurice Roche to my understanding of urban imaging strategies which are a major component of Chapter 6, and Keith Hollinshead for the opportunity to discuss ideas about the political dimensions of the representation of culture. Much of the original impetus for the book arose out of correspondence and discussions with Steve Britton, whose insights into the study of tourism are greatly missed.

For their 'infrastructural' and moral support during the writing of this book I would like to thank: Ann Applebee, Ross Annells, Nikki Bramley, Claire Campbell, Stuart Christopherson, Helen Gladstones, Bill Hanning, John and Kathy Jenkins, Tamsin Kerr, Simon McArthur, Treve McCarthy, Christine Petersen, Jacqui Pinkava, David Press, Brian and Delyse Springett, Brian Stoddart, Margot Sweeny, Bernie Walsh, Josette Wells and Sue Wright. The support of friends, particularly those in Canberra and Te Puke, was very much appreciated at a time when American international tourism policy was enough to bring me to tears. Bruce Cockburn, k.d. lang, *Indigo Girls*, *This Mortal Coil* and Jennifer Warnes also helped ensure that the book was completed.

I would like to express my very real appreciation to Iain Stevenson and everyone at John Wiley for their seemingly endless support, patience and professionalism. The provision of an Australian Research Council Grant and a Canadian Government Canadian Studies Award for research on visitor attractions and urban imaging strategies greatly assisted with the incorporation of urban tourism policy material into this book. Vanessa O'Sullivan and Kate Wright helped out cheerfully with the performance of onorous research tasks. John Jenkins and Vanessa O'Sullivan provided valuable comments on several drafts of the manuscript. Sandra Haywood, by various means, helped ensure that the manuscript was finished. Finally, my very special thanks go to my friends for their continued love and support.

C. Michael Hall
O'Connor
January, 1994

1

Introduction: The Politics of Tourism

In the real world, human societies are not composed entirely of rational and selfless people; people are not equal; people's needs and wants are not fully met; there are haves and have-nots; they contain limited resources. That is they contain a potential for conflicts for politics. (Jaensch, 1992, p.1)

Tourism is widely regarded as the world's largest industry. However, despite the significant role of tourism in national and regional economies, and its social and environmental effects, the political aspects of tourism are rarely discussed in the tourism literature. Given the vast seasonal intra- and international movements of people which modern travel represents and the impacts of tourism on many destinations, it must therefore strike the student of tourism that the rarity of academic research on the political dimensions of tourism is somewhat surprising.

So it was that this book came about. It is an attempt to identify the political dimensions of tourism and place them in the foreground of tourism studies rather than the academic backdrop that they presently occupy. Twenty years ago Matthews wrote, 'the literature of tourism is grossly lacking of political research' (1975, p.195). Today, the same comment still holds true. Despite the vast amount of research currently being conducted elsewhere in the social sciences on tourism-related subjects, the politics of tourism is still the poor cousin of both tourism research and political science and policy studies.

2 Tourism and Politics

The relationship between politics and tourism is *not* primarily concerned with political parties and elections and their influence on tourism policy, although this is, of course, an aspect of the politics of tourism. The study of politics is inexorably the study of power. *'Politics is about power, who gets what, where, how and why'* (Lasswell, 1936). There are five major elements to politics. First, it is concerned with the activity of making decisions in and for a collection of people, whether it be a small group, a community, an organisation or a nation. Secondly, it is about decisions and the various policies and ideologies which help establish the various choices which affect decisions. Thirdly, it is concerned with the question of who makes the decisions, one person or an élite, and how representative they are. Fourthly, politics is interested in the processes by which decisions are made and the various institutions within which they are made. Finally, politics is concerned with how decisions are implemented and applied to the community (Jaensch, 1992).

The mainstream of tourism research has either ignored or neglected the political dimension of the allocation of tourism resources, the generation of tourism policy, and the politics of tourism development. Not that political science has contributed much to the study of tourism. Apart from the notable efforts of Matthews (1978, 1983) and Richter (1983a, 1983b, 1989), political science has all but ignored the role of tourism in modern society. Defence, housing, health, energy, environmental issues and social policy have all been studied in depth by political scientists and policy analysts throughout the world, but tourism has rarely been touched upon.

There is a prevalence of prescriptive models of planning and policy making in the tourism literature which tend to indicate a clear, rational process to tourism development. For example, it would be hard not to agree with Edgell's (1990, p.1) laudable statement that 'the highest purpose of tourism policy is to integrate the economic, political, cultural, intellectual and economic benefits of tourism cohesively with people, destinations, and countries in order to improve the global quality of life and provide a foundation for peace and prosperity.' Edgell later observed: 'The political aspects of tourism are interwoven with its economic consequences . . . tourism is not only a "continuation of politics" but an integral part of the world's political economy. In short, tourism is, or can be, a tool used not only for economic but for political means' (1990, p.37). However, it must still be noted that Edgell's account of tourism policy presented a rational, prescriptive account of how tourism policy making should be conducted, not how it actually *is* conducted.

Tourism is not the result of a rational decision-making process. As Peck and Lepie (1989, p.216) noted, 'the nature of tourism in any given community is the product of complex, interrelated economic and political factors, as well as particular geographic and recreational features that attract "outsiders".' Decisions affecting tourism policy, the nature of government involvement in tourism, the structure of tourist organisations, and the nature of tourism development emerge from a political process. This process involves the values of actors (individuals, interest groups and public and private organisations) in a struggle for power. As Lindblom (1959, p.82) stated, 'one chooses among values and among policies at one and the same time.' Similarly, Simmons *et al.* (1974, p.457) noted that, 'It is value choice, implicit and explicit, which orders the priorities of government and determines the commitment of resources within the public jurisdiction.' To understand tourism and its related impacts we must therefore reach an understanding of its inherently political nature.

This book aims to discuss the inter-relationship between tourism and politics systematically at a number of levels, ranging from the international to the individual. It also seeks to highlight the contribution that some of the traditional concerns of political studies, such as ideology, institutional arrangements, interest groups, the appropriate role of government, political stability, the policy-making process and power, can make to an understanding of contemporary issues in the study of tourism.

This first chapter will introduce some of the issues that emerge in any analysis of the relationship between tourism and politics. It commences with a discussion of why the political dimensions of tourism have been grossly understudied and highlights the difficulties that students of tourism encounter in having their work regarded as 'serious' by their colleagues in the social sciences. The second section of the chapter notes some of the difficulties which arise in studying the politics of tourism and attempts to define the parameters of political analysis within the tourism context. The final section provides an outline of the remaining chapters of the book.

4 Tourism and Politics

POLITICAL STUDIES OF TOURISM: WHY THE POOR COUSIN?

> It would be nice, but we cannot expect tourism programs to think of political scientists, if political scientists themselves cannot foresee a role for themselves in analyzing tourism policy. (Richter, 1984, p.615)

As noted above, research into the political dimensions of tourism has received relatively little attention in the academic literature on either tourism or political science and policy analysis (Richter, 1983a; Hall, C., 1989a; Matthews and Richter, 1991). Several related factors can be recognised as accounting for this situation:

- there is an unwillingness on the part of many decision makers both in government and in the private sector to acknowledge the political nature of tourism
- there is a lack of official interest in conducting research into the politics of tourism
- tourism is not regarded as a serious scholarly subject
- there are substantial methodological problems in conducting political and administrative studies

The political nature of tourism at both the macro- and the micro-political level is not willingly acknowledged by individuals or institutions involved in the decision- and policy-making process. Indeed, 'Few organisations support serious inquiry into what happens when the world's largest industry grows with uncritical professional acceptance and without careful planning, routine monitoring, or an exploration of both its policy successes and its failures' (Matthews and Richter, 1991, p.122).

Given the lack of official interest in conducting research into the political arena, there is little incentive and/or financial support for students of tourism to undertake such research. As Ritchie (1984, p.10) has observed in the case of research into the political dimensions of event tourism, 'there are undoubtedly pressures in the opposite direction.' It is possible that the lack of research into the politics of tourism exists because tourism politics seldom generates sufficient controversy to become an issue on the political agenda and therefore attract the attention of politicians, political scientists or the media. 'Unlike the politics of abortion, equal rights, the environment, energy, or education—to name only a few examples—tourism politics evokes few strong feelings among established groups or citizens' (Matthews, 1983, p.303). Despite the apparent lack of interest in studies of the political and administrative dimensions of tourism by government and industry, and the community conflicts that occur in relation to tourism development, it is important to recognise that such research may be of an extremely practical nature. The results of such research may help facilitate and improve tourism planning through an increased understanding of decision-making processes (Murphy, 1985; Roehl and Fesenmaier, 1987; Gunn, 1988; Humphreys and Walmsley, 1991), and help maintain the long-term viability of a tourist destination (Hall and Selwood, 1989). As Heenan (1978, p.32) recognised:

> In their quest for viability and legitimacy, enlightened investors and community leaders must balance local and outside needs and interests . . . if the constructive impact of tourism is to be realized, collaborate approaches between diverse stakeholder groups will be needed. To survive and prosper in the decades ahead, tourism must develop some multiple constituencies.

Despite the growth of extensive research on tourism in the 1980s and 1990s, many people still do not regard tourism as a serious subject of study, often equating it with booking a holiday at a travel agency or learning how to pour a beer. Indeed, research on tourism is frequently seen as frivolous. The observation of Matthews (1983, p.304) that 'at a typical American university, a political scientist with a scholarly interest in tourism might be looked upon as dabbling in frivolity—not as a serious scholar but as an opportunist looking for a tax-deductible holiday', holds almost universal applicability. If one is to agree with Edgell (1990, p.xv) that 'a field of inquiry becomes a serious topic for policy analysis and research only when there is interest and recognition in the subject matter through the writing of articles, books, and documents', then while the economics, marketing or management of tourism is starting to become a topic worthy of serious discussion, then the politics of tourism remains in a (tragi-)comic state.

The lack of research on the policy implications of tourism is perhaps even more surprising given the emphasis by politicians on tourism as a means of economic and regional development (Mathieson and Wall, 1982; Williams and Shaw, 1988a; Pearce, 1989; Hall, D., 1991a; Hall, C., 1994a). However, as Richter (1984, p.614) has noted, 'it is journalists and marketing specialists who are hired for tourism developments', not the policy analyst with perhaps a vision of the wider implications of decision-making processes for tourism development. A review of the major international journals in policy studies, politics and public administration emphasises the dearth of information on the political dimensions of tourism. Similar to Smith's (1977, p.1) observations on the anthropology of tourism in the 1970s, it is a topic that appears to be thought of as unworthy of consideration by the serious scholar.

There are substantial methodological problems in conducting political and administrative studies. Problems have arisen because of the multiplicity of potential frameworks for analysis and the implicitly political characteristics of the results of the research process. Indeed, the very notion of 'power', one of the cornerstones of political analysis, is an ineradicably evaluative and 'essentially contested' concept (Gallie, 1955–56). Therefore, the lack of a clearly articulated or agreed upon methodological or philosophical approach to politics *per se*, let alone the politics of tourism, may create an intellectual and perceptual minefield for the researcher; particularly as, in the study of politics, the value position of the author will have an enormous bearing on the results of any research.

According to several authors, leisure and tourism policy research (Gray, 1984; Sessa, 1984) is in a relatively unhealthy state and is plagued by problems of 'lack of intellectual co-ordination and insufficient cross-fertilization of ideas among researchers; an inadequacy of research methodologies and techniques; and a lack of any generally agreed concepts and codes in the field' (Burton, 1982, pp.323–324). Indeed, Sessa (1984, p.285) goes so far as to state that the present deficiency in the understanding of the connection between tourism theory and policy formulation:

> is undoubtedly connected with the current state of tourism theory. Indeed, lack of research implies a weak theoretical framework. A weak theoretical framework implies poor teaching. This, in turn, results in faulty education, especially at the highest and not strictly professional level. Faulty education implies faulty development policies and faulty management. There is thus an entire chain of shortcomings observable everywhere tourism has developed.

However, the lack of agreed frameworks in tourism research or tourism theories cannot by itself be blamed for a failure to research the politics of tourism. For example, a failure of tourism researchers to arrive at a consensus of what actually constitutes tourism and a tourism industry does not appear to have harmed tourism studies (e.g. Smith, S.L.J., 1988; Leiper, 1990). In fact, the debate which marks such concepts should probably be seen as a sign of health and youthful vigour in an emerging area of serious academic study and should be welcomed and encouraged rather than regarded as a source of embarrassment.

The above comments by Sessa (1984) and Burton (1982) are relatively isolated critiques within the tourism literature. In the main, tourism studies have generally assumed a conservative, non-critical, value-free approach to their subject matter (Hall, C., 1989a). For example, in commenting on work undertaken by geographers in the tourism field, Britton (1991, p.451) noted that they have:

> been reluctant to recognise explicitly the capitalistic nature of the phenomenon they are researching . . . This problem is of funda-mental importance as it has meant an absence of an adequate theoretical foundation for our understanding of the dynamics of the industry and the social activities it involves.

In the tendency of many tourism researchers to focus on 'practical' or 'applied' studies, such as the economic dimensions of tourism or aspects of marketing, consumer research or visitor flows, little attention has been paid to the wider philosophical, political and societal implications of such work. Important aspects of political economy have been virtually ignored and it is perhaps ironic that, given the vital role of 'the image' in tourism, it is only recently that serious attention has been paid to the ideological nature of the tourist image (Roche, 1990; Urry, 1990a) and the way in which, for example, cities are being re-imaged in order to attract investment and the middle class employment market, where the focus of local and national governments on the economic benefits of tourism has 'reinforced the idea of the city as a kind of commodity to be marketed' (Mommaas and van der Poel, 1989, p.264). Furthermore, detailed tourism policy studies are few and far between (Richter, 1989; Pearce, 1992), and the few there are have tended to focus on notions of prescription, efficiency and economy rather than ideals of equality and social justice. If one agrees with Weber's (1968, p.1404) dictum that 'the essence of politics is struggle', then it can be safely stated that the vast majority of researchers in tourism have failed to detect it or have deliberately chosen to ignore it.

THE ANALYSIS OF THE POLITICAL DIMENSIONS OF TOURISM

The analysis of the political impacts of tourism is poorly developed. Political analysis or acknowledgement of the political dimensions of tourism have tended to be a by-product of social or economic research rather than an end in themselves (e.g. Forster, 1964; Smith and Turner, 1973; Butler, 1974; UNESCO, 1976; Smith, 1977, 1989; Runyan and Wu, 1979; Williams and Shaw, 1988a; Hall, D., 1991a). As noted above, political science has generally failed to see tourism as a legitimate topic of study. Yet, as Kosters (1984, p.612) observed, 'if a multi-disciplinary tourism science develops without the necessary ingredient of political analysis, it will remain imperfect and incomplete.' However, despite the espoused need for research on the political and administrative aspects of tourism, little basic research has been conducted while the research agenda itself remains somewhat unclear.

Matthews (1975, 1978), in his seminal studies on international tourism and political science research, identified three main dimensions of tourism as subjects of political research:

1. The politics of tourism in the marketplace, particularly in the metropolitan countries.
2. The politics of tourism in the developing host societies.
3. Ideological arguments about tourism, especially in developing states.

To varying degrees, the research issues outlined by Matthews have served as the focal points of politically oriented studies of tourism. Research on the politics of tourism are concentrated in several areas, including studies of individual countries' or regions' tourism development policies (e.g. Richter, 1980, 1989; Seymour, 1980; Richter and Richter, 1985; Williams and Shaw, 1988a; Hall, D., 1991a); the political economy of tourism development, particularly in developing economies (e.g. Nash, 1977; de Kadt, 1979; Hivik and Heiberg 1980; Richter, 1980; Britton, 1982a, 1982b, 1983; Jenkins and Henry 1982; Keller 1984; Britton and Clarke, 1987; Harrison,

1992a); the ideological nature of tourism (Thurot and Thurot, 1983; Uzzell, 1984; Ley and Olds, 1988; Urry, 1990a; Hall, 1992a; Hollinshead, 1992); and the creation of appropriate frameworks or methodologies with which to analyse tourism's political and administrative impacts (Getz, 1977; Ritchie, 1984).

Frameworks of analysis: political carrying capacity and impacts

Considerable attention has been given to the notion of carrying capacity in the recreation and tourism literature (e.g. Hall, J., 1974; Getz, 1983; Pearce, 1989). As Getz (1983, p.240) observed, 'discussion of the impact of tourism often leads to the question of capacity, yet actual measurement of capacity and the subsequent imposition of limits in tourism plans is rare.' The notion of capacity is of considerable interest to tourism planners because of the increased concern with the negative aspects of tourism and the long-term viability of tourist destinations. For example, in his influential article on the concept of a tourist area cycle of evolution, Butler (1980) contended that visitor numbers will decline as the infrastructural and social capacity of a destination to absorb tourists is exceeded. Consequently, according to Butler's arguments, tourism developments may need to be kept within capacity limits in order to sustain visitor numbers and the desired nett benefits of tourism.

The carrying capacity concept has been applied by Getz (1977) in the examination of political and administrative ability to absorb tourism (Table 1.1). The notion of capacity is of great importance in the study of tourism because of the need of tourist destinations to be able to cope with increased visitor numbers or changed visitor markets, and the resultant need for changes in the provision of physical and social infrastructure (Pearce, 1989). As Getz (1983, p.260) recognised, there is a need to 'encourage constant adaptation of the planning process through increased evaluation of impacts, and through research into the nature of the system. In particular, the determination of causal mechanisms and interrelationships . . .' In the case of the political and administrative components of measuring capacity, Getz (1977) identified components for measurement, possible capacity thresholds, and problems in the use of criteria. However, although Getz's (1977) framework may be of some value in the analysis and understanding of political impacts and capacity, it does not appear to

Table 1.1. Political/administrative criteria in the measurement of capacity to absorb tourism

Some components for measurement	Planning and administrative process Costs Efficiency Priorities for action and allocation of resources
Possible thresholds	Failure to cope Inability to achieve aims Costs cannot be recovered Priorities change
Problems in use of criterion	Difficult to obtain inter-level coordination Can always be made more efficient

Source: Getz, 1977, p.9.4

have been applied in any explicit manner to a case study (Hall, C., 1989a).

Ritchie (1984, p.10) established a framework for the measurement of specific variables and associated data collection and interpretation problems in the study of hallmark tourist events such as World Fairs or the Olympic Games (Table 1.2). The framework emphasises the important point that political impact should be studied at both a macro- and a micro-political level. However, Ritchie also acknowledges that there are severe problems in the conduct of political impact studies because of difficulties in obtaining appropriate data. As noted above, such difficulties may arise through the unwillingness of government and significant individuals within the policy-making process to be scrutinised and therefore to be held responsible for the decisions that they have made.

At the macro-political level Ritchie (1984) recorded the importance of the hallmark event as a means of enhancing images and ideology. A possible by-product of this may be the strengthening of the position of élites within local or regional power structures. At the micro-political level the event is seen to enhance careers and athletic opportunities. Although Ritchie's framework was not used in his subsequent study of the impacts of the 1988 Calgary Winter Olympics, it has proved influential in the analysis of political factors in the hosting and management of hallmark tourist events (e.g. Hall, C., 1989a, 1992a; Roche, 1990).

Table 1.2. Specific variables measured in political impact studies and associated data collection and interpretation problems

Category of data	Nature of variables measured	Associated data collection and interpretation problems
Macro-political	Image enhancement	Degree to which event improves awareness and status of city/region for commercial and tourism purposes
	Ideology enhancement	Degree to which event promotes awareness and status of a particular political ideology
Micro-political	Career enhancement	Degree to which event provides key individuals with high visibility and improved career opportunities
	Athletic enhancement	Degree to which event permits greater opportunity for local athletes to participate in and/or learn from activities

Source: Adapted from Ritchie, 1984, p.10

Ritchie's identification of ideology as a significant factor to be studied in tourism research has been similarly noted by Mings (1978), Thurot and Thurot (1983) and Matthews and Richter (1991), although consequent discussions of the ideological dimensions of tourism have been virtually non-existent. Ideologies are systems of belief about social and political issues that have strong effects in structuring and influencing thoughts, feelings and behaviour (Brown, 1973). Undoubtedly, state and individual ideologies do influence the pattern of tourism development (e.g. Williams and Shaw, 1988a; Hall, D., 1991a). Nevertheless, as Ritchie (1984, p.10) noted, 'it is difficult to obtain short-term, quantitative measures related to such goals as increased status or ideology enhancement from a diverse and dispersed international or national population.' Interestingly, this may well be a reason why the study of the impacts of a hallmark event such as the 1988 Winter Olympic Games does not include the analysis of political impacts (Ritchie and Aitken, 1984). However, it may also be because of the general inapplicability of positivist or prescriptive approaches to questions of ideology, power and structure. Nevertheless, it should still be possible to identify who benefits from tourism and the manner in which interests are engaged in tourism-related decision-making processes.

WHO BENEFITS?

> Politics is about control. At the local, regional and national levels, various interests attempt to affect the determination of policy, policy outcomes and the position of tourism in the political agenda. (Hall, C., 1991, p.213)

Tourism will have positive or negative effects depending on the scale of analysis and the perceptions, interests and values of those who are impacted and those who study such impacts (Hall, C., 1989a). Indeed, this should be a critical point in the study of the effects of tourism, as the question of for what and for whom these events are held should be central to the analysis of benefits and costs (Coppock, 1977, p.1.1). The benefits and costs of tourism are not evenly spread throughout a host community. Attention needs to be paid to the differential impact of tourism policies on desti-nation regions (Haveman, 1976; McDonald, 1986). As Greenwood (1976, p.141) observed in his study of the impacts of tourism on the Spanish Basque municipality of Fuenterrabia, 'only the local people have learned about the "costs" of tourism. The outside investors and the government have been reaping huge profits and are well satisfied.'

Greenwood's (1976) study is something of an exception within the tourism literature as he purposely concentrated on the struggle for power within the context of tourism development. The politics of place is all but ignored in tourism research. Nevertheless, as Thrift and Forbes (1983, p.247) declared, 'any satisfactory account of politics and the political must contain the element of human conflict; of groups of human beings in constant struggle with each other over resources and ideas about the distribution of resources.' For example, although they noted the significance of politics in tourism, the frameworks of Getz (1977) and Ritchie (1984) failed to come to terms with the importance of conflict and power relations within the political impacts of hallmark events and tourism in general. The attention that their frameworks placed on 'hard' data, measurement and thresholds reflects the quasi-positivistic, 'value-free' nature of much tourist research (Hall, C., 1992a). No attention was paid to the all-important notion of power in political research, nor was consideration given to the winners and losers of the political process. The vital questions of how, why and even whether people struggle within the political arena of tourism are not only unanswered, they remain unset. As Smith (1977, p.6) noted:

> Statistical analysis, the hallmark of the economist and the planner, frequently cites the gross profits to be derived from tourism but glosses over the real human costs of tourism residual in the disruption of locally-functioning economic systems without providing sustained, proven alternatives.

'All forms of political organisation have a bias in favour of the exploitation of some kinds of conflict, and the suppression of others, because organisation is the mobilisation of bias. Some issues are organised into politics while some others are organised out' (Schattsneider, 1960, p.71). Within the processes of tourism development and decision making, certain issues may be suppressed, relationships between parties altered, or inaction may be the order of the day. Those who benefit from tourism development may well be placed in a preferred position to defend and promote their vested interests. For example, in the case of the development of many large-scale hallmark tourist events such as World Fairs and Olympic Games, it appears commonplace that those who initially promote the hosting of a particular event do so because of the potential financial and political spin-offs (Hall, C., 1992a).

Politics is essentially about power. The study of power arrangements is therefore vital in the analysis of the political impacts of tourism because power governs 'the interplay of individuals, organisations, and agencies influencing, or trying to influence the direction of policy (Lyden, Shipman and Kroll, 1969, p.6). Power may be conceptualised as 'all forms of successful control by A over B—that is, of A securing B's compliance' (Lukes, 1974, p.17). The use of the concept of power is inextricably linked to a given set of value assumptions which predetermine the range of its empirical application (Bernstein, 1978). For instance, a pluralist conception of the tourism policy-making process, such as that which underlies the notion of community-based tourism planning (Murphy, 1985), will focus on different aspects of the decision-making process to a structuralist conception of politics (Britton, 1989, 1991), with each operating within a particular value and political perspective (see Chapter 6). However, given the policy analyst's 'need to understand the dominant groups and ideologies operating within a political and administrative system' (Jenkins, 1978, p.40), it seems reasonable to assume that the use of a wide conception of power, capable of identifying decisions, non-decisions and community political structure, will provide the most benefit in the analysis of the political dimensions of tourism.

Research on tourism's political impacts needs to connect the substance of policy, i.e. the general focus on data, with the process of policy making including the relationship between power, structure and ideology (see Sabatier, 1991, for a useful discussion of theories of the policy process). As Crenson (1971, p.181) has recognised, pluralism is 'no guarantee of political openness or popular sovereignty', and 'neither the study of [overt] decision-making' nor the existence of 'visible diversity' will tell us anything about 'those groups and issues which may have been shut out of a town's political life'. Studies of the political aspects of tourism should therefore attempt to understand not only the politically imposed limitations on the scope of decision making, but also the political framework within which the research process itself takes place. To do this will require acceptance of a far wider range of theoretical standpoints and academic traditions than that which has previously been the case in tourism research and, perhaps, encouragement of a dialectical approach to the analysis of political issues.

A CRAFT APPROACH TO THE STUDY OF THE POLITICS OF TOURISM

> . . . the policy process is complicated. Unless we are willing to make our assumptions about how it works and to subject these assumptions to empirical testing, we are unlikely to learn very much. As Pogo might say, 'Better to be clear and risk being wrong than be mushy and think you're always right'. (Sabatier, 1991, p.283)

As noted above, two of the main problems encountered in the study of the political dimensions of tourism are the essentially value-laden nature of political and policy analysis and the lack of an agreed methodological or theoretical base from which to conduct such research. The academic reception of tourism research is related to the emergence of a provisionally accepted body of knowledge in the field of tourism studies, which some commentators regard as heralding the development of a distinctive tourism discipline (Jafari and Ritchie, 1981). Such problems also exist in the world of political science. As Moon (1991, pp.46–47) has noted, political science is subject to an inevitable proliferation of approaches and theories for at least three reasons:

1. There are conflicting conceptions of politics.
2. Our understanding of political life, and what we take to be an understanding of political life, changes with crises of political life itself.
3. Social and political knowledge has a reflexive character: our understanding of politics can itself come to be part of the self-understanding of political actors, affecting their behaviour, and so altering the phenomena that political scientists study and the theories and approaches appropriate to them.

Political knowledge, as with tourism knowledge, is therefore social in character where even the 'most theoretical forms of knowledge presuppose an extensive matrix of personal judgements and practical skills' (Majone, 1980b, p.8). In terms of, for example, the analysis of tourism policy, 'the quality of research can be assessed in terms of two distinct but related criteria: internal-process oriented criteria of adequacy related to the technical competence of the work; and external, outcome-oriented criteria of effectiveness relating to the impact of analysis on the policy process' (Majone and Quade, 1980, p.1). The former lies in the domain of academic or professional notions of adequacy, while the latter is in the hands of the client or decision maker. Therefore, much research on the political dimensions of tourism is dealing with arguments concerning problem solution (Ostrom, 1976, 1977, 1982; Wildavsky, 1979; Paul and Russo, 1982; Majone, 1989), a conclusion which leads the analyst to the notion of political analysis as a form of craft work. As Ravetz (1973, p.75) observed: 'without an appreciation of the craft character of scientific work there is no possibility of resolving the paradox of the radical difference between the subjective, intensely personal activity of creative science, and the objective, impersonal knowledge which results from it.'

The notion of analysis as craft was first expounded by Aristotle in the *Nicomachean Ethics* (1976), which described the craftsperson's work in terms of four constituents of the task: material, efficient, formal and final. The material component is identified with the data, information and other conceptual inputs used in formulating the problem. The tools and methods of the analyst represent the efficient component, while the formal constituent is an argument in which evidence is cited and from which conclusions are drawn. The final constituent is the conclusion itself, with the related activities of communication and implementation (Ravetz, 1973; Holt and Turner, 1974; Becker, 1978; Majone, 1980a, 1980b, 1981, 1989).

According to Majone (1989, p.44), 'Craft knowledge—less general and explicit than theoretical knowledge, but not as idio-syncratic as pure intuition—is essential in any kind of disciplined intellectual inquiry or professional activity. It is especially important in policy analysis.' Craft knowledge is especially relevant to the analysis of the political dimensions of tourism because the researcher is dealing with policy arguments and value positions which cannot be proved in the sense that a theorem can be proved, or even in the manner of a proposition in natural science. The adequacy of an exercise in political analysis therefore depends on 'the quality of the data and limitations of available tools, on the time constraints imposed on the analysts, and on the requirements of the client' (Majone, 1981, p.17).

A craft approach to analysis is no less rigorous than formal hypothesis testing; however, it does explicitly recognise the role of values and social processes in the research task. Furthermore, in studying the politics of tourism, the idea of craft knowledge should also lead to us to realise that political analysis operates within a plurality of methodologies, techniques and values, each having the potential to be valid in terms of their results. However, the notion of touristic analysis as craft knowledge should also encourage students of tourism to cast their net for appropriate research methodologies and approaches far wider than has been the case in the past, and to place greater emphasis on some of those central aspects of society, such as power and values, which influence the patterns and processes of tourism development. As Majone (1989, p.183) noted, 'The need today is less to develop "objective" measures of outcomes—the traditional aim of evaluation research—than to facilitate a wide-ranging dialogue among advocates of different criteria.'

OUTLINE OF THIS BOOK

This book attempts to highlight some of the key fields of analysis in understanding the relationship between politics and tourism. Therefore, chapters are organised around a number of central political themes in tourism studies, for example, public policy and international relations, which are in turn related to the scale (international, national, regional/local, the individual) at which they occur (Figure 1.1). However, the various fields should not be seen as being mutually exclusive and the interconnection between key concepts in political analysis will be noted throughout. Indeed, as the final chapter discusses, one of the great challenges in tourism research is to relate patterns and processes of tourism development at the micro-scale to the social, political and economic processes which are occurring at the global level.

Chapter 2 discusses the tourism policy-making process and places particular emphasis on the role of the state in tourism. Government involvement in tourism is examined and a range of factors are identified as components of tourism policy involvement, including institutional arrangements, pressure groups, significant individuals, and their respective values and power relative to policy making and implementation.

Chapter 3 examines the politics of tourism in an international context and discusses the role that tourism plays in international relations and diplomacy. Several key issues are analysed, including the use of tourism as a mechanism to advance territorial claims, and tourism and free trade. The chapter concludes by questioning the popular notion that tourism is a force for peace between nations, a point taken up in further detail in Chapter 4 which looks at the relationship between tourism and political stability, with particular reference to revolution, terrorism and political violence.

Chapter 5 discusses the nature of tourism development at the national level with reference to both 'developed' and 'developing' countries. The viability of tourism as a tool for national development is discussed, as are the relationship between tourism and dependency and the potential to create plantation economies.

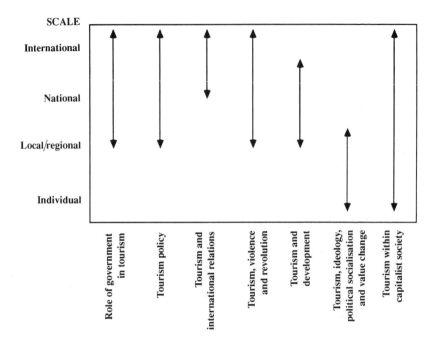

Figure 1.1. Major political dimensions of tourism

Chapter 6 examines the political role of tourism in the local state with specific discussions of the use of tourism as a re-imaging strategy, particularly in the urban context. Urban redevelopment projects and hallmark events associated with urban re-imaging strategies are often held to be empowering measures for local communities (Roche, 1993a). Community-based tourism planning is increasingly popular (Murphy, 1985; Hall, C., 1991). However, substantial questions remain about how representative the decision-making process is in terms of the power of local élites and their influence on tourism development.

Chapter 7 narrows the scope of analysis further by examining the relationship between tourism, culture and the presentation of social reality. Discussion is centred on issues of ideology, political socialisation and the use of tourism to present certain images of culture. The ideological dimensions of tourism, particularly in the form of the creation of images and stereotypes, are highlighted with reference to indigenous peoples. The chapter concludes with a discussion of the political significance of current interest in contemporary economic and cultural processes as indicated in the debate surrounding postmodernism and the notion of the 'tourist gaze'.

Chapter 8, the final chapter, attempts to provide an account of the position of tourism within capitalist society, highlights the manner in which tourism and leisure have become increasingly commodified on a global scale, and asks how the study of the politics of tourism will develop in the future. Particular attention is paid to the relationship between tourism and international capital and the way in which the global circulation of capital is marked out by tourism spectacles, the creation of tourism and leisure space in many major urban centres, and the commodification of the tourist experience. It is argued that the contextualisation of tourism within contemporary capitalist society provides for an account of tourism politics which integrates the interrelationship between public policy and power at the international, national, local and individual levels.

The chapter argues that much of the teaching and research in the tourism field does not address questions of power and values and instead examines tourism development issues, for example, from a technical–rational or managerial perspective which excludes substantive questions of politics. The chapter concludes that greater attention needs to be given to 'counter-institutional' or 'oppositional' approaches to the study of tourism which have the opportunity not only to articulate alternative policy settings in the tourism field, but also to broaden the debate over the value of tourism at all scales of development.

In the social science of tourism, political or public policy studies have received only little attention. Nevertheless, the continued growth of domestic and international travel, which is accompanied worldwide by increasing concerns over the potential impacts of tourism, has meant that the study of tourism is becoming ever more broad. Given the political nature of tourism development, examination of the political dimensions of tourism must clearly become one of the cornerstones of the analysis of tourism. As Matthews (1983, p.304) noted, 'the possibilities for political science contributions to the understanding of tourism are immense.' It is hoped that the present volume will contribute in some small way to the development of an understanding of the political nature of tourism.

2

Tourism, Government and the State: Tourism and the Policy-Making Process

The answer [to the question as to why governments should involve themselves with tourism] should not lie solely in economic reasons, for rarely in history has any society been a willing host to people from another culture or even another locality, yet in order to generate foreign exchange without having to exhaust assets which cannot be replaced, governments around the world are openly inviting tourists to visit their countries.

Every government must have a policy for tourism both at national and local level. To adopt a laissez-faire philosophy and stand on the sidelines is to court confrontation between hosts and guests leading to poor attitudes, bad manners and an anti-tourism lobby. Only the most determined tourists will visit those places where they are overtly made to feel unwelcome and where they perceive difficulties with regard to their personal safety.
(Wanhill, 1987, p.54)

The political dimensions of tourism occur at a number of different levels: international, national, regional, community and individual. Regardless of the level of analysis, the political process is dominated by the state. The state is an exceedingly complex structure which eludes precise definition (Held, 1989). Nevertheless, it is of 'crucial importance in understanding the contours of public policy ... because the state translates values, interests and resources into objectives and policies' (Davis *et al.*, 1993, p.19). The role of the state in a society is therefore one of the focal points of political studies and of the social sciences in general. However, it has not served the same function in the study of tourism.

The notion of the state is concerned with the idea of an:

> ensemble of agencies of legitimate coercion and as an amalgamated set of collective resources which intentionally and unintentionally produce policy outcomes. It is a structure of different political forces and institutions which attempt to justify chosen political directions and objectives. In policy terms, the state is a contingent political entity which reflects the interchanges of values, the outcomes of interest clashes, and accumulated patterns of resource usage. (Davis *et al.*, 1993, p.18)

It must be stressed that the state is not simply a reflection of the interests of the society in which it is situated, although clearly certain interests will exert greater power than others in influencing the nature of the state. The state has its own interests and values to pursue and will at times impose these value preferences even when they are in contrast with others that exist within the society. The state is a powerful, resilient, pragmatic, and reflexive social structure capable of sustained purposeful action across many areas of social activity of which tourism is only one. Nevertheless, 'It is not inherently a benevolent structure intent on social good; nor is it inevitably a modernising force working toward desirable forms of progress; nor is it singularly malevolent or motivated by self-interest' (Davis *et al.*, 1993, p.18).

'A state exists where there is a political apparatus ruling over a given territory, whose authority is backed by a legal system and by the capacity to use force to implement its policies' (Giddens, 1989, p.301). Similarly, Badie and Birnbaum (1983, p.105) define the state as a 'system of permanently institutionalized roles which has the exclusive right to the legitimate use of force, whereby it exerts sovereign power over a given territory.' The state serves four key functions: the maintenance of internal order, military concerns, the maintenance of communication infrastructures, and economic redistribution. All the functions of the state will affect tourism policy and development to varying degrees. However, the degree to which individual functions are related to particular tourism policies and decisions will depend on the specific objectives of institutions, interest groups and significant individuals relative to the political process.

This chapter will provide a discussion of the role of the state in tourism. Although, as will be noted below, the concept of the state is broader than that of 'government' or 'bureaucracy', for many tourism researchers the government *is* the state. This has meant that the analysis of state involvement in tourism has been somewhat restricted and has failed to appreciate the advantages of a broader conceptual category in the study of tourism policy and development. The first section of the chapter examines the various institutions of the state and describes how each of them relates to tourism policy and development. The second section discusses issues surrounding the appropriate role of the state in tourism and gives particular attention to the role of government as entrepreneur, the importance of political ideology and philosophy, and the coordinating function. This section also notes that most of the writing on government's role in tourism has failed to take into account the effect on tourism promotion and development of different political systems (e.g. unitary versus federal government systems and the degree of centralisation of power). The third and final section provides an analysis of the factors which influence tourism policy and decision making within the tourism policy environment, such as institutional arrangements, roles, interest and pressure groups, the influence of significant individuals and the critical roles of values and power in the tourism policy-making process.

TOURISM AND THE INSTITUTIONS OF THE STATE

[The international tourism industry] with its different branches in the originating and receiving societies should not be regarded as a system of action that can operate autonomously, independently of established political power. Numerous interactions exist between them. States are led to play an increasingly active part in this connection, not only because they have the task of defining tourist policy in the light of national objectives, but also because they assume an increasingly important role in promotion, co-ordination and planning, and provide financial backing. The tourist industry and the state should not be considered at odds with each other. In point of fact, it is difficult to draw a dividing line between the private sector and the public sector. Reciprocal interpenetration occurs. (Lanfant, 1980, p.25)

As noted above, while the state is extremely difficult to define, and is broader in extent than the idea of the government or the bureaucracy, an understanding of the relationship between tourism and the state can perhaps best be achieved by identifying the main institutions which constitute the state. Such an approach indicates the organisational composition of the state and its primary functions. 'The extent of the State's role in tourism varies according to the conditions and circumstances peculiar to each country (politico-economic-constitutional system, socio-economic development, degree of tourism development)' (IUOTO, 1974, p.67). Indeed, IUOTO (the forerunner to the World Tourism Organization) argued (1974, p.71) that tourism was such a key sector that in order to foster and develop tourism 'on a scale proportionate to its national importance and to mobilize all available resources to that end, it is necessary to centralize the policy-making powers in the hands of the State so that it can take appropriate measures for creating a suitable framework for the promotion and development of tourism by the various sectors concerned.' The main institutions of the state are: the central government, administrative departments, the courts and judiciary, enforcement agencies, other levels of government, government business enterprises, regulatory and assistance authorities, and a range of semi-state organisations (Deutsch, 1986; Davis et al., 1993).

The government, elected or unelected, is one of the central institutions of the state. Consisting of the ministers of the state and the head of state, government maintains political authority within the state. However, government legitimacy can only be provided through an electoral process. Therefore, parliamentary institutions provide the main forum for the articulation of alternative policies and acts as a decision maker in conjunction with cabinet, individual ministers and the head of state.

Despite the economic and social significance of tourism for many countries, tourism has only recently become an item on the political agenda of many national parliaments. Nevertheless, many countries have passed legislation which sets out the roles of national tourism organisations and which provides for assistance for the tourism industry. In addition, it must be recognised that even though government only occasionally enacts legislation primarily aimed at tourism development, the government will also set through its more general policy decisions the general economic and regulatory parameters within which the tourism industry operates. However, it should also be noted that the existence of democratic parliamentary procedures is certainly not a prerequisite for tourism development; indeed the opposite may well be the case. For example, in Greece 'greater emphasis on tourist development followed the imposition of dictatorial rule in 1967, involving construction, financing and promotion' (Leontidou, 1988, p.84), while similar events occurred in the Philippines in the 1970s when President Marcos sought to use international tourism as a means of gaining political legitimacy for his regime (Richter, 1989).

Tourism is often represented in non-elected administrative departments which are a component of the state bureaucracy. These administrative organisations are the state institutions primarily responsible for policy advice and implementation. In countries such as Australia and New Zealand, ministries of tourism responsible for policy have been separated from statutory authorities responsible for tourism marketing and promotion. However, it still tends to be the institutional norm that national tourism organisations unite policy and promotional concerns. According to Lickorish et al. (1991, p.145) the role of the national tourist organisation would normally include sections to cover the following functions:

1. Research
2. Information and promotion within the country
3. Regularisation of standards of lodgings and restaurants
4. Control of activities of private travel agencies
5. Publicity overseas
6. Technical and juridical problems
7. International relations
8. Development of selected tourist areas
9. Overall tourism policy and promotion

The judiciary and courts provide a third level of state decision making and often act to qualify the actions of other state institutions. The judiciary typically has little direct role in tourism development apart from enforcing industrial and business law. However, in a number of countries around the world the enactment of environmental protection legislation has given the courts a significant role in appraising the environmental impacts of tourism development projects.

A fourth arm of the state is formed by the enforcement agencies responsible for defence, public order and sanctioned behaviour.

Agencies such as the police or defence forces have little direct role in tourism, although the establishment of a safe environment appears important in attracting tourism development (see Chapter 4). As Allcock (1991, p.258) observed in the case of the former Yugoslavia and the changing nature of Eastern Europe, 'Tourists like to feel safe. Essential as it is to the economic stability of Yugoslavia, its tourist trade could readily be endangered by any serious deterioration in the conditions of internal order. In that respect also, therefore, Yugoslavia can be seen to be sharing a common destiny with the rest of Europe.' Agencies responsible for enforcing regulations in such areas as casinos, gambling and prostitution may also have an indirect relationship with tourism through the imposition of codes of behaviour.

One of the most significant aspects of the state is its political form, in particular the relative balance of power between central government and the regions. In many countries with unitary governmental systems, tourism planning and promotion are controlled by central government. The centralisation of political and economic control of tourism was especially significant under Stalinist regimes. For example, Hall (D., 1991c, p.49) has noted that 'the organisation of international tourism under state socialism comprised a central ministry out of which the role of a national tourism was devoted. Within that tourism organisation, regional and local branches would operate the various tourist services for their area, albeit subordinate to the national planning and organisational framework.' In contrast, many Western European governments have devolved state involvement to the regional and local levels. For example, in Italy national-level tourism planning and administration is not well organised and regional authorities were given greater powers in the fields of tourism planning and administration in the 1970s (King, 1988). Similarly, the Netherlands has no long-standing national strategy guiding tourist development (Pinder, 1988).

Different state levels will tend to have different sets of objectives to achieve via tourism development (Airey, 1983). As Williams and Shaw (1988b, p.230) observed, 'The study of policy formation is made more complex because the aims of the local state may diverge from those of the central state' (see Chapter 6 for a discussion of politics, tourism and the local state). Nowhere may this be more apparent than in federal political systems where there exist three or even four levels of the state: national, provincial or state, regional and local.

Federal structures will have a major impact on the relative importance attached to tourism development by the various levels of government. For example, central government involvement in tourism in Switzerland has been constricted because 'Switzerland has always been a country reluctant to adopt governmental, especially central government, measures even to guide let alone direct her economy. To do so is anathema to the Swiss view of federalism, local political power and free enterprise' (Gilg, 1988, p.137). However, the lack of central authority may also create difficulties in coordinating and controlling tourism development. In the Swiss case, de Hanni has argued that the quality and quantity of tourist development must be controlled in the interests of regional development, but he also noted that there is a lack of political will in the communes to curtail further development and concluded that 'the chances for an effective control of tourist development are not likely to improve significantly in the near future' (de Hanni, 1984, p.668, in Gilg, 1988, p.144). Similarly, in Germany national tourism policy is poorly articulated given the constraints of the federal structure (Schnell, 1988; Pearce, 1992), while in Austria the influence of the federal government is also limited (Zimmermann, 1988).

In federal systems such as Australia, Canada, India and the United States, states and provinces have built up substantial tourism administrations (Richter, 1989; Pearce, 1992), often with the division of powers between the various levels of the state being formally designated through intergovernmental agreements. For example, in Australia the division of responsibilities for tourism between the national and state governments was established in the Statement of Government Objectives and Responsibilities in Tourism set out in the Tourist Minister's Council Agreement of 1976 (Australian Government Inquiry into Tourism, 1987). Under the Agreement the national government's tourism agencies have prime responsibility for the international dimensions of tourism and for the formulation and implementation of policies which operate at a national level. The states and territories have the responsibility for promotion and marketing of state attractions and for the development of tourist facilities through such measures as land zoning, planning controls and licensing. However, it must be stressed that many responsibilities are shared and while the respective governments may have an official policy of maximising cooperation, this ideal situation is often not reached in the world of federal state relations, especially when parties of different political persuasions occupy government at the state and national levels (Hall, C., 1991).

A sixth institutional dimension of the state is the extent to which government business enterprises have extended the state into areas of commercial activity. Well-recognised examples of government tourism-related business enterprises include state-owned airlines and accommodation. While the level of state intervention in areas of commercial activity will often depend on the political ideology of the government, many governments around the world have shown themselves to be entrepreneurs in tourism development. For example, for most of its history the New Zealand Tourism Department has been involved in tourism through such commercial activities as running hotels, travel agencies and coach tours and operating as a booking centre for tourist activities, although it should also be noted that since 1984 the department has withdrawn almost completely from operational activities and instead has concentrated on marketing and promotion (Pearce, 1992). The tendency to privatise and, often, commercialise functions that were once performed by the state has been almost universal in Western nations since the late 1970s and has affected the nature of many national governments' involvement in the tourism industry. According to Davis *et al.* (1993, p.24) three principal reasons for this trend can be identified: 'governments are interested in reducing the dependency of public enterprises on public budgets, in reducing public debt by selling state assets, and in raising technical efficiencies by commercialisation.'

Commercialisation and corporatisation of state tourism agencies have also commenced in the former state socialist countries of Eastern Europe and Asia where former government agencies have had to become more entrepreneurial in their tourism role and have had to learn to adapt to international market forces rather than domestic ideology regarding the health of earners. Nevertheless, such a shift in roles will provide great challenges for former state agencies. As Hall (D., 1991b, p. 11) observed, 'The basic require-ment of a tourism industry, as understood in the West—the availability of a flexible, entrepreneurial service sector responsive to changing demands and fashions—was the very antithesis of the centralised socialist economy based upon heavy industry.'

A seventh aspect of the state, particularly in Western society, has been the establishment of a wide range of regulatory bodies and non-commercial statutory authorities. Several areas of the tourism industry, such as aviation and transport, labour relations, and hotels and resorts, are often subject to regulatory bodies. In addition, many tourism ministers around the world have non-commercial tourism advisory councils or committees which provide advice on tourism-related matters. In many ways, therefore, many of these regulatory bodies can be regarded as semi-state institutions, as a substantial proportion of their membership may come from the private sector.

Finally, in examining the state in its broadest sense, such components of society as political parties, trade unions and industry associations which receive funding from the state or which are state sponsored may be interpreted as being institutional elements of the state. Indeed, in many Western societies the formation of industry peak bodies, including tourism and hospitality, is often favoured by government as it has the potential to simplify communication and coordination across an industry.

As the above discussion indicates, the state has a number of institutional elements which will influence the tourism industry. However, although it has indicated the relationship of tourism to the state, it does not highlight the proactive role that government plays in tourism development. The next section will examine the various roles that the state, through government action, has in tourism and their impact on the pattern and nature of tourism development.

THE ROLE OF GOVERNMENT IN TOURISM

> While active governmental involvement in tourism development may serve to avoid or mitigate . . . potential problems, it may also serve to exacerbate them . . . the crucial question is not whether government plays a role in tourism development, but what kind of role is played. It is therefore important to give serious consideration to the types of policy choices faced by planners, and to their potential consequences. (Richter and Richter, 1985, p.203)

There is almost universal acceptance by governments around the world, regardless of ideology, that tourism is a good thing, with most tourism policies being designed to expand the tourist industry. As Smith (1989, pp.x–xi) noted, 'Government agencies at every level from the international down to small towns have adopted a progressively more active role in the use of tourism as a development tool ... government agencies currently promote tourism as a panacea for underemployment in economically depressed areas.' In commenting on the United Kingdom's experiences in tourism policy and tourism development, Shaw, Greenwood and Williams (1988, p.162) observed, 'it is against a background of wealth and job creation that successive UK governments have developed public policy towards tourism.' According to these authors (1988, p.174), a number of economic considerations have led to public sector involvement in tourism in the UK:

1. Improvements in the balance of payments
2. Fostering regional development
3. Diversification of the national economy
4. Increase in public revenue
5. Improvements in income levels
6. The creation of new employment

Similarly, in Spain 'tourism has been favoured by successive policymakers' with ideology seemingly having 'little influence on the importance attached to tourism and the policies developed for the industry' (Valenzuela, 1988, pp.39, 40). However, in recent years environmental and social concerns have also been incorporated into government tourism policies in response to the political power of environmental interest groups. The range of tourism issues noted in the tourism policies of several European governments is listed in Table 2.1.

The use by government of tourism as a tool in economic restructuring is not isolated to Western nations. Tourism is regarded as as economic escape route for the former state socialist countries of Eastern Europe and East Asia and for many of the less developed nations (Jenkins, 1980; Jenkins and Henry, 1982; Hall, D., 1991a). Indeed, 'the relatively labour-intensive nature of the tourism industry, and the limited scope for capital substitution in the production of tourism services ... may be particularly compelling for these societies which are experiencing, for the first time in a half a century, significant and increasing unemployment problems' (Hall, D., 1991b, p.4).

Table 2.1. Issues mentioned in European government tourism policies

Issues most frequently mentioned (in order of times mentioned)

1. Regional development
2. Seasonality
3. Consumer protection
4. Balance of payments
5. Social tourism
6. Rural/green tourism
7. Environmental protection

Other issues mentioned (unranked)

Increase/improve hotel capacity
Help for small hotels/budget hotels and self-catering
Provision of infrastructure
Help for small business
Vocational training and education
Youth tourism
Overseas aid for tourism
Action on currency and other restrictions
Coordination of government agencies involved in tourism
Public education on tourism issues
Community leisure and recreation needs
Control of casinos and gambling
Public access
Economic impact of tourism
Energy matters
Price control
Concern for traditional resorts and spas
Female holidays
Second homes
Employment in tourism
Development of computers and information technology
Levels of public transport fares (air, rail, coach)

Source: Airey, 1983, p.241. Reproduced by permission of Butterworth-Heinemann, Oxford, UK

No matter what type of political structure a country has, there is invariably some form of government intervention in tourism. Tourism is typically concentrated in both time and space: in time because of the seasonality of many tourism destinations, and in space because of the tendency for tourism flows to congregate in certain areas with suitable infrastructure and attractions. As Williams and Shaw (1988b, p.230) noted, 'the very nature of tourism—with its heavy spatial and seasonal polarisation—usually

requires some form of interventionism', whether it be for distributive or ameliorative purposes. Therefore, the issue is not whether
government should have a role but what the nature of that role
should actually be.

The question of the appropriate role of government in tourism is
illustrated by the debate which surrounded government tourism
policy in the United Kingdom in the mid to late 1980s. The
economic rationalists under Prime Minister Thatcher advocated
that the direct role of government in the industry should be
minimised and that government's task was instead to set the
broad economic parameters within which the industry could
operate and, of course, thrive. The economic rationalist perspective
is exemplified by Lord Young in his report on *Pleasure, leisure and
jobs*:

> It may be asked why the Government should involve itself directly
> in [tourism], which is primarily a matter for private enterprise.
> Indeed, the Government believes the best way it can help any sector
> of business flourish is not by intervening but by providing a general
> economic framework which encourages growth and at the same time
> removing unnecessary restrictions or burdens. (Lord Young of
> Graffham, 1985, para. 2, in Wanhill, 1987, p.54)

The idealism of Lord Young's paper stands in stark contrast to
the realities of government's relationship with tourism. Despite
government's undoubted role in setting the broad macro-economic
framework within which tourism operates, it would be extremely
difficult, if not impossible, for government to withdraw completely
from involvement with the tourism industry. Indeed, the Trade
and Industry Committee's response to Lord Young was that the
government did not know what to do and could not decide what
its role was:

> The Government minimises the appearance of involvement by
> reducing policy aims to statements of the obvious but maintains the
> fact of involvement in the tourist boards and the grants provided
> through them. The trouble is that this actual financial commitment is
> then left without there being any clear specific strategy to guide its
> use. More important still, the present legislature framework, creating
> as it does three independent and separately funded tourist boards in
> Great Britain, means there is no overall policy applied to developing
> tourism in the UK as a whole. There is no coordination of funding,
> so relative priorities are not assessed, nor is there any cohesion
> between strategies pursued by the boards. (Trade and Industry
> Committee, 1985, para. 73, in Wanhill, 1987, p.54)

The Trade and Industry Committee's response identifies the problems inherent in determining the appropriate role for government in tourism, problems which are repeated time and time again throughout the world (e.g. see Owen, 1992). As the next section discusses, the tension between government, industry and other interests as to the function of government in relation to tourism is seen in a number of different areas of government concern. Five main areas of public sector involvement in tourism may be identified: coordination, planning, legislation and regulation, entrepreneur, and stimulation (IUOTO, 1974; Mill and Morrison, 1985). To this may be added two other related functions, a social tourism role, and a broader role of interest protection. These seven functions of government are discussed below.

Coordination

> Since tourism is a manifold activity consisting of numerous units with divergent and often conflicting interests, it devolves on the State, which is concerned with the optimum promotion and development of tourism in the national interest, to harmonize and coordinate all tourist activities. This coordinating role of the State is expanding with the complex problems arising from the fast growth of tourism. (IUOTO, 1974, p.68)

Of all the roles of government in tourism, probably the most important is that of coordination. This is because the successful implementation of all the other roles will, to a large extent, be dependent on the ability of government to coordinate and balance their various roles in the tourism development process. The need for a coordinated tourism strategy has become one of the great truisms of tourism policy and planning (e.g. Smyth, 1986; Lamb, 1988; Jansen-Verbeke, 1989; McKercher, 1993). For example, Lickorish et al. (1991, p.vi) argued that 'There is a serious weakness in the machinery of government dealing with tourism in its co-ordination, and co-operation with operators either state or privately owned. Government policies or lack of them suggest an obsolescence in public administration devoted to tourism ... Political will is often lacking.' Similarly, at the local government level in the Netherlands, Jansen-Verbeke (1989, p.240) noted that:

> The fragmentation of the municipal organization over numerous departments, all dealing with different aspects of tourism and recreation, is very much seen as an obstacle to that construction of

an overall development plan. The more people involved, the greater the risk is that no consensus can be obtained, that views of decision-makers will differ from one another, or that establishing a community of interests is unrealistic and that departmentalism will prevail.

However, although considerable attention has been given to the importance of a coordinated approach to tourism, particularly as it relates to government involvement in the tourism industry, many commentators have failed to indicate exactly what is meant by the concept.

Coordination is necessary both within and between the different levels of government in order to avoid duplication of resources in the various government tourism bodies and the private sector, and to develop effective tourism strategies. '"Co-ordination" usually refers to the problem of relating units or decisions so that they fit in with one another, are not at cross-purposes, and operate in ways that are reasonably consistent and coherent' (Spann, 1979, p.411). However, there are two different types of coordination covered under this definition: administrative coordination and policy coordination. The need for administrative coordination can be said to occur when there has been agreement on aims, objectives and policies between the parties that have to be coordinated, but the mechanism for coordination is undecided or there are inconsist-encies in implementation. The necessity for policy coordination arises when there is conflict over the objectives of the policy that has to be coordinated and implemented. Undoubtedly, the two types of coordination may sometimes be hard to distinguish, as coordination will nearly always mean that one policy or decision will be dominant over others (Hall, C., 1991).

Coordination is a political activity, which is why it can prove extremely difficult, especially when, as in the tourism industry, there are a large number of parties involved in the decision-making process. As Edgell (1990, p.7) observed, 'there is no other industry in the economy that is linked to so many diverse and different kinds of products and services as is the tourism industry.' However, it must be noted that perhaps the need for coordination only becomes paramount when coordination is not occurring. Most coordination occurs in a very loose fashion that does not require formal arrangements (Parker, 1978). In addition, a good case could be argued that a situation of conflict can also be productive in the formulation of new ideas or strategies for dealing with problems.

The need for coordination will also be issue specific. Nevertheless, the continued calls for a coordinated strategy for tourism development would tend to indicate that there are problems in the tourism industry that may require both administrative and policy measures.

Planning

Planning for tourism occurs in a number of forms (development, infrastructure, promotion and marketing); structures (different government organisations); and scales (international, national, regional, local and sectoral). In several nations, such as Israel, national tourism development plans have been drawn up in which government decides which sectors of the industry will be developed, the appropriate rate of growth and the provision of capital required for expansion (Mill and Morrison, 1985). As in most forms of economic planning, it is desirable to balance the development of supply (attractions, facilities and infrastructure) with the promotion of demand (the number of tourists). However, planning is rarely exclusively devoted to tourism *per se*. Instead, planning for tourism tends to be 'an amalgam of economic, social and environmental considerations' which reflects the diversity of the factors which influence tourism development (Heeley, 1981, p.61). Nevertheless, the emergence of public concern over externalities and the recent worldwide interest in the search for more appropriate and sustainable forms of tourism have led to demands for improved planning for tourism, in the belief that this will help ameliorate the negative impacts of tourism development. As Burkart and Medlik (1981, p.235) commented, 'All tourism activity is increasingly regulated in the interests of the consumer; physical planning and development are increasingly regulated in the interests of the tourist as well as the resident. The need for physical planning has come to be widely recognized, if not always readily accepted.'

Tourism planning has tended to mirror broader trends within the urban and regional planning traditions (Murphy, 1985; Getz, 1986, 1987). Moreover, planning for tourism will reflect the economic, environmental and social goals of government at whichever level the planning process is being carried out. Therefore, in many ways planning may be regarded as going hand-in-hand with tourism policy. Nevertheless, as in the formation of policy, planning is an essentially political process, the results of which may be indicative of the dominance of certain stakeholders' interests and values over other interests and values.

In Western nations, planning for tourism has traditionally been associated with land-use zoning or development planning at the local government level. Concerns have typically been focused on site development, accommodation and building regulations, the density of tourist development, the presentation of cultural, historical and natural tourist features, and the provision of infra-structure including roads and sewage. However, in recent years tourism planning at all levels of government has had to adapt its programme to include environmental considerations, concerns over the social impacts of tourism, demands for greater community participation and, somewhat paradoxically, demands for 'smaller government'. The latter trend has led to government often becoming entrepreneurial in its involvement with tourism in order to increase the financial contribution of tourism to government income. Therefore, government has increasingly been involved in the promotion and marketing of destinations, and in the joint development of tourist attractions or facilities with the private sector. However, such activities are often carried on outside the statutory powers of government (Pearce, 1989). For example, in Australia, while the New South Wales Tourism Commission is charged with development and marketing, it has no statutory authority to intervene in the planning process (which is instead the responsibility of the New South Wales Department of Environment and Planning) (Hall, C., 1991).

Prior to the break-up of the state socialist nations of Eastern Europe in the late 1980s, tourism planning had been highly centralised within state agencies. According to Hall (D., 1991c, p.50), 'The administration of tourism under socialism . . . has . . . implicitly acted both to contain and to concentrate tourism—and especially foreign tourism—within very specific spatial para-meters.' Although state centralisation of tourism primarily served state ideological interests and helped ensure that leisure and tourism were in line with broader state objectives (see below for a discussion of social tourism functions in Eastern Europe), Hall (D., 1984, p.542) suggested that 'there could be a number of ways in which a socialist development strategy could subordinate inter-national tourism to Stalinist economic priorities':

1. It should provide assistance in the implementation of policies seeking the equal distribution of goods, services and opportunities across the state area.
2. It should be used as a catalyst to improve economic performance and stimulate economic development.
3. Infrastructural improvements and elaborations should follow in its wake to benefit the indigenous population as well as, if not to a greater degree than, foreign tourists.
4. The natural environment should not be adversely affected, and wherever possible, should be positively enhanced by the process of tourism development.
5. The much needed hard currency brought by foreign tourists should be employed for the purchase of essential imports to improve the country's qualitative and quantitative performance.
6. A preclusion, within the tourism performance, of alien influences should be secured—whether of an ideological, cultural or economic nature likely to affect those coming into contact with foreign visitors or likely to cause significance economic 'leakages' from the country.
7. International peace and understanding, as defined by the state socialist society itself, should be promoted.
8. Visitors' ideological appreciation should be enhanced by imbuing them with a sense of the superiority of the socialist system in general, and of the host country's own interpretation of socialist development in particular.
9. Tourism should thereby be employed to project a deliberately constructed, self-conscious image of the host country to the outside world. (Hall, D., 1991d, pp.83–84)

All the above objectives could only be achieved with an extremely high degree of state control and a notion of planning which encompassed social, ideological and political goals as well as economic objectives. Therefore, in the former state socialist countries of Eastern Europe, tourism planning was completely subservient to the interests of the state, while in Western, liberal-democratic nations, tourism planning is more often focused on land-use issues within a political arena of stakeholder interests.

The lack of a single authority responsible for all aspects of tourism development within a state may lead to substantial confusion between central government, local authorities and private industry over roles within the tourism development and planning process. Even in the former state socialist countries of Eastern Europe, government is still recognised as having a significant role. For example, a Ministry of Tourism was established in East Germany in late November 1989 'to face the challenge of a massive influx of visitors, and the pent-up urge of east German citizens to travel abroad. Its role was to prepare the shift from state-monopoly to a mixed or free enterprise infrastructure, prior to unification with the Federal Republic' (Mellor, 1991, p.142). Furthermore, the diverse structure of the industry has meant that coordination of the various elements of the planning process has been extremely difficult. It is the very nature of the industry which makes planning so important. As Gunn (1977, p.85) observed, because of the fragmented growth of the tourism industry 'the overall planning of the total tourism system is long overdue . . . there is no overall policy, philosophy or coordinating force that brings the many pieces of tourism into harmony and assures their continued harmonious function.' More recently, Lickorish *et al.* (1991, p.70) argued that 'without governments' involvement in tourism planning, development of the industry will lack cohesion, direction, and short-term initiatives might well jeopardise longer-term potential.' Government tourism planning therefore serves as an arbiter between competing interests. Nevertheless, while planning is recognised as an important element in tourism development, the conduct of a plan does not guarantee appropriate outcomes for the interested stakeholders. Pearce (1992, pp.12–13) reported that a 1980 World Tourism Organization study of tourism plans 'revealed that about one-third of the more than 1,600 plans inventoried were not implemented, that many plans lacked social and environmental considerations and failed to integrate tourism within broader socio-economic objectives':

> *a desire to plan* exists in the tourism sector, but . . . few countries have been in a position to follow a policy of continuity regarding tourism development. Furthermore, the virtual absence of legislation seems to prejudice applying a directive plan. (World Tourism Organization, 1980, p.22, in Pearce, 1992, p.13)

Legislation and regulation

Government has a wide range of legislative and regulative powers which directly and indirectly impinge on the tourism industry.

Government involvement ranges from policies on passports and visas, which may in some instances act as a travel deterrent, to international aviation agreements regarding the passage, landing and pick-up rights of international carriers, to land-use, labour and wages policy. At both the local and national levels, general measures such as industry regulation, environmental protection and taxation policy will significantly influence the growth of tourism.

The nature and scope of governmental regulatory and legislative powers will depend on the national political system within which a government is situated. In Western nations, the level of government regulation of tourism is a major issue for the private sector which often calls for deregulation, increased competition, and for free market forces to be allowed a full rein. As Bramham *et al.* (1989b, pp.2–3) have noted with respect to leisure policy in Western European cities:

> The particular model of welfare policy adopted in the liberal democracies of Western Europe varies considerably, but together they represent instruments to mediate unequal market opportunities in access to consumption services, such as education, housing, medicine, cultural, and leisure provisions. In recent years welfare policies in much of Western Europe have been subject to attack, particularly from neoconservative governments which have proclaimed a renewed belief in the liberating power of the market.

The exception to this is, of course, when individual business operations, labour organisations or even industries feel threatened by competition, then the private sector often demands government intervention in order to protect business interests and/or employment. Undoubtedly, while the private sector recognises that government has a significant role to play in tourism development, particularly when it comes to the provision of infrastructure, marketing or research, the predominant global argument is that the industry must be increasingly deregulated. The comments of Wright (1988, pp.29, 33) are indicative of this approach: 'regulation must exist but in a greatly reduced form and must be supportive rather than prohibitive . . . All unnecessary regulations must be removed to enable industry to operate successfully in the highly competitive world tourism arena.' Perhaps the greatest advocates for a reduced level of government regulation of the tourism industry are peak industry bodies who represent the interests of significant sections of the industry. For example, the Australian Tourism Industry Association in their *Tourism 2000 Strategy* document demanded that the various Australian federal and state governments reduce impediments to tourism development: 'The problem is that governments get in the way. They over-regulate industry. The industry requires them to get out of the way, in the national interest—if not their own' (cited in Wright, 1988, p.31). However, while governments face demands from most of the tourism industry for deregulation, governments themselves have simultaneously called for increased regulation of tourism. Probably the most prominent source of demands for tourism industry regulation is from the environmental lobby (Bramwell and Lane, 1993).

As tourism is an industry predominantly driven by the private sector, tourism development decisions by enterprises must be geared to function at a profit, resulting 'in preference for investment in profit centres (such as swimming pools) rather than in cost centres (such as sewage systems) . . . Mitigation protection programmes will receive lower priorities, unless there is an opportunity for profit generation or a legislative imperative forcing such investment' (McKercher, 1993, p.10). Therefore, 'the very nature of the tourism industry makes voluntary compliance with environmental programmes virtually impossible' (McKercher, 1993, p.10), thereby creating a regulatory vacuum in which government must operate in order to establish clear environmental guidelines. Although the relationship between tourism and the environment has the potential to be symbiotic, control of undesirable tourism activities becomes essential if certain aspects of the environment are to be protected from tourists and associated facilities. Environmental lobbyists, particularly in environmentally sensitive areas such as national parks or the coastal zone, will often seek the extension of government regulation to ensure that tourism remains 'controlled'. The regulatory conflict does not so much exist over whether controls should be in place, but over what the nature of the controls should be. Industry often seeks to place the locus of control on itself, to be self-regulating, while environmentalists will typically seek to have control placed in a government body, such as an environmental protection authority, which is distinct from the tourism industry.

Government as entrepreneur

Government has long served an entrepreneurial function in tourism. According to Pearce (1992, p.11), 'because of the scale of development and the element of the common good, provision of infrastructure is a widely accepted task of public authorities and one which can greatly facilitate tourist development and selectively direct it to particular areas.' However, governments may not only provide basic infrastructure such as roads and sewage, but may also own and operate tourist ventures including airlines, hotels and travel companies. For example, in order to maximise indigenous control of tourism resources and economic returns, the government of Vanuatu established its own airline, Air Vanuatu, in 1981, thereby securing its own international air services. More recently it acquired a major shareholding in a local tour and sightseeing operator, Tour Vanuatu, to further indigenous employment in the tourism industry (Hall, C., 1994a). While in many developing countries the role of government in tourism is relatively unquestioned because of the need to maximise scarce economic resources, in Western countries the direct entrepreneurial role of government in tourism is undergoing revision, given the need to reduce foreign debt and to encourage greater private sector participation in what is essentially a private sector area. For example, since the mid-1980s the former New Zealand Tourist and Publicity Department (NZTP) has undergone massive restructuring which has meant a reduction in staff, disposal of its travel offices as the 'government moved out of commercial tourist operations', the sale of hotel corporation properties, and the privatisation of the national carrier, Air New Zealand (Pearce, 1992, p.166).

In the former state socialist countries of Eastern Europe and south-east Asia all tourist resources were owned by the state. However, the former state tourism bureaucracies are increasingly being dismantled in order to encourage tourism development, improve the quality of tourist services by creating competition, maximise employment opportunities, encourage entrepreneurship, gain foreign currency and reduce the level of national debt (Hall, D., 1991a). For example, the Civil Aviation Administration of China (CAAC) announced in November 1988 that it would be broken up into six regional state-owned airlines in order to encourage competition and to maximise economic returns from the growing domestic and international travel market (Tisdell and Wen, 1991).

The role of the state (government) as entrepreneur in tourist development is closely related to the concept of the 'devalorisation of capital' (Damette, 1980). This is the process by which the state subsidises part of the cost of production, for instance by assisting in the provision of infrastructure or by investing in a tourism project where private venture capital is otherwise unavailable. In this process what would have been private costs are transformed into public or social costs. The provision of infrastructure, particularly transport networks, is regarded as crucial to the development of tourist destinations. There are numerous formal and informal means for government at all levels to assist in minimising the costs of production for tourism developers. Indeed, the offer of government assistance for development is often used to encourage private investment in a particular region or tourist project, for instance through the provision of cheap land or government-backed low-interest loans (Hall, C., 1991).

Stimulation

According to Mill and Morrison (1985) governments can stimulate tourism in three ways. The first way is financial incentives such as low-interest loans or a depreciation allowance on tourist accommodation. However, 'in general terms for both developed and developing countries their introduction often reflected both the scarcity of domestic investment funds and widespread ambition to undertake economic development programmes' (Bodlender and Davies, 1985, p.3, in Pearce, 1992, p.11). The second possibility is sponsoring research for the general benefit of the tourism industry rather than for specific individual organisations and associations. Thirdly, tourism can be stimulated by marketing, promotion and visitor servicing, generally aimed at generating tourism demand, although it can also take the form of investment promotion aimed at encouraging capital investment for tourism attractions and facilities. According to Middleton (1988) marketing and promotion are the dominant functions of national tourist administrations, that is 'the authorities in the central state administration, or other official organization, in charge of tourism development at the national level' (World Tourism Organization, 1979, in Pearce, 1992, p.7). Tourism demand generation has been one of the primary areas in which governments at all levels have had a high profile (Ascher, 1982) although, given demands for smaller government in Western society in recent years, there have been increasing demands from government and economic rationalists for greater self-sufficiency by industry in tourism marketing and promotion

(Jeffries, 1989). The political implications of such an approach for the tourism industry are substantial. As Hughes (1984, p.14) noted, 'The advocates of a free enterprise economy would look to consumer freedom of choice and not to governments to promote firms; the consumer ought to be sovereign in decisions relating to the allocation of the nation's resources.' Such an approach means that lobbyists in the tourism industry may achieve more by shifting their focus on the necessity of government intervention to issues of externalities, public goods and merit wants rather than employment and the balance of payments. 'Such criteria for government intervention have a sounder economic base and are more consistent with a free-enterprise philosophy than employment and balance of payments effects' (Hughes, 1984, p.18).

Tourism promotion by government agencies has developed because of the perceived need to promote destinations and establish a distinct destination identity and image in the market-place. However, as Pearce (1992, p.8) has recognised, 'general destination promotion tends to benefit all sectors of the tourist industry in the place concerned; it becomes a "public good". . . The question of "freeloaders" thus arises, for they too will benefit along with those who may have contributed directly to the promotional campaign.' The public good argument has been used by industry representatives in New Zealand to justify continued government responsibility for tourist promotion. The New Zealand Business Round Table and the New Zealand Tourism Industry Federation (1990, p.8, in O'Fallon, 1992, p.11) argued that individual operators would not be likely to be able to 'capture a sufficient return to justify their own promotional expenditure overseas because too much leakage of the benefits to rival firms would occur . . . international promotion is seen as having a strong public good element in it.' The continued support for government sponsorship of tourism promotion around the world has also been justified by the argument that the tourist industry should be 'rewarded' for the income it brings into the economy and specifically to government through taxation (Jeffries, 1989; O'Fallon, 1992).

One of the more unusual features of tourism promotion by government tourism organisations is that these have only limited control over the product they are marketing, with very few actually owning the goods, facilities and services that make up the tourism product (Pearce, 1992). This lack of control is perhaps testimony to the power of the public good argument used by industry to justify continued maintenance of government funding for destination promotion. However, it may also indicate the political power of the tourism lobby (e.g. Craik, 1990) to influence government tourism policies.

Social tourism

Social tourism can be defined as 'the relationships and phenomena in the field of tourism resulting from participation in travel by economically weak or otherwise disadvantaged elements of society' (Hunzinger, quoted in Murphy, 1985, p.23). Social tourism involves the extension of the benefits of holidays to economically marginal groups, such as the unemployed, low-income households, single-parent families, pensioners and the handicapped. The International Bureau of Social Tourism defines social tourism as 'the totality of relations and phenomena deriving from the participation in tourism of those social groups with modest incomes—participation which is made possible or facilitated by measures of a well defined social character' (Haulot, 1981, p.208).

According to Murphy (1985, p.24), 'Social tourism has become a recognized component and legitimate objective for modern tourism. By extending the physical and psychological benefits of rest and travel to less fortunate people it can be looked upon as a form of preventative medicine.' European governments have had a long tradition of providing holidays for the disadvantaged, for example those provided by the Swiss Travel Saving Fund. Indeed, in the case of Switzerland it could be argued that their national tourism policy is heavily influenced by principles of social tourism. The overriding principle of Swiss tourism policy is 'that tourism is a vital attribute of a healthy and sane society' (Gilg, 1988, p.139), with national tourism policy identifying social, economic and environmental objectives for tourism:

> Global Objective: 'To guarantee optimal satisfaction of the needs of tourists and individuals from all walks of life in effectively grouped facilities and keeping the environment healthy'
>
> Partial Objectives:
> Social Objective: 'Create the best possible social conditions for both tourist and locals'
> Economic Objective: 'Encourage a tourist industry that is both competitive and efficient'

Environmental Objective: 'To ensure the relaxing quality of both natural and man-made countryside'.
(Commission Consultative Fédérale pour le Tourisme, 1979, p.60, in Gilg, 1988, p.139)

However, the Swiss situation is perhaps unique within the Western European tourism policy environment. In recent years, with government cutbacks on welfare expenditure and perhaps also because of perceptions that social tourism carries the hallmarks of socialist ideologies, the level of Western European government support for social tourism has diminished.

Undoubtedly, state-sponsored tourism was a central element of the perspective on leisure activities adopted by the former state socialist countries of Eastern Europe. Under the state socialist nations, 'Domestic tourism . . . was often a major social or welfare role of trade unions, although other organisations and individual arrangements played an important part' (Hall, D., 1991c, p.49). Within the former state socialist countries, tourism was seen as a form of creative leisure and served a socio-economic function by restoring the health and well-being of the industrial workers through youth camps, holiday homes, educational tourism, trade union sponsored tourism and subsidised holidays (Hall, D., 1991d). For example, in Poland (Ostrowski, 1986, 1987) and the former Czechoslovakia, the main social function of tourism was seen as the 'reproduction of the physical and mental forces of the working population' (Demek and Strída, 1971, in Carter, 1991a, p.161).

In Romania tourism was regarded as central to a 'multilaterally developed socialist society' (Turnock, 1991, p.209). In Romania tourism under state socialism was also contrasted with that of the capitalist West, the collectivism of socialist man overcoming the individualism of tourism in Western nations. Therefore, in Romania tourism often had an educational element with workers being encouraged to examine global issues and the possible relationship of tourism to alpinism and health in state communist countries (Turnock, 1991). Similarly, in the former German Democratic Republic (East Germany) tourism served an important ideological function for the state with 'the considerable emphasis on group recreation and holidays in accommodation provided by the workplace or trade union. . . designed to build social coherence and an esprit-de-corps, besides allowing recreation time to be mixed with political indoctrination' (Mellor, 1991, p.149). The size of such state support for tourism was substantial, leading to relatively high rates of domestic travel: 'Under the old regime, well over half the east German population, perhaps as high as three-quarters, made at least one holiday visit each other year, usually of the order of 10–14 days' (Mellor, 1991, p.149).

Now that there has been a shift from state socialist to mixed economies in Eastern Europe, the former welfare function of tourism in those countries has been severely undermined as scarce financial resources have been shifted to more immediate social and economic concerns (Hall, D., 1991a). The changed circumstances of Eastern Europe have also perhaps led to suspicion by Western governments of the ideological functions of state tourism. Nevertheless, perhaps social tourism should be seen within a more universal perspective on the nature of human rights. As Haulot (1981, p.212) has so admirably stated: 'Social tourism . . . finds justification in that its individual and collective objectives are consistent with the view that all measures taken by modern society should ensure more justice, more dignity and improved enjoyment of life for all citizens.'

Government as interest protector

The final role that government plays in tourism is that of interest protector. Although not tourism specific, such a role may have major implications for the nature of tourism development. The defence of local interests has traditionally occupied much government activity, particularly as government has had the role of balancing various interest and values in order to meet national, rather than narrow, sectional interests, such as that of a specific industry like tourism. This is, of course, not to deny that interests are not represented within the structure of government. 'Statutory authorities and a myriad of state agencies were established to protect sectional groups, to represent key interests in the policy process, and to protect the social order via welfare provisions to many sections of business and society in general' (Davis et al., 1993, p.26). Nevertheless, tourism policy needs to be considered as potentially subsumed beneath a broader range of government economic, social, welfare and environmental policies. Ideally, policy decisions will reflect a desire to meet the interests of the relevant level of government, i.e. national, provincial/state or local, rather than the sectionally defined interests of the tourism industry.

GOVERNMENT AND TOURISM POLICY

The above discussion has illustrated the diverse ways in which government is involved in tourism. Lickorish *et al.* (1991, p.64) have identified two roles of government in tourism policy formulation: first, active, 'a deliberate action by government introduced to favour the tourism sector'; second, passive, 'government undertakes an action which may have implications for tourism, but is not specifically intended to favour or influence tourism development.' Such a distinction, while perhaps simple in terms of distinguishing between policy outcomes, does not indicate the complexity of either tourism policy or the nature of the tourism policy-making process.

Policy analysis is 'concerned with understanding and explaining the substance of policy content and policy decisions and the way in which policy decisions are made' (Barrett and Fudge, 1981, p.6), where public policy is the 'structure or confluence of values or behaviour involving a governmental prescription' (Kroll, 1969, p.9). This definition of policy is broad enough to distinguish 'between that which is stated, that which is implied, that which is perceived, and that which is done' (Aucion, 1971, in Mitchell, 1979, p.295) in the tourism policy process.

Much of the commentary on tourism policy is essentially prescriptive in nature (see Chapter 1). For example, Lickorish *et al.* (1991, p.67) argue that 'What is required is an acceptance of the notion that tourism policy must include considerations of economic and non-economic factors, international and domestic tourism, and that without agreed aims and objectives, formal development planning is likely to be uncoordinated and unsatisfactory', and go on to state that 'The optimisation of tourism's potential contribution is clearly linked to the need to: 1. Develop objectives for the tourism sector, and 2. Formulate a policy to implement those objectives' (Lickorish *et al.* 1991, p.70). From a managerial perspective such statements may have some pertinence and most people reading this book will probably agree with them. However, they give no indication of the political environment and the policy process which must be encountered to give such statements effect in the real-world of tourism policy making.

Unfortunately, the contemporary discussion of tourism policy development, apart from some notable exceptions (e.g. Richter,

1989; Greenwood, Williams and Shaw, 1990), has failed to illustrate the political dimensions of tourism policy and the action or implementation of policies in the form of specific tourism developments. Most writing on tourism policy has instead concentrated on government tourism organisations and their actions. Nevertheless, such a perspective is inadequate to explain the nature and pattern of tourism policy formulation or outcomes. As Freedman (1976, pp.446–7) observed:

> To view organisations as unitary wholes with consistent objectives may be to neglect the dynamics of organisational life. In particular, it may gloss over the shifting patterns of interest of groups that make up the organisation . . . what is downgraded is the power structure, a limited set of groups and individuals all concerned in some way with a specific policy-making process. Thus the outputs of the policy-making process can be said to reflect the relative strengths of those involved, so that stability in a power structure will result in a certain stability of policy . . . If the policy output appears to have a coherence and substantive context that might justify the description 'rational', then this reflects the ability of a particular group to dominate proceedings.

To argue that the formulation of tourism policy at an organisational level is not influenced by various interests and values is to also ignore that government involvement in tourism is political. As Held and Krieger (1984, p.18) noted, 'State power expresses at once the intentions and purposes of government and state personnel (they could have acted differently) and the parameters set by the institutionalized context of state–society relations.' Therefore, the next section will discuss the nature of tourism policy analysis and identify some of the key elements which determine the direction of tourism development and tourism policy formulation.

THE ANALYSIS OF TOURISM POLICY

Public policy is troublesome as a research focus because of its inherent complexity, 'specifically because of the temporal nature of the process, the multiplicity of participants and of policy provisions, and the contingent nature of theoretical effects' (Greenberg et al., 1977, p.1532). As Lyden, Shipman and Kroll (1969, p.156–157) observed:

Altogether the realistic working assumption is that a public decision is an amalgam of a variety of contributions—public attitudes amongst them—fed into a network of social interactions. The interaction path rarely shows a constant, unchanging structure; instead it develops, evolves, and changes shape and form over time. One of the primary reasons why the public policy process has always appeared to be such a mystery to many people is this fluidity, this refusal to remain within the confines of institutional structures designed to deal with public issues.

This situation has given rise to a wide and diverse body of theory. As Jenkins (1978, p.ix) noted, 'the study of policy has become an interdisciplinary field, [however] popularisation of the field has not led to a great deal of theoretical cohesion . . . interpretations . . . may differ sharply depending on the pedigree of the analyst.' Different models exist to interpret the same events, leading in many cases to different conclusions (Allison, 1971; Fagence, 1979).

The majority of references to policy and decision making in the tourism literature have tended to utilise a prescriptive model which demonstrates how tourism policy and decision making should occur relative to pre-established standards (e.g. Sessa, 1976; Murphy, 1985; Gunn, 1988; see Chapter 1). The prescriptive-rational approach assumes that a dichotomy exists between the policy-making process and administration and the existence of 'Economic Man [sic]', whereby individuals can 'identify and rank goals, values and objectives', and can choose consistently among them after having collected all the necessary data and system-atically evaluating them (Mitchell, 1979, p.296). This 'scientific' or 'rational' approach to policy analysis, management and adminis-tration is centred on two objects, 'to discover . . . what government can properly and successfully do', and 'how can it get to do these things with the utmost possible efficiency and at the least possible cost either of money or of energy' (Wilson, 1941, p.481). Prescrip-tive or rational approaches to the analysis of tourism policy may be useful in distinguishing certain characteristics of human behaviour, although they cannot fully explain the richness and complexity of the policy-making process. Prescriptive models serve as a guide towards specific ideals. However, such ideals cannot be reached without an understanding of what actually does happen in the formulation and implementation of tourism policy.

Descriptive models of policy making, through their emphasis on the policy-making *process*, represent a refutation of the rational, policy/administration dichotomy that characterises prescriptive approaches to policy analysis. 'Without process, the mainstream [rational] model is static . . . Without process, there is no attention to the complex and uncertain character of relationships . . . without process the mainstream model is unintelligible: we simply cannot grasp how one element is mystically transformed into another' (Munns, 1975, pp.649–650). Similarly, Jenkins (1978, p.16) argued, 'for many process is a central, if not the central, focus, to the extent that they argue that a conceptual understanding of the policy process is fundamental to an analysis of public policy.' Therefore, for the descriptive analysis of tourism policy:

> to explain policy maintenance and policy change, one needs to explore the socio-political conditions in which the political system operates, examining in particular the extent to which outputs are conditioned by external influences. Thus . . . the vital task of the policy analyst is to explore the links between the environment, the political system and policy outputs and impacts. (Jenkins, 1978, pp.26–27)

'Policy making typically involves a pattern of action *over time* and involving *many decisions*' (Anderson, 1975, p.10). Much consideration of the policy process has been in terms of an adapted input–output model of the political system derived from the work of Easton (1957, 1965). The focus of Easton's approach is the dynamics and processes of a political system operating in its policy environment (Figure 2.1). The model differentiates between:

1. *Policy demands*: demands for action arising from inside and outside the political system.
2. *Policy decisions*: authoritative rather than routine decisions by the political authorities.
3. *Policy outputs*: what the system does, thus, while goods and services (such as tourism) are the most tangible outputs, the concept is not restricted to this.
4. *Policy outcomes* (or *impacts*): consequences intended or unintended resulting from political action or inaction.

The four components of the policy-making process relative to specific tourism policy issues are indicated in Figure 2.2. Each particular policy development should also be set within the context of a policy arena in which interest groups (e.g. industry associations, conservation groups and community groups), institutions

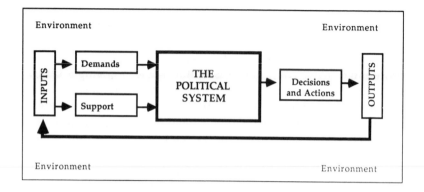

Figure 2.1. Easton's simplified model of the political system. Source: Easton, 1965, p.32, reproduced by permission of the University of Chicago Press

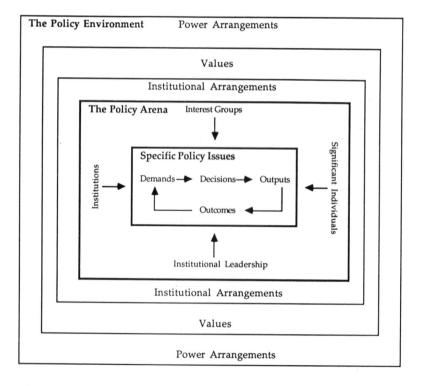

Figure 2.2. Elements in the tourism policy-making process

(e.g. government departments and agencies responsible for tourism), significant individuals (e.g. high profile industry representatives) and the institutional leadership (e.g. Ministers responsible for the tourism portfolio and senior members of government departments) interact and compete in determining tourism policy choices. However, in highlighting the competing aspirations of the actors within the policy-making process one is also forced to recognise the existence of the broader environment within which policy making occurs and which includes institutional arrangements, values and power arrangements.

As noted in Chapter 1, when selecting certain tourism policies, decision makers are also choosing between different sets of values. Therefore, government bodies delegated the task of regulating and determining the nature of tourism development are involved in the process of value choice.

Values are 'ends, goals, interests, beliefs, ethics, biases, attitudes, traditions, morals and objectives that change with human perception and with time, and that have a significant influence on power conflicts relating to policy' (Henning, 1974, p.15) and have received increasing attention in the study of tourism development, particularly as regards 'sustainable' or 'appropriate' tourism (e.g. Richter, 1989; Hall, C., 1991; Bramwell and Lane, 1993). Much tourism policy only stresses the benefits of tourism rather than the potential negative impacts. As Shaw, Greenwood and Williams (1988, p.172) observed in the British situation, 'it is an oft-repeated dictum that government policy towards tourism in the United Kingdom is at best nebulous, in the sense that little official policy actually exists save to emphasise that "tourism is a good thing"'. Nevertheless, 'there is a need . . . to look not just at tourism but at the opportunity costs of its development, and the alternative strategies which could be pursued by a region or community' (Williams and Shaw, 1988b, p.238). However, in order to assess the selection of potential tourism development alternatives, the significance of the power arrangements which determine policy selection must be recognised.

A consideration of actors and the system of constraints that impinges upon these actors is central to an understanding of the behaviour and performance of tourism organisations. Indeed, Crozier (1964, p.107) argued that 'the behaviour and attitudes of people and groups within an organisation cannot be explained without reference to the power relationships existing among them.'

Similarly, Crenson (1971, pp.156–157) noted, 'political issues have an organizational aspect'. Hence attempts to connect the *substance* of tourism policy to the *process* of tourism policy making 'require the adoption of analytical techniques that merge organisational analysis with policy analysis' (Jenkins, 1978, p.47). Therefore the study of power arrangements is a vital part of the analysis of tourism policy because power governs the interaction of individuals, organisations and agencies influencing, or trying to influence, the formulation of tourism policy and the manner in which it is implemented. In the case of British tourism policy, for example, 'the agenda for tourism is largely covert in the sense that it is made at sub-governmental level and implemented by private sector operations largely divorced from these structures' (Shaw, Greenwood and Williams, 1988, p.174). One is forced to recognise that in the development of tourism policy certain issues may be suppressed or interests ignored, relationships between individuals and agencies may be altered, or inaction may be the order of the day (Nozick, 1972).

The fragmented structure of the tourism industry makes it harder to form a strong lobby to encourage government to formulate policies in favour of the industry (Wanhill, 1987). In Australia and the United States (see below) relatively strong industry-based interest groups have been able to exert reasonable influence on government policy. However, in the case of tourism in Thailand, for example, the fractured nature of the tourism industry has lessened its ability to lobby government for the allocation of resources in comparison with other industry groups. According to Elliot (1987, p.225), 'tourism does not have the power of the military or organized agriculture groups to endanger governments or the ambitions of politicians. Its influence is lessened because it is not a large industry in terms of number of people involved, nor is it well organized or an influential lobby group.' Indeed, it was economic imperatives rather than any intrinsic power base for tourism that has led the Thai government to embrace tourism as a tool for economic development:

> It is the nature of governments to respond to powerful pressures. Tourism does not have such power, and therefore it has been given minimal real support and subject to almost benign neglect. Now, because of strong economic pressures, the role and input of the Thai government is becoming more dynamic and responsive. (Elliot, 1987, p.225)

INTERESTS, POWER AND TOURISM DEVELOPMENT

An indication of the role that power plays in tourism development was provided by a study of recreational tourism on three coastal communities in North Carolina: Bath, Oriental and Harkers Island. Peck and Lepie (1989, p.203) examined the hypothesis 'that both the rate (magnitude and speed) of development and the amount of community involvement and control (power) over the change would affect the amount and distribution of payoffs and tradeoffs associated with increased tourism.' Power was defined as including the ownership of land, financial sourcing, input from local people, and the relation of local traditions to tourism development projects. From an examination of tourism development in the three communities the authors developed a typology of touristic development which related rates of growth to the allocation of power and the respective trade-offs which each community made (Table 2.2). Peck and Lepie (1989, p.221) argued that the differentiating factor in determining the positive or negative impact of tourism development on the host community was the source of regulatory power, 'that is, whether or not the host community had access to that power.' For example, in the case of the town of Oriental they noted that the impact of new-comers on traditional lines of authority can cause resentment towards tourism development. Such a conclusion is significant because it illustrates the need for tourism planners to consider the allocation of power among the range of interests involved in the tourism development process.

While the factors leading to certain patterns of tourism development may be somewhat difficult to determine in community tourism studies, more 'open' procedures of tourism policy formation have emerged in recent years in Western countries with the establishment of committees or commissions of inquiry (Craik, 1990). Such inquiries may provide valuable insights into the nature of the policy-making process and the relative 'power' of participants and interest groups in the process.

In 1988–89 the Australian Industries Assistance Commission (IAC) conducted an inquiry into travel and tourism in Australia. 'Public submissions were invited to advise the IAC about aspects of the industry and about its national context. Unfortunately, little of this input was evident in the Final Report' (Craik, 1990). The IAC (1989) received a large number of submissions on the

Table 2.2. Typology of touristic development

Rate of Change	Power Basis	Payoffs and Tradeoffs
Rapid Growth	• 'Bedroom' communities • Summer residents • Specialized commerce (outside financing)	• Rapid change of local norms • New power structure and economy
Slow Growth	• Individual developments • Local ownership • Expanding local commerce (local financing)	• Slow change of norms • Stable power structure • Expanding local economy
Transient Development	• Pass-throughs • Weekenders • Seasonal entrepreneurs (local financing)	• Stable norms • Individual mobility within power structure and economy • Little overall change in local economy

Source: Peck and Lepie, 1989, p.204, reproduced by permission of the University of Pennsylvania Press

Australian tourism industry with particular reference to the environmental and social impacts of tourism as well as a number of industry submissions (Table 2.3). However, in a classic example of clientelism, the conclusions of the report were closely allied to the submissions of the government departments, industry associations and the Australian Tourism Industry Association (ATIA), the peak industry body. The latter appeared to have substantial influence. The extent of the clientelism and the apparent political weight of sections of the tourism industry can be gleaned from the changes which took place between the draft report and the release of the final report. According to Craik (1990):

> recommendations in the Draft Report, concerning questions of industry incentives, tax conditions and the principle of 'user pays', were significantly revised or renounced in the Final Report after intensive industry lobbying. The biggest about-face concerned the future of the Australian Tourist Commission, the federally-funded promotion body. Whereas the draft Report recommended that funding be phased out over five years and national promotion be

Table 2.3. Breakdown of submissions to the Industries Assistance Commission inquiry into travel and tourism

Source of Submission	No. of Submittees	No. of Submissions
Government		
Federal	24	46
State	15	24
Local/Regional	8	11
Other	3	5
Sub-total	50	86
Private Sector		
Peak Bodies	18	40
Regional Associations	12	15
Transport & Travel	21	33
Accommodation	16	16
Other	30	34
Sub-total	97	138
Public Submissions		
Conservation Groups	15	24
Community Groups	7	8
Educational Institutions	9	11
Unions	4	4
Individuals	35	36
Sub-total	70	83
Total	217	297

Source: Industries Assistance Commission, 1989, pp.B1–B5.

taken over by the private sector, the Final Report quoted an ATIA submission almost verbatim recommending that funding continue and be reviewed in five years time.

The degree to which the IAC met the needs of ATIA is also witnessed in the change of tune by Sir Frank Moore, Chairman of ATIA, towards the inquiry. At the beginning of the inquiry, he denounced it as a 'Treasury stooge' wanting to impose further taxes on the tourism industry. 'After the final report, he declared that the tourist industry welcomed attention from the IAC because it was "neutral" and had "no pre-conceived ideas". The IAC was, he said "dispassionate", "divorced from self-interest", and had a "balanced view of industry"' (Craik, 1990).

The conflict between interest groups in tourism policy formulation was most clearly seen in this instance in concerns over social and environmental issues. Social issues received two pages of discussion in the final report, while the issue of the environment was assigned the penultimate chapter. However, the report examined such issues purely in terms of land use and competing users and uses, and failed to deal adequately with non-economic factors. Longer-term social and environmental concerns were, therefore, all but ignored in the final report. According to Craik (1990), 'ATIA now regards the IAC Report as "the bible of the industry". Others see it as a blueprint that endorses narrow self-interests at the expense of public interests.' In terms relevant to the above discussion of the relationship between policies and values, she concluded, 'It is high time that the "too hard" basket of cultural and environmental factors was restored to a central place in the process of policy analysis and not just occasionally sampled as a humanist afterthought.'

One further example of the value of examining tourism policy formulation within the framework of power, values, institutional arrangements and interests discussed above is the study by Hayes (1981) of the influence of the United States Congressional Travel and Tourism Caucus (TTC) on American national tourism policy. The TTC provides a network for the channelling of information from the tourism industry, political negotiations, and the formation of compromises in legislative decision making. It also acts as a mechanism for industry to influence policies which affect their interests. Hayes (1981, p.132) concluded that the TTC 'with more than 250 members—the largest informal group in the House—the Caucus' enjoyed 'a broad base of support, its "sphere of influence" radiating in many directions.'

The influence of the TTC operated in two main directions. First, it established relationships with institutional actors such as the House Transportation and Commerce Subcommittee and the Department of Transportation. Second, it achieved the passage of relevant legislation, such as a national tourism policy, or the defeat of legislation which would harm tourism industry interests, such as a plan for gasoline rationing. In both cases the Caucus served to further the interests of sections of the tourism industry through its congressional activities (Hayes, 1981).

The TTC is also subject to lobbying from private sector tourist interests. The size of industry influence is substantial. Airey (1984, p.271) noted that 'most airlines, hotel companies and bus operators etc maintain full-time Washington DC representation. In addition, in 1981, 22 travel-related trade associations had headquarters in the capital. Seven had Washington-based government relations offices, and 11 were represented there by law or public relations firms.' Furthermore, the political influence of the tourism industry on Congressmen and the Administration is also translated into the provision of political funds. 'In the 1979/80 elections a total of 62 travel industry political action committees disbursed over $1.5 million to candidates' (Airey, 1984, p.271).

The above three examples of tourism policy making are useful case studies of the manner in which tourism policy or tourism development decisions are actually made. However, they are rarities in the study of tourism. As noted in Chapter 1, appropriate tourism policy decisions are dependent on a knowledge of how such decisions are made in the real world of policy and how they are, in turn, implemented. It therefore becomes vital, if students of tourism are to contribute to improvements in the tourism policy-making process, that further studies are undertaken which illustrate how policies are made and whose interests they favour.

TOURISM, THE STATE AND TOURISM POLICY

> Tourism is, by now, too important and pervasive an activity for governments to ignore. Any government that accepts a degree of responsibility for the pattern and pace of economic activity of its country must be conscious of the emergence of the 'post-industrial society' or 'service economy' and for the need to meet the new challenges of such changes. (Hughes, 1984, p.19)

This chapter has provided an overview of the relationship between the state and tourism, the different types of government involvement in tourism, and the nature of tourism policy making. It has been noted that the institutions of the state provide the framework within which tourism operates. Unfortunately, the activities and role of the state have been ignored in much contemporary tourism research, although recent studies (e.g. Bramham *et al.*, 1989a; Urry, 1990a; Britton, 1991; Roche, 1992) are starting to redress this situation. More attention has been given to the role of government in tourism. However, even here good case study material is relatively scarce (see Williams and Shaw, 1988a; Richter, 1989; Hall, D., 1991a; Pearce, 1992). Therefore, most of the discussion of tourism policy making has tended to concentrate on what government should do rather than examining the manner in which decisions have actually been made. While prescriptive policy studies do have some utility, they do not highlight the political dimensions of tourism, nor ask the critical questions of whose interests and values are being served by particular policy settings.

Undoubtedly, tourism policy making is a complex phenomenon, but that should not deter students of tourism from examining it. Indeed, it is essential that the 'real world' of policy analysis is analysed if improvements are to be made to tourism management and planning and if sustainable and appropriate forms of tourism are to be encouraged. Tourism analysts must be forced to recognise the 'questions of political theory and political values' which 'underlie explicitly or implicitly, public policy decisions' (Stillman, 1974, pp.49–50). Different analytical frameworks contain different strengths and weaknesses, and the analyst chooses between theoretical approaches in order to attack issues of policy. Nevertheless, by focusing on critical elements in the tourism policy-making process, such as institutional arrangements, power, actors, interests and values, it should be possible to improve our current poor understanding of the formulation and implementation of tourism policy and the various activities of the state in tourism development.

3

International Tourism Policy and International Relations

International tourism is political, since the state must be involved in foreign relations, the expenditure of large quantities of capital, and large scale planning. (Crick, 1989, p.320)

INTRODUCTION: INTERNATIONAL TOURISM AND INTERNATIONAL RELATIONS

By its increasingly international nature, tourism is inseparable from the field of international relations. Tourism is as much an aspect of foreign policy as it is a commercial activity, and the global tourism infrastructure now forms an important component of international relations (Mowlana and Smith, 1990). 'To admit foreign visitors and to facilitate their travel within a nation's borders is a political action. It is also an action which, to some extent, is bound to have an impact on domestic politics' (Edgell, 1978, p.171). The political relationship between nations, and the policies of nations towards foreign nationals travelling to, from and within their country, are essential to an understanding of contemporary tourism. As Urry (1990a, p.48) observed, the 'internationalisation of tourism means that we cannot explain tourist patterns in any particular society without analysing developments taking place in other countries.'

The encouragement of travel flows between nations may be evidence of a positive political relationship. For example, travel was encouraged between the former state socialist nations of Eastern Europe in order to support notions of communist solidarity. Conversely, travel flows between nations may be suspended if political relations are poor. For example, the prohibition since the early 1960s on Americans wishing to travel direct to Cuba, or the dramatic fall in American travel to the Soviet Union following the invasion of Afghanistan and the shooting down of flight KAL 007 by Soviet jet fighters. Restrictions in travel flows may be deliberately imposed in order to further political objectives:

> While tourism may be a relatively risk-free weapon by which superpowers vent their displeasure with each other, the time is rapidly approaching when travel trade restrictions on the part of one country may in fact constitute an act of war against a small nation heavily dependent on the tourist trade. In some geographic regions, like the Caribbean, this is already the case. Cuba, Jamaica (under Manley), Nicaragua, and even Grenada discovered that the United States as a government has considerable leverage over the tourism industry. Add to that the US travel industry's clout, particularly in terms of airlines and hotels. The result for small destinations is a formidable combination. (Richter, 1984, p.614)

Travel flows between nations may also encourage economic interdependence. However, the uneven flow of tourists in developed countries to Third World regions has also been criticised for creating economic dependence (Britton, 1982b). However, from the perspective of the tourism-generating country such dependence may be politically useful, as it may create conditions for influencing the foreign policy of the host country (Edgell, 1978; Francisco, 1983). Matthews (1978, p.79) has put this kind of dependency argument in the following terms (see also Chapter 5):

> The intermingled foreign policies of metropolitan governments and their own corporations lead to suspicions within developing countries that corporate tourism has hidden motives. Profit is the apparent goal of the corporation. Political influences exercised through those companies by parent governments causes fears that tourism has become a means of political and economic domination of host countries. This influence often is interpreted as direct. That is, metropolitan diplomacy in host countries is highly focused upon the welfare of the metropolitan business in those states.

While concerns over dependency may lead to conflicts between nations, tourism is also seen as a mechanism to achieve improved international harmony and act as a force for peace. The inherent logic of this is that the greater the contact between nations and cultures, the greater will be the level of international under-standing. The more cynical may argue that such a situation has not particularly helped in areas such as the former Yugoslavia. Nevertheless, tourism may be used as a mechanism to reinforce certain ideas and belief systems.

Despite the existence of a number of international tourist organisations, the most notable being the World Tourist Organiz-ation based in Madrid, Spain, there is 'little in the way of supranational regulation of tourism services' (Williams and Shaw, 1988b, p.231) except in the area of air transport. Tourism has received little attention in the General Agreement on Tariffs and Trade (GATT), although the overall liberalisation of the services area agreed to in the 1993 conclusion to the Uruguay Round of the GATT will undoubtedly have some spin-offs for tourism.

International tourism also has a distinct ideological component. For example, recent European Union interest in tourism has come about not only because of tourism's economic and employment potential, but also because it is seen as a means of reinforcing the process of Europeanisation (Airey, 1983; Lee, 1987; Pearce, 1988; Lickorish, 1991; Kearney, 1992). Similarly, tourism is a substantial part of the integration of Eastern Europe with the European Community and the development of economic and political linkages (Hall, D., 1991b).

Ideology may have a dramatic bearing on international travel. Many of the former state socialist countries of Eastern Europe had restrictions on travel both within the country and, especially, to Western nations for fear of ideological contamination. For example, there were substantial restrictions on Poles travelling to Czecho-slovakia during the 'Solidarity' period in the early 1980s for fear that they might spread many of the ideas of the Solidarity Union within the Czech state (Carter, 1991a). As Vuoristo (1981, p.241) commented with respect to travel in Eastern Europe in the 1970s and early 1980s, 'The ideological boundary is thus like a semi-permeable membrane: it allows penetration from one side but not from the other.' However, with the collapse of the state socialist systems in Eastern Europe, travel in that part of the world is rapidly shifting from being driven by state communist ideology to following the necessities of economic development and the expression of new foreign policies. In the case of Hungary, for example:

The downgrading of tourism from the countries that comprised Communist Eastern Europe until late 1989 has been deliberate as Hungary has positively sought to attract visitors from the West by relaxing bureaucratic and monetary constraints. Initially, the motive was the country's desperate need for hard currency, but it is now part of the process of political liberalisation and an assertion of Hungary's independence. (Compton, 1991, p.188)

The changes taking place in the European Community and Eastern Europe indicate the manner in which tourism is a substantial component of international relations. This chapter will examine the relationship with respect to four major issues. First, it will consider the manner in which tourism becomes part of international diplomacy, national foreign policy agendas and international trade. Examples of the implications of international tourism policies for tourism growth and development will be provided with reference to a number of countries, including Japan, Korea, the People's Republic of China (mainland China), the Republic of China (Taiwan) and the United States of America. The second issue is the way in which tourism may be utilised as a means to gain international legitimacy and respectability for authoritarian regimes; and the third, the manner in which tourism is used as a mechanism for making territorial claims. Fourthly, the chapter will address issues of whether or not tourism is a force for peace. This final section will also serve to introduce some of the issues which will be raised in the following chapter, which discusses the relationship between tourism and political stability and the implications for tourism of revolution, terrorism and political violence.

TOURISM, FOREIGN DIPLOMACY AND TRADE

The numbers and to a lesser extent nature, of tourist flows can be comprehensively influenced by administrative and bureaucratic controls and impositions. These can cover such areas as visa regulations, currency exchange controls and proscriptions, on tourist movements and activities. In other words, constraints may be imposed before, at and subsequent to the tourist's point of entry. (Hall, D., 1991c, p.53)

Since the Second World War tourism has become an important component of international diplomacy and foreign policy initiatives. The United Nations Conference on International Travel and

Tourism in Rome in 1963 highlighted the role of tourism in economic development and in improving international relations, with the conference considering 'that it is incumbent on governments to stimulate and coordinate national tourist activities' (1963, p.17). Despite the economic significance of tourism to many countries and to the global economy as a whole, the establishment of trade regimes for tourism has not had the high profile of the agricultural or manufacturing sectors. This is most probably because of tourism's position as a service industry and as an 'invisible' export or import in many countries' trade balances. As Williams and Shaw (1988c, p.2) stated, 'In most countries it is "statistically" invisible and usually, only the most obvious sectors or those devoted exclusively to tourists are enumerated in official tourism data. Inevitably, this tends to be the accommodation sector, and perhaps, cafés and restaurants.' Such a situation meant that for many years tourism was not taken seriously as a priority area for policy development. For example, in the case of the European Community, Kearney (1992, p.35) noted, 'European tourism has long suffered from the benign neglect of governments which have still to recognize its economic and social importance in modern economies increasingly dominated by the services sector.' Indeed, Lickorish (1991, p.179) argues that 'there has never been an explicit European tourism policy.' Similarly, Tuppen (1988, p.193) observed with respect to France, 'The attitude of the French government to tourist development is somewhat ambivalent. The fact that over time the minister responsible for tourism has been frequently moved from one ministry to another might indicate the relatively low priority accorded to this activity.' However, the growth of recognition in Western economies of service industries, including telecommunications and finance, for economic development and employment purposes has increased interest in tourism (McCoy, 1982). Indeed, the Uruguay round of the GATT, concluded in December 1993, gave substantial attention to mechanisms to encourage freer trade in the area of services.

International tourism trade issues are usually dealt with on either a bilateral or multilateral basis, although unilateral action may be taken by governments when they feel that their interests are being impeded. Many bilateral trade agreements relating to tourism are in the area of transport (e.g. air transport agreements) or investment (e.g. protection for foreign investment under most-favoured-nation status). Multilateral negotiations are often conducted under the auspices of international organisations. Three international trade organisations with an interest in tourism are the International Monetary Fund (IMF), the Organisation for Economic Cooperation and Development (OECD) and the General Agreement on Tariffs and Trade (GATT). Organisations with a more specific interest in tourism activities include the World Tourism Organization (WTO), the International Civil Aviation Organization (ICAO), the International Maritime Organization (IMO), the Customs Cooperation Council (CCC) and regional bodies such as the Tourism Council of the South Pacific (TCSP) and the Tourism Program of the Organization of American States. In examining obstacles to international travel and tourism, Ascher (1984, p.3) has identified a number of government-imposed restrictions which affect tourist trade:

- Government attention to tourism is focused more on promotion of inbound tourist business rather than on a more general approach that deals with reduction or removal of restrictions to tourism on a worldwide basis.
- Governments have not fully assessed the 'tourism impact' of their laws and regulations.
- Government policies concerning international relations— political, economic, monetary, financial—often conflict with, and override, tourism policy.
- For the most part, the international organizations that address problems of tourism deal with them mainly in piecemeal fashion and not with tourism as an integral unit.
- Although there is some coordination among international organizations on tourism matters, greater cooperation would improve their effectiveness.
- There is a lack of general, internationally accepted rules and principles for dealing with new problems as they arise, and of a mechanism for dispute settlement.

The Ad Hoc Working Party on Obstacles to International Tourism for the OECD's Committee on Tourism identified 40 specific obstacles to international travel and tourism in five different areas (Table 3.1): first, those affecting companies providing services to facilitate travel (e.g. travel agents); second, those affecting companies providing transportation (e.g. airlines, coach

Table 3.1. Types of obstacles to international tourism

I. Obstacles affecting the individual intending to travel

1. Imposed by the home country.
   a) Currency restrictions imposed upon residents.
   b) Conditions and procedures for issue of travel documents.
   c) Customs allowances for returning residents.
   d) Restrictions on overseas travel.

2. Imposed by the host country.
   a) Currency restrictions imposed upon visitors.
   b) Entry visas, identity documents, limitations on duration of stay.
   c) Formalities concerning entry of motor vehicles, pleasure boats or other craft.
   d) Formalities concerning applicability of drivers' licences, car insurance, etc.
   e) Restrictions on acquisition of property by non-nationals (e.g. holiday flats).
   f) Taxes on foreign visitors.

II. Obstacles affecting companies providing services to facilitate travel (e.g. travel agents, tour operators)

3. Limitations on foreign investment/equity participation.
4. Restrictions on the establishment of foreign owned entities (branches and subsidiaries).
5. Requirements for qualifications for operating professionally which are either directly discriminary or more difficult for non-nationals to acquire.
6. Restrictions on non-national personnel and employment (e.g. visas, work permits).
7. Difficulties in obtaining licences to operate.
8. Relevant restrictions on transfer of funds in and out of the country (not covered under *I* above).
9. Restrictions upon the ability of non-established foreign companies to solicit for custom, advertise or sell direct to clients without locally established intermediaries.
10. Distinction in EEC countries between EEC and non-EEC nationals with regard to the above items.

III. Obstacles affecting companies providing transportation (e.g. airlines, railways, coach operators, cruise liners)

11–18. Categories as under *II* (3–10)
19. Restrictions on non-national airlines, coach operators or cruise liners.
20. Limitations on movements of passengers by foreign airlines or cruise ships.
21. Discriminatory landing dues, taxes or port charges.

continued overleaf

Table 3.1. *(continued)*

22.	Lack of reciprocal recognition of qualifications (e.g. air crew, site guides, coach drivers).
23.	Requirements for government employees to use national airlines/ferry services.
24.	Discriminatory access to special terms from state enterprises (e.g. airlines, railways), including differential commissions.
25.	Limitations on access to reservation systems.

IV. Obstacles affecting companies providing reception facilities (e.g. hotels, resorts, car hire firms)

26–33.	Categories as under *II* (3–10).
34.	Restrictions on imports of essential goods.
35.	Requirements for placing of contracts (e.g. for site development) with local enterprises.
36.	Discriminatory tax regimes for foreign entrants (including tax holidays not available to nationals).
37.	Restrictions on ownership by non-nationals (e.g. leasing only permitted) and problems related to security of tenure or repatriation of investments.
38.	Limitation on access to reservation systems.

V. Other obstacles

39.	Discriminatory regulations on health inspection/consumer protection, etc.
40.	Compulsory use of centralized governmental/municipal organizations or middlemen.
41.	Others.

Source: Ad Hoc Working Party on Obstacles to International Tourism for the OECD's Committee on Tourism, in Ascher, 1984, 'Obstacles to International Travel and Tourism', *Journal of Travel Research*, vol. 22, p.14. The *Journal of Travel Research* is published by the Business Research Division at the University of Colorado at Boulder.

operators); third, those affecting companies providing reception facilities (e.g. hotels); fourth, obstacles affecting the individual intending to travel (e.g. currency restrictions, restrictions on overseas travel); and fifth, other obstacles such as discriminatory regulations (Ascher, 1984).

Obstacles to tourism can be further classified according to whether they constitute tariff or non-tariff barriers. Non-tariff barriers include travel allowance restrictions, restrictions on credit card use, limitations on duty-free allowances, and measures such as advance import deposits (e.g. compulsory deposits prior to travel). Tariff barriers include import-duty measures, airport departures or airport taxes, and subsidies, for example a consumer subsidy measure such as an official preferential exchange rate for foreign tourists or price concessions. Although tourism tariff barriers may be lowered by specific tourism agreements, tariffs are usually dealt with under broader multilateral negotiations on tariff reductions on trade in goods and services (e.g. the GATT, or negotiations within a specific trading bloc such as the European Union, the Association of South East Asian Nations (ASEAN) or the North American Free Trade Agreement (NAFTA)) or through bilateral agreements (e.g. the Closer Economic Relations (CER) agreement between Australia and New Zealand). The implications of the CER for tourism are discussed below.

The Closer Economic Relationship between Australia and New Zealand: implications for travel and tourism

> A single market requires the abolition of all restrictions on travellers and on the transport of goods and services within the area, that is, the abolition of the customs control at the frontier . . . There can be little doubt that the removal of Trans-Tasman restrictions . . . would increase this form of arbitrage. (Sir Frank Holmes in Lloyd, 1985, 28)

The growing integration of the world economy has led to increasing attention on the implications of the development of regional trading blocs for travel and tourism. However, while international interest has generally been focused on the economic integration of Europe and North America, the implications of the integration of the Australian and New Zealand economies for tourism has received little attention. Although the combined number of visitor arrivals in Australia and New Zealand accounts for less than 2 per cent of total world tourism arrivals, these countries have had some of the fastest growing tourism arrival rates in the OECD in the past decade and are major destinations in the Pacific Rim. Tourism arrivals are expected to more than double by the end of the century, with both countries putting substantial emphasis on tourism as a means of economic development and for employment generation (Hall, C., 1991; New Zealand Tourism Board, 1991; Commonwealth Department of Tourism, 1992).

The Australia New Zealand Closer Economic Relations Trade Agreement (CER) came into force in 1983. The goal of CER is to establish a single trans-Tasman market within which tariff and other trade barriers are abolished, relevant business laws and administrative practices are harmonised and free trade is encouraged in goods and services. CER is not designed to be exclusive and the governments of both countries have stressed that CER is part of a strategy to encourage a lessening of protectionism in the region and also to assist Australian and New Zealand companies to improve their links with Asia (Hall, C., 1994a).

CER has undeniably hastened a natural convergence of the two economies. Capital and labour inter-migrate with much more ease than between any two members of a supposedly integrated Europe. CER has been especially beneficial to New Zealand. In terms of gross domestic product, New Zealand's economy sits behind that of the Australian states of New South Wales, Victoria and Queensland; while in population terms Australia's population of almost 18 million people has become far more accessible to New Zealand businesses who only have a domestic market of 3.5 million people. Since 1983, New Zealand has become Australia's fourth largest market and Australia is New Zealand's most important trading partner. Trade between the two countries has increased from NZ$2600 million in 1983 to NZ$5960 million in 1989–90 (Murphy and Reid, 1992). Although initially only affecting goods, CER has now been extended to include aviation and tourism.

The extension of CER to include aviation services and to merge the Australian, New Zealand and trans-Tasman aviation markets into a single deregulated market has considerable benefits for tourism, not only between the two countries but also in promoting Australia and New Zealand as a single destination package. In addition, the creation of a single market for travel will clearly have substantial implications for the manner in which Australian destinations market themselves to the New Zealand market and vice versa. According to the joint study commissioned by the two governments into the formation of a single Australasian aviation market (Commonwealth of Australia and Government of New Zealand, 1991), both countries would benefit through lower fares and more flights, but with a larger consumer gain in Australia because it was a bigger market. Nevertheless, in proportional terms, the New Zealand tourism industry would have more to gain because of its improved access to the much larger Australian population.

Under the study's model, any benefits to consumers from a removal or relaxation of barriers would come in the form of reduced fares and an improvement in the quality of air services. A 'net welfare gain' was also calculated by subtracting the costs incurred by the airlines in producing the additional output stimulated by the changes. The results of the single market model suggested that Ansett Airlines' entry into the Tasman and limited added competition from Qantas and Air New Zealand on the domestic Australian market would generate a net welfare gain of A$53 million. The total consumer gains would be A$93 million but airline profits would reduce this by A$40 million, with Australia gaining A$35.9 million, New Zealand A$9.7 million and other countries A$7.1 million (Commonwealth of Australia and Government of New Zealand, 1991).

At the same time as trans-Tasman aviation has become liberalised, expanded 'beyond' rights have also become available to Australian and New Zealand airlines. The rights are especially valuable to New Zealand because of the larger Australian market and should bring in significantly extra arrivals to New Zealand (Kissling, 1993). Air New Zealand is scheduled to gain access to the Australian domestic market by November 1994. Air New Zealand will also be progressively entitled to pick up and set down passengers and cargo in Australia *en route* between New Zealand and up to nine cities in Asia and Europe (Field, 1992). The opening up of trans-Tasman passenger services will enable the former domestic carrier Ansett Airlines to integrate its Australian and New Zealand operations and to provide an improved service for its newly developed approved routes into East Asia and Japan. This will strengthen the promotion of Australia and New Zealand as a joint destination package in the high growth Asian market. As the managing director of Air New Zealand's Australian operations commented, 'our marketing strategy is entirely based on creating demand through promotion of inbound tourism into the southwest Pacific region and in that, we do not separate Australia and New Zealand' (New Zealand Herald, 1993, p.2).

The relationship between tourism policy formulation and the activities of interest groups (see Chapter 2) is highlighted by the fact that the New Zealand Tourism Industry Federation and the Australian Tourism Industry Association have been lobbying their respective governments to create a single entry destination between the two countries since 1990 (Coventry, 1990). The two organisations have also engaged in joint marketing campaigns and the Australian Tourism Commission and New Zealand Tourism have conducted a joint market segmentation study in Asia, Europe and North America. However, there is considerable debate over whether the two destinations should be marketed jointly. Organisations such as Air New Zealand and the McDermott Miller Group have been arguing for the development of a 'Destination South West Pacific' concept, including Australia and New Zealand, which would establish a regional tourism alliance in much the same way as 'Visit ASEAN Year' and the European Travel Commission (McDermott Miller Group, 1991; Hall, C., 1994a). Although the development of joint marketing campaigns seems inevitable, particularly as the extension of CER virtually establishes a single domestic tourism market, the desire to maintain national identity will probably override regional promotion in the short term. Nevertheless, the CER does indicate the potential implications of trade agreements for the removal of barriers to international tourism trade and for international tourism policy formulation.

RESTRICTIONS AND RESTRAINTS

Travel allowance restrictions are internationally widespread with, according to Edgell (1990), more than 100 countries imposing such travel restrictions. The imposition of travel allowance restrictions is usually undertaken in an attempt to retain scarce financial resources. For example, in 1984 the Thai government imposed a tax on Thais travelling abroad in order to save foreign currency at a time of economic crisis in the country (Elliot, 1987).

Sometimes such restrictions may strike the Western traveller as being extremely excessive; for example, in the case of Bulgaria 'each Bulgarian visiting abroad, unless in an official capacity, has been allowed to take only $20 out of the country' (Carter, 1991b, p.234). However, the removal of restraints is seen as having positive economic benefits. For example, according to the European Community 'the phasing out of customs controls, the abolition of checks on vehicles at frontiers and the introduction of the European passport constitute major boosts to tourism not only for tourists from the member states but also for those from elsewhere' (Kearney, 1992, p.36). (See the example of South Korea below for a further discussion of the effects of the removal of travel restrictions on growth in outbound travel.)

Constraints on tourists' movements come about for a variety of economic and political reasons: for example, the retention of foreign currency, improvements in the balance of payments, security measures, or restriction of contact between hosts and guests for fear of the introduction of social and political values deemed undesirable by the government in power. The majority of the constraints discussed above operate at the international level. However, national constraints, such as through the explicit closure of tracts of a country's territory to foreigners, or local constraints, 'through verbal or other more explicit indications, precluding movement in areas of economic, political, administrative, military or ethnic sensitivity' (Hall, D., 1991c, p.56), may also impinge on international relations.

Countries enter tourism agreements for a variety of economic, diplomatic and political reasons. For example, in the case of the United States, the tourism agreements entered into by the American government:

- aim to increase two-way tourism
- support efforts by the National Tourism Organization travel promotion office(s)
- improve tourism facilitation
- encourage investments in each other's tourism industry
- promote the sharing of research, statistics and information
- recognize the importance of the safety and security of tourists
- suggest mutual cooperation on policy issues in international tourism
- provide for regular consultations on tourism matters
- acknowledge benefits from education and training in tourism
- enhance mutual understanding and goodwill (Edgell, 1990, p.43)

However, the current positive nature of American attitudes toward promoting international tourism is only a recent development. During the 1950s the Eisenhower administration 'recommended that no federal funds be spent on tourism promotion. By 1960, a travel deficit developed accounting for nearly 30% of the total US balance of payments' (Hayes, 1981, p.124). The 1961 International Travel Act saw the commencement of efforts to develop an international tourism policy and promotion strategy for the United States, although it was not until the passage of the National Tourism Policy Act in 1981 that tourism policy gained a credible position within the Department of Commerce. Under the Act the principle mission of the United States Travel and Tourism Administration (USTTA) 'is to develop travel to the USA from abroad as a stimulus to economic stability and to the growth of the US travel industry, to reduce the nation's travel deficit, and to promote friendly understanding and appreciation of the USA abroad' (Edgell, 1984, p.67). The Act and the activities of USTTA were specifically designed to provide a much more active involvement by government in the tourism industry. As Edgell (1983, p.433) stated:

> There are only two basic options with respect to international tourism policy: to maintain a stance of laissez-faire toward the U.S. international travel industry, or to use diplomatic and other governmental channels to advance the cause of U.S. tourism interests and create an environment in which U.S.-owned firms can compete more effectively for the world's international tourism business. Obviously, the course taken should be the second option.

The American situation regarding the twinning of economic and diplomatic goals within international tourism policy is repeated throughout the world. However, while in most countries tourism is seen as a means to generate income, in some cases, such as Japan and Taiwan discussed below, international tourism is utilised as a mechanism to reduce embarrassing foreign trade surpluses.

Japanese international tourism policy

Unlike many other countries in the Pacific Rim, tourism is not an important item in Japan for economic development and the generation of foreign exchange. This function was significant during the 1950s and 1960s but was rapidly eclipsed by other export industries and by the country's strong domestic economy. Instead, outbound tourism is encouraged by government as a means of reducing trade imbalances with other nations in the region and to serve broader educative, diplomatic and political goals (Hall, C., 1994a). As Tsuneaki Iki, executive vice-president of the Japan National Tourism Organisation (JNTO), stated, 'My aim is for foreigners to gain an understanding of Japan, not how much revenue is earned' (quoted in Jeffrey, 1991, p.34).

A good example of the changed significance of tourism in Japanese government policy formulation is the shift in roles for the JNTO. Originally established in 1959 as the marketing organisation

Table 3.2. Japanese trade and travel-related expenditures balance, 1980–1990 (US$m)

Year	Trade Balance	Travel-Related Expenditures Balance
1980	2 125	−4 913
1981	19 967	−5 046
1982	18 079	−4 518
1983	31 454	−4 756
1984	44 257	−4 952
1985	55 986	−4 981
1986	92 827	−7 416
1987	96 386	−11 356
1988	95 012	−19 468
1989	76 917	−24 416
1990	63 528	−27 339

Source: Adapted from The Bank of Japan, in Japan Travel Bureau, 1991, p.3

responsible for attracting foreign tourists to Japan and the promotion of domestic tourism, the JNTO has also been charged, since 1979, with offering services to facilitate the travel of Japanese overseas. Japan has used promotional schemes, for example the Ten Million Programme (see below), changes to tax exemptions for corporate travellers, increases in duty-free allowances, and development assistance to destinations in order to encourage increased outbound travel (Hall, C., 1994a).

Travel-related expenditures are the third largest import category in Japan behind mineral fuels and machinery and equipment. In 1990 the number of Japanese travelling abroad reached 10.997 million travellers, ensuring that the plan to increase overseas travel known as the 'Ten Million Programme', launched in 1987, had reached its target a year ahead of schedule. The programme was designed by the Ministry of Transport as a means to reduce Japan's large trade surplus, thereby avoiding the potential for conflict with major trading partners such as the United States and the European Union. Table 3.2 indicates the Japanese trade balance and the travel-related expenditures balance. In 1989 Japan became the country with the highest deficit travel account balance in the world ahead of Germany (Japan Travel Bureau, 1991). In 1990 the travel trade balance of payments (balance of total travel and passenger fares) had a deficit of US$27.3 billion, a figure equivalent to 43 per cent of the total trade surplus (Japan Travel Bureau, 1991).

Taiwanese international tourism policy

The traditional primary objective of international tourism policy, to earn foreign exchange, has also diminished in importance to the Republic of China (Taiwan) due to its massive accumulation of foreign exchange reserves. As with Japan, the emphasis in international tourism policy has now shifted toward outbound tourism that improves the image of the ROC, strengthens substantive international relations, and meets broad diplomatic objectives (Republic of China Tourist Bureau, 1992a). Taiwan has also utilised overseas tourism to ease pressure on its own domestic recreational resources and to improve economic and political relations with its major trading partners. As the Republic of China Tourist Bureau (1992a, p.7) has stated: 'Although the ROC government has not introduced any special incentive packages encouraging travel abroad, the high annual growth rate for overseas travel from the ROC has achieved some of the results sought by Japan's tourism policy.'

Taiwan has only recently reduced the restrictions on its nationals travelling overseas following a period of martial law. As of July 1988, the number of allowable overseas trips for tourism purposes increased from two to three per year; the age range during which males were prohibited to travel was shortened from 16–30 to 16–26 years; and the fee for tourist exit and entry permits was halved from NT$4000 to NT$2000 (Wieman, 1989).

The lessening of travel restrictions, combined with increased spending power, has made the Taiwanese one of the most sought-after markets in the Asia-Pacific region (Hall, C., 1994a). Table 3.3 indicates the numbers of Taiwanese travelling overseas and their destinations for the period 1980 to 1991. Extremely high growth rates have existed since 1987 when travel restrictions were being eased.

Given the economic and diplomatic emphasis of Taiwanese tourism policy, it is perhaps not surprising that inbound tourism has received very little attention. Consequently, Taiwan is one of the few destinations in the Pacific Rim which is experiencing difficulties in maintaining inbound tourism growth. Indeed, international visitation to Taiwan has been dropping steadily since 1989 because of a combination of factors including the attraction of mainland China, the appreciation of the Taiwanese currency, and visa restrictions on inbound travellers. As Asia Travel Trade

Table 3.3. Destinations and numbers of Taiwanese outbound travel for selected destinations, 1980–1991

Main or First Destination	1980	1982	1984	1986	1988	1989	1990	1991
Hong Kong	63 812	81 558	109 975	121 427	621 864	810 977	1 245 764	1 368 295
Japan	173 581	260 414	292 127	253 524	340 488	474 245	591 495	653 242
South Korea	76 995	67 002	73 008	81 644	100 569	133 867	221 454	284 902
Singapore	19 563	24 124	29 648	30 831	45 989	70 924	96 607	153 811
Malaysia	4 418	8 996	12 974	30 841	42 251	59 938	57 074	79 820
Thailand	14 956	21 726	22 619	63 271	154 853	258 668	355 962	346 310
Total Asia	402 244	522 434	584 752	627 134	1 374 976	1 915 893	2 669 545	3 039 090
United States	69 448	98 995	132 692	153 462	183 402	157 565	239 325	267 584
Total Americas	73 754	104 135	139 104	162 137	193 304	159 408	241 519	284 062
Europe	4 830	7 786	11 498	16 772	22 279	18 549	17 869	20 281
Total	484 901	640 669	750 404	812 928	1 601 992	2 107 813	2 942 316	3 366 076

Source: Adapted from Republic of China Tourism Bureau, 1992b, p.47

(1989, p.41) observed: 'The mainland is not only cheaper and has far more scenic and cultural attractions than Taiwan, but its visas are also easier to obtain. Taiwan has diplomatic relations with few countries; in others, visas or letters of recommendation exchangeable for visas on arrival are issued by agencies that go by a variety of names [e.g. Sun Yat-sen Centers].' The Taiwanese government eased strict visa requirements for foreign visitors at the beginning of 1994 in a bid to reverse the decline in tourism arrivals and obtain visa concessions from other nations. Taiwan had maintained tough visa regulations from its martial-law period which ended in 1987. Citizens of 12 nations—Australia, Austria, Belgium, Britain, Canada, France, Germany, Japan, Luxembourg, the Netherlands, New Zealand and the United States—can now visit Taiwan for five-day periods without visas. Previously, almost all foreigners had to apply for visas before going to Taiwan.

One of the most fascinating aspects of Taiwanese international tourism policy is the relationship of Taiwan (the Republic of China) to mainland China (the People's Republic of China). The lifting of travel restrictions in October 1987 for travel to mainland China to visit relatives meant that many Taiwanese could now visit the mainland, both to see relatives and to experience the greater China of which Taiwan is still culturally a part. The diplomatic impasse between China and Taiwan has meant that no direct air or sea services exist between the two countries. The official statistics of Taiwan do not even recognise the existence of the People's Republic, with many Taiwanese travellers visiting Hong Kong and Japan as stopovers *en route* to the mainland. Officially, only residents with close relatives on the mainland are allowed to travel there and then only for the purpose of visiting those relatives, not for pleasure or business activities (Wieman, 1989). However, the restriction is universally ignored by government and tourists alike, because of the political benefits (for both Chinas) and the economic benefits (for the mainland).

South Korean international tourism policy

The international tourism policy of South Korea makes an interesting comparison with that of Taiwan. As in the case of Taiwan, South Korea is still technically in a state of civil war in a divided country. South Korea has also undergone massive economic transformation in recent years, to the stage where it has one of the fastest rates of economic growth in East Asia. However, while the South Korean economy is reasonably healthy, the country has not built up foreign reserves to the same extent as Taiwan, and therefore uses tourism to serve quite different economic goals.

Although North Korea still retains strict control over the domestic and international travel of its residents (Hall, D., 1990b), the South progressively lifted its restrictions during the 1980s (Hall, C., 1994a). South Korea had two main reasons for imposing travel restrictions: first, for security during a period of superpower and regional tension and because of the continuing poor North–South Korean relations; second, in order to retain foreign exchange for its economic development.

Until 1983 Korean citizens were not allowed to travel overseas except for business, employment, study or some other activity that was deemed to benefit the national interest. In 1983 overseas leisure travel was permitted for those aged 50 and older but only for spouses travelling together. Furthermore, people over the age of 50 could only holiday overseas if they deposited 2 million won with the Korea foreign exchange bank for one year. The effect of these restrictions is evidenced by the fact that only half a million South Koreans travelled overseas annually between 1981 and 1987. In September 1987 the deposit was waived, with the age limit being dropped from 50 to 40 in January 1988. In April 1988, shortly before the hosting of the Seoul Summer Olympics, the Foreign Minister announced that the age restriction on overseas travel would be removed as of 1 January 1989, and as an intermediate step the age limit was lowered from 40 to 30 as of 1 July 1988. According to the Assistant Foreign Minister, Hong Soon-Young, 'The liberalisation of overseas travel is designed to meet the growing trend of internationalisation of people's lifestyles, at the same time a new government is inaugurated' (in Crean, 1988, p.30). In 1989, the first full year without restrictions, 1.2 million South Koreans travelled overseas. The figure is expected to rise further as the Korean economy continues to grow, with a prediction of 3.6 million travellers in 1996 and 5.4 million by the year 2000 (Hamdi, 1991).

Tourism has played a significant role in the Korean government's search for foreign exchange with which to fund economic development. Between 1981 and 1990 receipts from

Table 3.4. Korean tourist trade balance, 1970–1991 (US$000s)

Year	Tourist Receipts	Travel Expenditure	Balance
1970	46 772	12 424	34 348
1971	52 383	14 808	37 575
1972	83 011	12 570	70 441
1973	269 434	16 984	252 450
1974	158 571	27 618	130 953
1975	140 627	30 709	109 918
1976	275 011	46 234	228 777
1977	370 030	102 714	267 316
1978	408 106	208 019	200 087
1979	326 006	405 284	−79 278
1980	369 265	349 557	19 708
1981	447 640	439 029	8 611
1982	502 318	632 177	−129 859
1983	596 245	555 401	40 844
1984	673 355	576 250	97 105
1985	784 312	605 973	178 339
1986	1 547 502	612 969	934 533
1987	2 299 156	704 201	1 594 955
1988	3 265 232	1 353 891	1 911 341
1989	3 556 279	2 601 532	954 747
1990	3 558 666	3 165 623	393 043
1991	3 426 416	3 784 304	−357 888

Source: The Bank of Korea, in Ministry of Transportation, 1992, p.85

tourism grew from US$448 million to US$3559 million and these have contributed significantly to Korea's balance of payments (Table 3.4). For example, there was a positive tourism trade balance of US$393 million in 1990, although it should be noted that this was considerably lower than the peak of US$1911 million in 1988, the Seoul Olympics year (McGahey, 1991, p.47). However, the explosion in overseas travel by Koreans following the ending of travel restrictions has impacted on the balance of tourism receipts, with the nation recording its first deficit in tourist trade of US$380 million in 1991. The tourist trade deficit has brought warnings against 'excessive consumption' by government officials, while the government's austerity campaign 'includes provisions to punish travel agencies which the government concludes "abet or induce overseas travellers to indulge in excessive spending"'

(Do-sun, 1992, p.57). Nevertheless, while the government will undoubtedly utilise a range of measures to keep outbound travel within reasonable limits, it will be impossible to reimpose travel restrictions while the economy and the ensuing consumer and political expectations continue to grow (Hall, C., 1994a).

INTERNATIONAL TOURISM POLICIES IN STATE SOCIALIST COUNTRIES

The political ideology of a state will influence its foreign policy outlook, including those policies relating to international tourism. The former state socialist nations had very clear political and economic objectives for international tourism which differed substantially from that of the West with its quite different notions of individual freedom and the role of the state. Hall (D., 1984, p.542; 1990a, p.11) identified a number of objectives for a state socialist approach to tourism:

1. Assist the implementation of policies seeking the equal distribution of goods, services and opportunities across the state area.
2. Help improve economic performance and stimulate rapid economic development.
3. Stimulate infrastructural improvements for the benefit of the host population.
4. Aid environmental improvement.
5. Project a favourable image of the host country to the outside world.
6. Promote international peace and understanding, as defined by state socialist dogma.
7. Enhance visitors' cultural and ideological awareness by the host country convincing them of the superiority of socialism.
8. Avoid introducing 'anti-socialist', 'revisionist' or 'capitalist' influences to 'turn the heads' of the indigenous population working in the tourist industry and coming into contact with foreign tourists.

Although the doctrines of state socialism have lost much of their tarnish in recent years because of the political upheavals in Eastern Europe, several states such as the People's Republic of China, North Korea, Albania and Cuba still follow, to varying degrees,

socialist principles in the determination of their policies regarding
international tourism.

The People's Republic of China and international tourism

> China's interest in tourism historically has had primary political
> motivations. The rapid expansion of tourism since 1977 under the
> leadership of Deng Xiaopeng has been the result of both political
> and economic motivators. By quickly linking with the international
> business community in terms of joint ventures in hotel development,
> imports of tourist transport, and ties with the international travel
> industry, tourism has become an increasingly active policy sector
> allied to Deng's 'Four Modernizations' campaign. (Richter, 1983b,
> p.441)

Although the first travel service handling overseas tourists was set
up by the People's Republic of China over 30 years ago, it is only
since 1978 that there has been a major expansion in inbound
tourism. Until that time tourism was regarded almost solely as a
diplomatic tool to encourage international goodwill and focused on
visitors from other communist countries and friendly third world
or non-aligned nations. Since the shift by the Chinese government
in 1978 to an 'open door policy' in its relations with non-
communist countries and the promotion of the doctrine of a
'socialist market economy', tourism has been regarded as an
important element in the modernisation of China and a means to
earn foreign exchange (Richter, 1983b, 1989; Choy, 1984; Reynolds,
1990; Hall, C., 1994a). As Zhao Ziyang stated at the Thirteenth
National Congress of the Communist Party of China in 1987:

> Our capacity to earn foreign exchange through export determines, to
> a great extent, the degree to which we can open to the outside world
> and affects the scale and pace of domestic economic development.
> For this reason, bearing in mind the demands of the world market
> and our own strong points, we should make vigorous efforts to
> develop export-oriented industries and products that are competitive
> and can bring quick and high economic returns. (quoted in Tisdell
> and Wen, 1991, p.55)

The potential of tourism to net foreign exchange for the Chinese
government is substantial. For example, in 1988, the year before the
political unrest of T'ian-an-men Square (see Chapter 4), 3.17 million
overseas tourists visited China, almost 18 times the number of
visitors who arrived in 1978. China's accumulated foreign
exchange earnings from international tourism between 1978 and

1988 were estimated to be US$11.65 billion. At the end of 1988, there were 1496 hotels with 478 000 beds, and 1.57 million people owing their employment to tourism with 400 000 being directly employed (Tisdell and Wen, 1991). Nevertheless, despite the economic benefits that international tourism has provided for China, there is concern from some conservative Communist Party members and government officials over the role that foreign tourism has in the spread of Western ideology and values in China (Hall, C., 1994a). For example, following the events in T'ian-an-men Square in 1989, 'China's estimated 620 000 tourism workers underwent compulsory political indoctrination that aimed to cleanse their socialist minds, deepen their love of the Communist Party and, alarmingly, to cultivate their suspicions of foreigners, presumed by paranoid leaders to be bent on sundering communist rule' (Parker, 1992, p.47).

Tourism has also been blamed by some commentators for the introduction of unwelcome practices at odds with the principles of the Chinese socialist state. For example, in 1983 Dichen and Guangrui argued that tourism had brought:

> 'unhealthy' and 'uncivilised' influences . . . into China. Some weak-willed Chinese, youngsters in particular, could not withstand such influences and blindly pursue the way of life of the foreigners. Also smuggling, contraband trafficking, divulging state secrets and other offences occurred. These have violated the decency and image of socialist China and should not be tolerated. (1983, p.78)

Six years later, the negative social impacts of tourism had not declined in significance for the Chinese authorities, with the effects of tourism on Chinese socialist values remaining a major concern:

> Following a few years of tourism development many undesirable practices have arisen, e.g. asking for an exorbitant payment and unreasonable commission, accepting (or demanding) bribes, prostitution, and illegal selling and buying of foreign currencies. These hardly existed even during the cultural revolution but have emerged in most tourist areas. Accepting tips, contrary to socialist ethics, was rampant for a time among tourist guides and service people. The practice was so serious that in August 1987 the SATT [State Administration for Travel and Tourism], with the approval of the State Council, issued special regulations to stop the practice of tipping. (Guangri, 1989, p.61)

Concerns over the social and political impact of tourism in China indicate the extent to which international tourism is intricately connected with foreign policy formulation and the fostering of ideologies. Even though China wants to develop tourism in a 'Chinese Way', in that the 'government's experimenting with "capitalistic" ideas such as individual incentives, competition, and private enterprises are attempts to develop a system suitable for China's situation but still maintain a socialist system' (Choy, 1984, p.619), it is still clearly influenced by economic and social forces external to the Chinese mainland. Tourism is inseparable from the transmission of ideas between nations. Even though some tourists travel in a 'glass bubble', the values which those tourists may appear to represent to the host community, particularly perhaps in terms of individual freedom and wealth, may still impact on political and social aspirations.

Nevertheless, ideology may spread in both directions and the host country may seek to use visits by international tourists to show specific images to the outside world. For example, working holidays in Cuba and Nicaragua were utilised by the governments of those countries to help promote socialist values amongst supporters in the West. Similarly, Israel has used kibbutz-based holidays to assist in gaining support for the Israeli state among visiting Western youth (Stock, 1977). However, efforts to restrict the influx of unwanted ideologies by outsiders tend to be more strident than the promotion of political values. For example, fear of ideological contamination strongly influenced Albanian tourism policy, which implemented a group visa system which allowed screening of undesirables and greater control of foreign tourists (Hall, D., 1991e). Indeed, such were the restrictions on international tourists that 'up to the early 1980s the country rigidly adhered to the notion that tourists should conform to a particular dress sense. Albania's points of entry thus had resident barbers and tailors whose role was to "advise" new arrivals on Albanian notions of sartorial appropriateness' (Hall, D., 1991e, p.269).

The actions of the Albanian government perhaps indicate a more extreme use of tourism to achieve ideological ends. Nevertheless, as noted in this book from the outset, tourism is inherently political because of the manner in which it interacts with notions of power and values. The uses of international tourism to achieve political objectives are manyfold. The next section provides an examination of the way in which foreign tourism can be used to provide international respectability for authoritarian and illegitimate regimes.

TOURISM AND INTERNATIONAL RECOGNITION

The promotion of tourism is closely connected to image making. From a political perspective international tourism allows a host government the possibilities of offering a positive image of itself to the outside world, which in turn may improve its international standing and create favourable climates of public opinion for it in other nations. For this reason, travel and tourism are often primary areas for the enforcement of sanctions within the international community. For example, many countries did not allow their national carriers to fly direct to South Africa in protest at the apartheid policies of the South African government and for fear that tourist visitation would be seen as an endorsement of such policies. This situation had a substantial impact on the country's tourism industry. Indeed, Sun International, a South African multinational with tourism development interests (see below), was quarantined in its international operations to those African states which either were 'economic or political satellites of South Africa or, in the case of the "independent" Bantustans, were creations of apartheid' (Rogerson, 1990, p.353). Similarly, Libya has been subject to aviation sanctions in light of the alleged involvement of the Libyan government in the Lockerbie air disaster.

An illegitimate or authoritarian government does not by itself mean that international tourism will not be encouraged. The investment by Southern Sun, a multinational hotel and casino company based in South Africa, in casinos in the nominally independent South African Bantustans of Transkei, Bophuthatswana, Venda and Ciskei (Rogerson, 1990), gave 'considerable weight' to the South African government's 'attempts to legitimise Bantustan independence in the international forum' and allowed the South African state 'to replace a considerable portion of the costs of subsidizing the Bantustan strategy with private capital' (Crush and Wellings, 1987, p.107).

In many cases, international powers will support repressive regimes if it furthers their foreign policy interests. For example, the United States has supported authoritarian regimes in Latin America and the Caribbean for most of the twentieth century in order to further its national interests. Authoritarian regimes do not of themselves deter tourists; instead, as the following chapter highlights, it is political instability which drives off tourists and foreign investment in the tourism industry. Indeed, perhaps somewhat paradoxically, the political stability provided by an authoritarian regime may even serve to encourage the development of a tourism industry. As Hall (D., 1990a, p.15) observed, 'the perceived nature of a political regime as repressive may not necessarily deter international tourism: both Spain and Portugal developed their very considerable international tourism industries under what many would regard as fascist dictatorships.'

By their very nature, authoritarian regimes do not have to go through the public consultation measures which are in place in most Western democracies. Therefore, tourism development can be fast-tracked through any local, provincial or national planning system that is in place. In the case of Portugal, 'the transformation of the . . . tourist industry has been accompanied by major shifts in the priority attached to it in government policy' (Lewis and Williams, 1988, p.119), with emphasis being given to tourism in government development plans in the late 1960s and early 1970s in order to attract foreign tourists and up-market tourism. Similarly, in the case of Spain, special laws were passed to facilitate the creation of new tourist settlements in the zones most favoured by spontaneous tourism (Valenzuela, 1988).

According to Edgell (1978, p.171), 'International travel tends to have a moderating effect on the internal policies of foreign governments. An authoritarian regime knows it is being watched and judged by foreign tourists.' Such a situation may also be described as the 'Amnesty effect', that is, the international attention given by campaigning organisation Amnesty International to political prisoners has often assisted in the latter's release because they have come to the attention of foreign governments. Whether international tourism moderates more than the worst excesses of an authoritarian regime is debatable, particularly as tourism destinations may well become political showcases. In addition, tourist centres will often be located away from those areas in which the worst oppression actually occurs.

The opening up of areas to outsiders in order to legitimise occupation or governance can potentially be a two-edged sword for the regime in power. For example, the opening up of Tibet to Western visitors through the reforms of the Chinese government in 1979 had a number of unintended effects. Rather than support Chinese-backed tourism developments and images of Tibet as part of China, the policy only served to reinforce indigenous and refugee motivations to free Tibet from China, and to heighten the sacredness of the country for Westerners:

> As distorted presentations of Tibet crafted by Chinese agencies appeared increasingly incredulous to many Westerners, the official tourist infrastructure built at great expense by China was increasingly ignored. Westerners wanted to experience Shangri-La, and Tibetans were more than happy to share their vision of the sacred landscape. Lost on the tourist audience was the Chinese managed impression that Tibet has been, since the days of Khubilai Khan, an integral part of the motherland. (Klieger, 1992, p.124)

The use of international tourism to create conditions of support for illegitimate regimes is well illustrated in the case of the Philippines under President Marcos in the 1970s and early 1980s. However, the high profile of international tourism also served to lessen the level of international support for the President. As Richter (1989, p.52) commented:

> No regime has more blatantly used tourism policy for political leverage than that of ex-President Marcos of the Philippines. Although tourism contributed to many of the regime's political and economic objectives, it achieved those gains at enormous cost to the Filipino economy. As time went on, the insensitive development of tourism in the midst of deteriorating economic and social conditions spawned a counter use of tourism—opposition violence against the tourist industry. Thus one finds in the case of the Philippines a microcosm of the political uses and abuses of tourism.

International tourism and the Philippines under Marcos

Ferdinand Marcos was elected President of the Philippines in November 1965, and won a second term of office four years later. On 21 September 1972, amid increasing unpopularity, he imposed martial law declaring that the country was faced with a serious communist insurgency. Until the declaration of martial law tourism had been a low priority of the government. However, 'within eight months of the declaration of martial law, tourism was a priority industry eligible for a variety of tax incentives and customs concessions' (Richter, 1989, pp.54–55). Four main reasons can be provided for the Marcos government's sudden interest in tourism development, two of which related primarily to international political factors. First, tourism could be utilised by the regime to create a favourable image of the country and the Marcos government for international tourists and for foreign governments. Secondly, international tourist visitation could be held up by the regime to be an endorsement of its activities and of martial law in particular, thereby providing legitimacy for its undemocratic activities. Thirdly, tourism was a means by which Marcos could provide rewards to his supporters by giving them favourable consideration in development projects and by providing government finance. Finally, the president's wife, Imelda Marcos, had her own ambitions regarding the development of the Philippines as an international tourist destination (Richter, 1989; Hall, C., 1994a).

In an effort to maintain the legitimacy of the Marcos regime with overseas governments and investors, the government launched a vigorous tourism development programme. The regime used such high profile events as the Miss Universe contest and the 'Thriller in Manila' world heavyweight title fight between Mohammed Ali and Joe Frazier to improve the international image of the country. The hosting of the 1976 International Monetary Fund (IMF)—World Bank Conference led the regime to fast-track the construction of twelve luxury hotels, the Philippine International Convention Center and the Philippine Center for International Trade and Exhibitions, all for the conference and all at enormous cost to the government. As Richter (1989, p.56) commented: 'The tantalizing prospect of hosting 5,000 VIPs, even for just a week led to a rush to complete 12 luxury hotels within 18 months, though the tourism master plan had not expected such accommodation needs for at least a decade.' The size of the government commitment to the project was enormous (US$410–545 million) and was completely out of proportion either to the infrastructure requirements of the Filipino tourism industry or the economic and social needs of the country. The expenditure on hotel financing was between 30 and 40 times the amount that the Marcos government had spent on public housing. 'The relative size of this commitment . . . was between one-seventh and one-fifth of the government's total proposed 1976 expenditures of $3.05 billion. It was more than the nation's total 1976 borrowing from the World Bank of $315 million' (Richter, 1989, p.57). Nevertheless, the conference was a political success for the Marcos government and economic and military aid to the country was increased from both the United States and the IMF–World Bank (Hall, C., 1994a).

TOURISM AND TERRITORIAL CLAIMS

Sovereignty is a key concept in international law and politics. Sovereignty has four related meanings: first, as a distinctive characteristic of states as constituent units of the international legal system; second, as freedom of action in respect of all matters with regard to which a state is not under any legal obligation; third, as the minimum amount of autonomy which a state must possess before it can be accorded the status of a 'sovereign state'; fourth, as the plenary international authority to administer territory (Crawford, 1979, pp.26–27). There are several ways in which territorial sovereignty may be acquired: 'occupation of *terra nullius*; prescription, by which title is gained by possession adverse to the abstract titleholder; cession, or transfer by treaty; accretion, where a gradual deposition of soil changes the shape of the land; and, finally, conquest' (Triggs, 1986, p.2). Touristic activity is intimately related to the first manner by which sovereignty may be acquired, as it may serve as an example of effective occupation. Furthermore, tourism may serve as an economic linkage between the disputed territory and the claimant state, thereby giving further weight to any argument of effective occupation.

Tourism is currently being used to support territorial claims in three areas of the globe, the Arctic, Antarctica and the Spratly Islands. In the Arctic the creation of national parks by the Canadian government, and the development of special-interest tourism activities in these parks, may be seen as a means to reinforce Canada's territorial claims to the northern islands and to the surrounding waters (Hall, C. and Johnston, 1995).

The Spratly Islands are a group of islands in the South China Sea. Although many of the islands are too small for human habitation, they possess strategic significance, and they provide potential access to mineral (oil and gas) and fish resources. The islands are disputed by several countries including Brunei, China, Malaysia, the Philippines and Vietnam. They have already been the source of military conflict between Vietnam and China, while all the claimant states, except Brunei, have had a military presence on the islands. In 1992 Malaysia sought to run ecotourism tours to the southern islands in order to assist the economic dimension of its claim. However, it has since discontinued the tours as the military situation in the region remains very tense and the safety of tourists could not be guaranteed.

Tourism and sovereignty in Antarctica

No nation has legal sovereignty over any part of Antarctica. Several states (Argentina, Australia, Chile, Ecuador, Great Britain, France, New Zealand and Norway) claim territory but these claims are not generally recognised by the international community (Auburn, 1982; Triggs, 1986; Farmer, 1987). The legal status of the lands and resources of the continent are subject to the conditions of the Antarctic Treaty which was signed on 1 December 1959 and came into effect on 23 June 1961. Although the Antarctic Treaty makes no specific reference to tourism, measures and recommendations relating to tourism and non-government expeditions have been adopted at almost every biennial Antarctic Treaty Consultative Meeting (ATCM) since the 1966 meeting in Santiago, while more recently debate is occurring about whether to establish a specific protocol or convention to regulate tourism within the Antarctic Treaty framework (Nicholson, 1986; Hall, C., 1992b; Hall, C. and Johnston, 1994). However, from the perspective of claimant nations, tourism in Antarctica also offers a potential mechanism to justify territorial claims and a possible source of funds to subsidise stations and scientific research (Reich, 1979).

In the Antarctic context, tourism may be defined as all existing human activities other than those directly involved in scientific research and the normal operations of government bases. Such a definition covers the activities of commercial tourism operations, non-government expeditions and the recreational activities of government personnel. Tourism is the only activity presently which commercially utilises the land-based resources of Antarctica. Tourist activity is concentrated in cruise ship and flight operations in the Antarctic peninsula and, to a lesser extent, the Ross Sea (Hall, C., 1992b). Tourist activity on the Antarctic peninsula is given the greatest support by Argentina and Chile. Although this is in part because of their geographical location, the primary reason for their sanction of tourism in their territorial areas, including use of airbases, is that it provides support for their territorial claims to the peninsula.

Australia is also using tourism, and control of tourist activity, as a means of maintaining its claim. In the absence of organised and regular tourism to the Australian Antarctic Territory (AAT), the Australian government tended to take a generally neutral position on tourism and non-government expeditions to the territory until the late 1980s (Bergin, 1985; Hall, C., 1992b). However, the pressure on the Australian government by conservation groups to act on a variety of Antarctic environmental issues, the negotiations on the renewal of the Antarctic Treaty, the rise of commercial interest in the tourism opportunities provided in the AAT, and the need to maintain a viable Australian presence in Antarctica have led to the first steps being taken towards the development of an Australian Antarctic tourism policy within the context of Australia's broader Antarctic policy objectives. These include, significantly, to 'preserve its sovereignty over the [Australian Antarctic Territory], including rights over the adjacent offshore areas' (HRSCERA, 1989, p.2).

TOURISM: A FORCE FOR PEACE?

In recent years, substantial profile has been given to the notion of tourism as a force for peace, including the hosting of international conferences on the subject. Undoubtedly, tourism can lead to improved understanding between individuals, cultures and nations; however, it can also lead to substantial misunderstanding.

The Conference on Security and Cooperation in Europe continued throughout the 1970s and early 1980s and included all the European nations, except Albania, as well as Canada and the United States. The conference had the general goals of 'peace, security, justice and cooperation' and was aimed at achieving a basic objective of promoting better relations among the signatory countries. The Final Act of the Conference encouraged the development of tourism on both an individual and collective basis as a means of achieving the above ends. Separate sections on tourism included its promotion, travel for personal and professional reasons, and the improvement of conditions for tourism (Ronkainen, 1983). In the human rights section of the Final Act of the Conference on Security and Cooperation in Europe (known as the 1975 Helsinki Accord), with specific reference to tourism, the signatories to the Accord:

a) expressed their intentions to 'encourage increased tourism on both an individual and group basis',
b) recognised the desirability of carrying out 'detailed studies on tourism',

c) agreed to 'endeavour, where possible, to ensure that the development of tourism does not injure the artistic, historic and cultural heritage in their respective countries',

d) stated their intention 'to facilitate wider travel by their citizens for personal and professional reasons',

e) agreed to 'endeavour gradually to lower, where necessary, the fees for visas and official travel documents'

f) agreed to 'increase, on the basis of appropriate agreements or arrangements, cooperation in the development of tourism, in particular, by considering bilaterally, possible ways to increase information relating to travel to other related questions of mutual interest', and

g) expressed their intention 'to promote visits to their respective countries' (in Edgell, 1990, p.40).

Despite the grand-sounding elements of the Final Act, progress was slow and tangible results were extremely limited, with the vagueness of the wording having little effect on countries' international tourism policies. As Ronkainen (1983, p.425) concluded:

> it is quite apparent that the Helsinki declarations are being ignored by many of the Eastern bloc signatories. A perfect example of this is provided by the highest official of the German Democratic Republic, Eric Honeker, who, upon return from Helsinki, declared that the final act notwithstanding, there would be no immediate easing of East German travel restrictions.

The Helsinki Accord was a political child of its time and was testimony to the easing of Cold War tensions. However, its practical effect on peace through tourism was negligible. In the case of the countries of Eastern Europe, for example, it took the demise of state socialism rather than international agreements to improve the freedom of individuals to travel to Western Europe. The optimism of the World Tourism Organization's motto 'Tourism: passport to peace' has not been matched by the reality of world affairs. As the next chapter discusses, political stability is a critical element in sustaining tourism development: 'The tourist, unlike some entrepreneurs, does not need to go to a particular destination, and when there is a hint of insecurity, they do not' (Richter, 1983b, p.409). Therefore, perhaps the WTO motto should read 'peace: passport to tourism' (Edgell, 1990). In addition, the notion of tourism as a force for peace fails to appreciate the broad political dimensions within which tourism occurs. For example,

Matthews' (1975, p.201) statement that 'tourism in many Third World countries is little more than whorism' reflects the need to consider tourism development within ideas of dependency and cultural control, a point which will be returned to in Chapters 5 and 6. Therefore, the idea that tourism is a force for peace is an overly simplistic interpretation of the complexities of tourism and international relations. Such gross simplification of the political dimensions of tourism may serve to provide a platform for politicians and consultants to launch nice-sounding statements, but it does little to improve our understanding of tourism's position in the political environment.

4

Tourism and Political Stability: The Implications of Revolution, Terrorism and Political Violence for Tourism

Most of the evidence on tourist motivations points to fear and insecurity as a major barrier to travel and thus a limitation on the growth of the industry. In addition to the openly stated fear there is often an expression of lack of interest in travel, which can mask an underlying fear. In these circumstances the possibility of terrorism, however remote, will have an effect on the tourist demand of a large number of potential tourists. (Buckley and Klemm, 1993, p.191)

Political stability is one of the essential prerequisites for attracting international tourists to a destination. Violent protests, civil war, terrorist actions, the perceived violations of human rights, or even the mere threat of these activities, will serve to cause tourists to cancel their vacations. Undoubtedly, travellers have been in danger of attack by brigands and robbers since the time of the Romans. Many pilgrims to the Holy Lands in the Middle Ages, for example, travelled in fear of their lives and belongings. Indeed, the origin of the word 'travel', to travail, to overcome adversity and hardship, gives evidence of the difficulties which the many travellers faced. However, the overt connection between tourism and political violence is clearly a phenomenon of the late twentieth century.

This chapter will discuss the relationship between tourism and political stability, with particular emphasis on the impacts of political violence, terrorism and war on tourist behaviour and tourism development. The first section will note the manner in which war, coups and revolutions, even if they are of a relatively peaceful nature, serve to damage not only tourist infrastructure and arrivals but also the longer-term image of a destination. The second part of the chapter will examine the direct and indirect impacts of terrorism on tourism.

WAR, COUPS AND REVOLUTIONS: THEIR IMPACTS ON TOURISM

Political stability is a fundamental precondition to the successful establishment of a tourist industry. As Richter and Waugh (1986, p.231) observed:

> tourism may decline precipitously when political conditions appear unsettled. Tourists simply choose alternative destinations.
>
> Unfortunately, many national leaders and planners either do not understand or will not accept the fact that political serenity, not scenic or cultural attractions, constitute the first and central requirement of tourism.

Political stability is important not only for the development of the infrastructure that is required for tourism but also because of the central role that images play in tourism marketing and promotion. Given the requirement of many travellers to feel 'safe' when they visit a destination, perceptions of tourist safety become vital in attracting international and domestic travellers. Safety can be perceived in terms of the dangers presented by physical disasters, health concerns, crime and the potential for political violence. While all these safety concerns are important for the traveller, the present chapter will only examine the implications of political violence on tourism.

Political violence can take several forms. Lea and Small (1988) identify five different dimensions of political violence and international tourism: wars, coups, terrorism, riots and strikes. Warfare is clearly disastrous for tourism. Apart from the dangers which war presents to the individual, military activity can also damage tourist infrastructure. For example, in the Middle East, years of civil war and conflict with neighbouring Syria and Israel have severely harmed Lebanon's once thriving tourist industry. Much of former Yugoslavia's tourism infrastructure and attractiveness as a tourist destination have been all but destroyed by the ethnic conflict between Serbs, Croatians and Muslims. Similarly, in the case of Northern Ireland, Smyth (1986, p.120) noted, 'as an industry, tourism is particularly susceptible to certain exogenous factors and when civil unrest culminated in violence with subsequent media coverage, visitor numbers and expenditure fell.' Military coups may have a substantial effect on tourist arrivals. Following the change of regime in Afghanistan, the number of tourists fell by 60 per cent between 1978 and 1979. In the case of an attempted coup in the Gambia in July 1981, the number of visitors dropped from 21 327 in 1980/81 to 16 962 in 1981/82 (Cater, 1987, p.212).

Warfare may also have long-term impacts on the image of a destination. For example, South Korea's tourism industry has long been harmed by the Korean War and conflicts between North and South Korea. A study by Jeong (1988) indicated that the 1988 Summer Olympics in Seoul were perceived as a means to overcome the poor image of Korea in the international tourism market, particularly the United States, because of such factors as MASH (the highly popular television series based on the fictionalised exploits of an American field hospital during the Korean War), the devastation of the Korean War, the shooting down of Korean Airlines flight 007 in the early 1980s, and the ongoing political instability between North and South Korea. Nevertheless, experience from other destinations such as Cyprus (Andronicou, 1979), Sri Lanka (Richter and Waugh, 1986) and Zambia (Teye, 1986) indicates that tourism can recover rapidly following the cessation of conflict. In the case of Zambia, for example, international tourist arrivals increased threefold after the civil war finished in neighbouring Zimbabwe (formerly Rhodesia) and a black majority government came to power (Teye, 1986).

Tourism does appear to have amazing resilience in the face of potential violence in destination areas. In the case of Northern Ireland, the predominant feature in tourism development has been the adverse impact of the activities of the Irish Republican Army (IRA) and Protestant extremist groups. Until the civil unrest of 1968 tourist arrivals had shown a steady increase since the late 1950s. The decline in visitor numbers was particularly hard on the holiday market, with the consequence that by 1973 holiday travel accounted for only 7 per cent of all visitors (Smyth, 1986). The effects of the civil unrest in Northern Ireland led the *Financial Times* (4 July 1978, in Smyth, 1986, p.120) to state, 'Apart from whatever else they have done, the bombings, shootings and other horrors which go under the general rubric of "the troubles" have in the past decade virtually wiped out the Northern Ireland tourist industry.' Nevertheless, apart from a major decline in 1981, at the time of the violence and tension which accompanied the IRA hunger strike, tourism numbers showed a slow but steady increase over the remainder of the decade. With, as at the time of writing, the prospects for peace in Northern Ireland being as good as at any time in the past decade, it would seem likely that, should peace talks succeed and the rate of political violence decrease, Northern Ireland would almost certainly witness a major increase in tourist arrivals (Witt and Moore, 1992; Buckley and Klemm, 1993).

An additional element of the impact of political unrest and wars on tourism is the degree to which political violence can affect regional tourism as well as the particular destination in which the violence actually occurred. For example, the Gulf War was widely credited for downturns in tourist visitation in a number of East Asian nations, because of a perception in tourist-generating regions such as Japan and North America that it was generally unsafe to travel overseas because of the possibility of terrorist attack (Hall, C., 1994a). Tourism in India and the Maldives has suffered because of the civil war and associated terrorism in Sri Lanka. The actions of Basque separatists have, at times, damaged the tourism industry in northern Spain. 'Even Switzerland, the pre-eminent symbol of domestic tranquility and political neutrality, has seen tourism drop as a consequence of terrorist attacks in Italy, France, Austria and FR Germany' (Richter and Waugh, 1986, p.232). Similarly, in 1985 political unrest by the indigenous Kanaks who were seeking independence from France in neighbouring New Caledonia was associated with Vanuatu. 'Unfortunately, as very little image building had been done there was confusion in many tourism source countries over whether Vanuatu was or was not a part of New Caledonia and Vanuatu's tourism industry suffered accordingly' (National Tourism Office of Vanuatu, 1990, p.3). In 1986 arrivals from Australia were the lowest for nine years. As Lea and Small (1988, p.9) commented in relation to the effects of political violence on tourism in the region, 'the main lesson for South Pacific destinations is that trouble in one country means trouble for the region.'

Undoubtedly, political violence can be short-lived, but the longer-term implications for tourism may last for many years, affecting the confidence of not only tourists, but also potential investors in the tourism industry. In the highly competitive global tourism marketplace, destination substitution is becoming increasingly possible. For example, for three decades, India promoted Jammu and Kashmir as 'Paradise on Earth', where luxury hotels float in a vast fresh water lake at Srinigar and where a Maharaja's Palace serves as a hotel for the up-market visitors to Kashmir. However, political and religious violence in paradise has warned off many tourists. The reduction in visitor arrivals to Jammu and Kashmir, stemming from a dispute between Muslims and non-Muslims concerning the secession of Kashmir from India, has shifted some arrivals to other areas of the Himalayan region catering to adventure tourists (Seth, 1990, p.65).

Tourism managers and planners therefore need to become far more sophisticated in their approach to crisis management and be more aware of the political dimensions of tourism development. At present, 'when problems arise, the only response the industry knows is to market more vigorously, regardless of the likelihood of success' (Richter and Waugh, 1986, p.232). However, as the following short case studies illustrate, the sheer scope of the implications of political violence for tourism requires a far more sophisticated understanding of the nature of the international traveller's response to political instability and perceived threats to tourist safety.

Political unrest and Chinese tourism: the effects of T'ian-an-men Square

> The sight of tanks rolling into the Square; the violent battles between students and troops; the steadfastly uncompromising attitude of the Chinese authorities; it was all watched by the world on prime-time television. And most people living in free societies felt revulsion and anger; those planning holidays to China cancelled, while those with a vague notion of visiting the country put it on hold for the distant future—if ever. (Graham, 1990, p.25)

On 4 June 1989, much of the Western world watched with horror the images of tanks and troops marching to quell what had been perceived by the West as a peaceful pro-democracy protest in Beijing's T'ian-an-men Square. The political protests at T'ian-an-men Square and throughout many of China's cities at this time dramatically impacted on the country's tourism industry, as well as affecting China's relationship with many Western nations.

By late 1989 many of Beijing's hotels were almost empty. Occupancy levels in the hotels were 'below 30 per cent at a time when closer to 90 per cent would have been expected . . . 300 tour groups totalling 11,500 people were cancelled in May' (Lavery, 1989, p.96). As Gartner and Shen (1992, p.47) noted, 'occupancy rates of 15% were considered high in the months shortly after the conflict.' The low occupancy rates reflected many hotels' reliance on business travellers. Business visits were affected both by perceptions of stability which affected business confidence and also by the formal and informal sanctions that were imposed on corporations conducting business in China. However, the perception of risk affects all aspects of the tourism market.

Tourism is one of China's main sources of foreign exchange and is regarded as a significant element in the country's economic modernisation (Hall, C., 1994a). In 1988 China earned US$2220 million from foreign tourists but this fell by US$430 million the following year due to the effects of the political unrest during May and June (Tisdell and Wen, 1991). While a substantial loss of foreign exchange was experienced, it was nowhere near as bad as some commentators had forecast (Table 4.1). For example, *Travel and Tourism Analyst* estimated that 'receipts from foreign tourists will fall by 75 per cent in 1989, reducing earnings to around $550 [million], or, to put it another way, recording a loss of $1.9 [billion] over expected levels' (Lavery, 1989, p.96). Following the political unrest of mid-1989, the Taiwanese market was unaffected, the Japanese are coming back but the insurance-conscious American market is still substantially affected (Hall, C., 1994a).

Research by Roehl (1990) on American travel agents and Gartner and Shen (1992) on mature travellers indicated a negative shift in attitudes toward visiting China as a result of the events at T'ian-an-men Square. Given time and a run of favourable images in the travel press and the general media, China's tourist image may slowly revert to that held before the political unrest of 1989. As Cook (1989, p.64) argued, 'The massacre of Chinese students and civilians in T'ian-an-men Square put a temporary end to

Table 4.1. China's international tourism receipts, 1978–1992

Year	Receipts US$million	% Growth rate
1978	262.90	–
1979	449.27	70.9
1980	616.65	37.3
1981	784.91	27.3
1982	843.17	7.4
1983	941.20	11.6
1984	1 131.34	20.2
1985	1 250.00	10.5
1986	1 530.85	22.5
1987	1 861.51	21.6
1988	2 246.83	20.7
1989	1 860.48	−17.2
1990	2 217.58	19.2
1991	2 844.97	28.3
1992	3 946.87	38.7

Source: Adapted from National Tourism Administration of the People's Republic of China, 1993, p.122

international tourism in China. As history is rewritten in China, however, and as the events of Spring 1989 become back-page news around the world, tourists will return to China. In fact, the number of travellers to China is expected to increase dramatically throughout the 1990s.' Indeed, China's inbound tourism appears to have returned to the growth rates of pre-1989. Nevertheless, overseas attitudes towards the Chinese occupation of Tibet (Klieger, 1992), human rights issues, and the transfer of Hong Kong to Chinese sovereignty will clearly continue to colour foreign tourists' perceptions of China as a destination and therefore influence their decision making.

Fiji: The effects of the 1987 coups

We get cyclones, fires, floods, tidal waves, so what's a couple of coups. (resort manager, in Coventry, 1988, p.91)

As with many countries of the South Pacific, tourism is one of the mainstays of the Fijian economy. In 1990 tourism accounted for about 22 per cent of gross foreign exchange earnings, with nett earnings estimated to be about 65 per cent of gross (Fiji Ministry of

Tourism, 1992, p.7). The hotel and restaurant sector accounts for about 4 per cent of gross domestic product (GDP), although tourism expenditure through multiplier effects is estimated to contribute between 12 and 15 per cent of GDP. Tourism is also the major source of employment in Fiji (22 per cent) (Fiji Ministry of Tourism, 1992). However, the development of tourism in Fiji has been severely affected by the political disturbances of the late 1980s.

Tourism numbers to Fiji had risen substantially between 1984 and 1986, but the 1987 military coup by Major Sitiveni Rambuka over Prime Minister Timoci Bavadra's democratically elected government severely damaged the country's image in its main markets of Australia and New Zealand. Although tourists were not harmed in the coup, the storming of an Air New Zealand jet by Fiji's military did give an impression of danger to potential visitors. On 13 May 1987, tourism in Fiji was up 10 per cent on the same period for the previous year. On 14 May the industry collapsed as the newly elected Bavadra government was over-thrown. According to Lea and Small (1988, p.4), 'By 23 May, headlines in Australian newspapers stated "Tourism in tatters as visitors check out" and "Coup cuts off tourism, Fiji's economic lifeblood".'

Japanese visitation was halved during June, and dropped further during July and August. Tourist arrivals from Australia, New Zealand and the United States were cut by almost 75 per cent. From the 85 000 visitors in April, arrivals fell to 5000 in June. The Australian and New Zealand governments advised their nationals not to travel to Fiji and the occupancy rate in Fiji dropped to approximately 10 per cent (Armstrong, 1988; Fiji Visitors Bureau, 1988). Further implications of the coup for tourism were the suspension of Air New Zealand flights to Fiji until December 1987 following the attempted hijack at Nadi, and the imposition of bans by Qantas unions in protest at the coup and in concern over safety. As Lea and Small (1988, p.7) observed, 'These bans and those threatened after the second coup . . . had the effect of reinforcing opinions that it was unsafe for Australians to travel to Fiji and raised extra uncertainty in people's minds about problems in returning home if they did decide to go.'

The immediate reaction of the Fijian tourism industry, aided by the devaluation of the Fiji dollar, was to slash holiday prices. By August 1987 there was an increase in Australian and New Zealand arrivals of 9.6 per cent, and by September these markets were up 40 per cent. Then on 28 September a second coup occurred, leading to a further 30 per cent drop in arrivals. The Fijian response to the second coup was to launch a promotional campaign with the theme 'I wonder whether Fiji is still a paradise?' with the emphasis 'that all is normal and "ordinary Australians" are featured to reassure potential visitors that the destination is safe' (Lea and Small, 1988, p.8).

Nevertheless, despite the best efforts of marketers, the instability of Fijian politics has continued to have an impact on tourist arrivals, with the 1986 visitor arrival total not being reached again until 1990 (Fiji Visitors Bureau, 1992; Table 4.2). Given the potential substitutability of tropical tourism destinations it appeared that both Bali and north Queensland benefited from the coups. Indeed, 'several destinations used the Fijian coups to highlight the appeal and safety of their own resorts: "Golden beaches, coconut palms and *no* coups!", was the message used to attract visitors to Magnetic Island [Queensland] in October 1987; and "War in the Solomons ended in 1945. Why risk Fiji?"' (*Times on Sunday*, 31 May 1987, in Lea and Small, 1988, p.9). Cut-price fares and accommodation were only a short-term solution to the problems posed by the coups. As Armstrong (1988, p.43) observed, tourists 'who spend $20 a day instead of $100 cannot make the country solvent.' Therefore, the coups have had a substantial longer-term impact not only on visitor arrivals but, given the dependence of Fiji on tourism, on the overall pattern of the country's economic and social development.

Thailand: the May 1992 coup

In Thailand the military has long had a major role in determining the fates of governments. The military has been the main constant in the system of shifting allegiances within the political élite and has been a factor behind the short life spans of most Thai governments since the Second World War. The military coup rather than the ballot box has been the most common method of achieving office. Fortunately, however, coups in Thailand have generally been bloodless and the omnipresent state bureaucracy has managed to maintain an image of stability which has continued to attract both tourists and investors (Elliot, 1983, 1987; Richter, 1989). Nevertheless, the rapid economic growth of recent

Table 4.2. Visitor arrivals into Fiji by country of residence 1982–1991 (000s)

Country	1982	1983	1984	1985	1986	1987	1988	1989	1990	1991
Australia	95.46	85.03	101.40	89.46	86.29	65.38	75.26	96.99	103.54	86.63
New Zealand	28.30	24.05	26.80	19.54	22.72	16.20	21.51	28.13	29.43	30.63
United States	23.21	25.64	37.29	49.56	69.71	47.04	42.14	34.43	36.93	31.84
Canada	13.70	13.04	16.52	18.91	23.65	16.82	16.88	16.54	18.44	15.24
Japan	18.03	14.4	14.86	12.6	11.8	5.49	3.43	13.84	21.62	27.80
United Kingdom	4.33	5.89	8.57	7.71	9.97	8.51	8.46	11.40	16.77	16.56
Continental Europe	6.11	8.33	11.28	12.67	15.08	14.73	20.50	23.92	27.21	26.23
Pacific Islands	9.97	10.59	13.18	11.94	12.81	11.22	14.22	18.06	17.53	16.23
Other Areas	4.53	4.66	5.32	5.80	5.77	4.49	5.75	7.26	7.53	8.16
Total All Arrivals	203.64	191.62	235.23	228.18	257.79	189.87	208.16	250.57	279.00	259.35
% Change	7.21	-5.90	22.76	-3.00	12.98	-26.35	9.63	20.37	11.35	-7.04

Source: Adapted from Fiji Visitors Bureau, 1992, p.6

years and the consequent emergence of an educated middle class has also led to calls for greater public participation in political affairs, a reduced role for the military in politics and increased anti-corruption measures.

In May 1992 the disenchantment exploded with the army shooting and beating up demonstrators as part of a clamp-down on political protest and anti-government marchers, and it was only with the involvement of the monarchy that the situation became calm. The images of the violence in the streets of Bangkok were relayed around the world, deeply harming the tourist trade and also damaging the perceptions of political stability that had been so crucial for the attraction of foreign investment. Many tourists cancelled their trips while the meetings industry was also badly damaged. For example, the Australian Federation of Travel Agents decided to proceed with the holding of its annual convention in Bangkok in late July 1992 only after receiving assurances from the government, and with the Tourism Authority of Thailand (TAT) underwriting the convention. Hotel occupancies during the time of the convention were low. The Thai Hotels Association estimated that the average occupancy rate among its member hotels in Bangkok, Phuket and Chiang Mai was between 30 and 35 per cent, compared to the normal low-season level of 50 to 55 per cent (Asia Travel Trade, 1992).

The coup has had both short- and long-term impacts on the Thai tourism industry. In the short term, inbound tourist numbers slumped dramatically. Accommodation suffered from low occupancy rates of between 10 to 30 per cent and the tourism industry as a whole suffered from heavy discounting, with overall loss estimates by Bangkok Bank and other tourist enterprises ranging between 10 billion and 30 billion baht (US$400 million to 1.2 billion) (Hail, 1992). In the longer term, the marches and the subsequent violent response has led to altered tourist perceptions of the safety and stability of Thailand akin to travellers' responses to the massacre at T'ian-an-men Square in Peking in 1989 (see above). The sustainability of Thai tourism growth will therefore be dependent on the government and TAT reestablishing a positive image of Thailand in the international marketplace; an image that has already been substantially affected by sex tourism, the threat of AIDS and other sexually transmitted diseases, and concerns over the quality of the environment (Hall, C., 1994a).

The need for political stability

As the various examples above illustrate, tourism is extremely susceptible to perceptions of political instability, particularly when such instability is tied to military activities, whether it be a coup, as in Fiji, or a crackdown on political unrest, as in China. Tourism in these examples is merely an incidental victim of broader political activities. However, in the case of the effects of terrorism on tourism which we examine in the next section, tourism is often a direct and deliberate target of political violence.

TERRORISM AND TOURISM

A favourable image is an essential requirement of any tourist destination. The problem with any kind of civil unrest is that unfavourable images are beamed across the world, so that even those who are not afraid of terrorism will be discouraged from taking a holiday there. It is not so much that the area is dangerous; more that it does not look attractive. (Buckley and Klemm, 1993, pp.193–194)

Terrorism in all its varied forms is a fact of modern life. For example, images of hijacked aircraft or the taking of hostages are a common element in television news. Indeed, the media profile given to terrorist activities is probably critical in its occurrence given that 'terrorism is a form of communication, of both the threat or reality of violence and the political message' (Richter and Waugh, 1986, p.230).

Terrorism as a form of political violence undoubtedly has a long history. However, in recent times the profile of terrorist activities has increased because of the internationalisation of the media and greater political and economic interdependence. Tourism is affected by terrorism through two means. First, terrorist activities can damage a destination's or country's tourist industry by creating an image of lack of safety. Second, tourists or tourist facilities, such as airport terminals or aircraft, may themselves be subject to attack. 'Tourist facilities are logical targets of terrorist violence because they afford opportunity and relative safety for terrorists to act' (Richter and Waugh, 1986, p.233). Although the actual risk of terrorist attack is quite low, it is perceptions that count and the effects of such perceptions on travel decisions can be substantial (Conant et al., 1988). For example, Richter and Waugh (1986, p.230)

Richter & Waugh (1986) Terrorism + tourism
as logical companions, Tourism management,
Dec 230 - 238.

104 Tourism and Politics

reported 'preliminary estimates indicating that 1.8 million Americans changed their plans for foreign travel in 1986, following American raids on Libya and terrorist attacks on several European airports.'

Attacks on tourists or tourist facilities can be used by terrorists to achieve a range of tactical, strategic and ideological objectives. One of the most common reasons for terrorist attacks is to gain publicity for the terrorist cause. For example, the hijacking of airliners in the early 1970s by the Palestine Liberation Organisation (PLO) was used to gain publicity for the Palestinian cause. More recently, in eastern Turkey in 1993, members of the Kurdistan Workers' Party seeking the establishment of a separate Kurdish state kidnapped a number of tourists. Australian, French and British tourists were abducted and held hostage in order to raise the profile of the Kurdish separatists in the world media.

Terrorist attacks on tourists can also be used to punish nationals of a country which supports the government which the terrorists are trying to overthrow or which is in opposition to their own activities. For example, in the mid-1970s the Moro National Liberation Front, a Muslim secessionist group in the southern Philippines, kidnapped a number of Japanese nationals, both to gain publicity for their cause and to take action on the Japanese government's support for the Marcos regime (Richter, 1980). Similarly, Richter and Waugh (1986) noted that attacks on American tourists may be viewed as a form of punishment of the United States government for its foreign policy decisions and military actions.

Events which are used by governments to enhance their legitimacy can also be utilised by opposition groups to undermine support for government and to focus attention on government activities. As Richter and Waugh (1986, p.238) noted, 'Uncompromising positions taken by authoritarian leaders in their own states or self-righteous world leaders, often backfire when they cannot enforce their policies and when terrorists view the policies as challenges to be overcome.' For example, the 1980 American Society of Travel Agents (ASTA) Conference in Manila, which had over 6000 delegates in attendance, was seen as a means to enhance the profile of the Marcos government in the domestic and international media. However, just minutes after Marcos had given the opening address a bomb exploded, missing the President but injuring several delegates. The ASTA Conference caused irreparable damage both to the standing of the Marcos regime in the United States and to the attraction of the Philippines as a destination. Tourist arrivals dropped by 10 per cent immediately following the bombing protest and they continued to decline for the remainder of the Marcos reign. This trend was exacerbated by the assassination of opposition leader Benigno 'Ninoy' Aquino in late 1983 at Manila International Airport in front of the world's media (Richter, 1989).

Tourists and tourist facilities can also be targeted by terrorist organisations in an attempt to achieve ideological objectives and to strengthen claims to political legitimacy by making the incumbent government appear weak. For example, tourists in Egypt were deliberately targeted in 1992 by Muslim militants who are fighting to turn the country into a purist Islamic state, marking a change in previous political tactics. Sheikh Omar Abdel-Rahman, associated with the Palestinian militant Muslim group Hamas, was suspected of giving his religious blessing to the extremist attacks on tourists in Egypt in late 1992 and early 1993, which had seriously damaged the country's US$4 billion tourist industry, cutting the tourism trade by almost half.

Islamic fundamentalists perceive tourism as a soft target on which to wage their mission, and are aware of the role tourism plays in the Egyptian economy and in the regional economy of destinations such as Luxor. Many Islamic fundamentalists are also concerned at the contradiction between the values of mass tourism and Islam. According to Sheikh Abdel-Rahman, 'Tourism is legal in Islam . . . but tourism is not gambling or dancing in nightclubs or drinking liquor' (Time Australia, 1993, p.37).

The bomb attack on a Cairo coffee shop in February 1993 which killed four people, two Egyptians, a Turk and a Swede, appeared to be targeted at tourists. The blast ripped through the coffee shop at peak time, about four hours after Muslims ended their daytime fast during the holy month of Ramadan. Although Egypt's most active fundamentalist group, the El-Gama'a el-Islamiya (Islamic Group), which was responsible for most of the attacks on tourist attractions at the end of 1992, denied they had any responsibility for the attack, they had been warning foreign tourists to stay away from Cairo and Upper Egypt. According to the group: 'The Gama'a has carried out about 20 operations targeting the tourist industry and the casualties among the tourists themselves were negligible, in accordance with our policy of "tourism not tourists"'

(Reuter, 1993, p.7). In response, the Egyptian government has attempted to imprison many of the leaders of the fundamentalist movement and has used military forces to help protect convoys of tourist buses, particularly in the south of the country. However, the latter action, while helping to ensure tourist safety, does not enhance tourist perceptions of Egypt as a safe destination.

The above examples illustrate the extent to which terrorism can impact tourism. However, as Richter and Waugh (1986, p.238) have recognised, 'the relationship between terrorism and tourism is important not because the problem is new but because the political and economic ramifications are immense and likely to grow larger.' Because of its international visibility tourism is a ready-made target for terrorist groups who are seeking to gain publicity for their objectives. The challenge for tourism managers and planners is therefore to develop ways of preventing terrorist attacks against tourists, without giving tourists the impression that a serious threat is present, otherwise there is a likelihood that they will alter their choice of destination or, at least, undertake a different range of activities once at the destination.

POLITICAL STABILITY AND TOURISM

This chapter has illustrated the various means by which political instability and political violence can impact tourism. The effects of political violence can be both direct and incidental, and may have repercussions far beyond the immediate location in which the violence occurs. By driving tourists away political instability can have major effects on the local economy and on employment. For example, the tourist economy of Kashmir in India has been all but wrecked by the conflict between the Indian military and the Islamic separatist movement. In 1990, following a period of major political unrest in the region, only 1200 visitors entered the Valley of Kashmir in the first eight months compared with 45 000 in the same period in 1988 (Seth, 1990). Similarly, the economies of the Philippines, Fiji, Vanuatu, Egypt and Sri Lanka have all been damaged to varying degrees by political violence in recent years.

Continuing political instability, particularly in the Balkans and the Soviet Union, has also had a deterrent effect on tourism in the former state socialist countries of Eastern Europe, at a time when those countries are most in need of the foreign exchange and economic development benefits of tourism. As Hall (D., 1991f, p.287) accurately predicted in the case of tourism in the former Yugoslavia:

> While the 1989 revolutions had unique novelty value for attracting visitors to the region, long-term political uncertainty and short-term political upheaval could act as deterrents. For example, during one week in August 1990 which witnessed an armed uprising of minority Serbs, the Croatian tourism industry suffered losses estimated at $200 million as a result of cancelled holiday bookings and physical damage to roads and public transport.

Attacks on tourists or political instability in general can also lead tourists to avoid destinations. Damage to the tourist image of a destination may take years to overcome, or given favourable media coverage may be overriden relatively quickly. In addition, political instability can affect tourism development by reducing the likelihood of both foreign and domestic investment in tourist infrastructure and by increasing the costs of insuring such investments. Finally, it must be recognised that the internationalisation of tourism makes it increasingly subject to the effects of political instability and political violence. Therefore, tourism planners need to take greater heed of the political context within which tourism development occurs and to establish policies which negate the likelihood of destinations being the subject of political violence. Undoubtedly, it is impossible to insulate tourism completely from the effects of political instability. However, wherever possible proactive measures can be taken to ensure that the overall political environment is favourable to tourism development.

[handwritten margin note: other effects of terrorism]

[handwritten note: non offensive to anyone.]

5

Policy, Dependency and Tourism: The Politics of Tourism Development

Ultimately tourism in less developed countries, or anywhere else, is justified by its many participants, 'host' or 'guest', according to the alleged benefits it brings. And whereas modernisation is a more or less objective process, usually emanating from Western Industrialised countries, with specific and describable patterns of economic, social and political change, the evaluation of costs and benefits belongs to the sphere of development. The point is worth emphasising: defining development necessarily involves assessment and evaluation. Furthermore, what specific individuals, groups or classes consider progress, or development, may or may not coincide with the empirical reality of modernisation. (Harrison, 1992b, p.10)

Tourism development is one of the most commonly used, but least understood, expressions in the tourism lexicon. Development means different things to different people. As Friedmann (1980, p.4) observed, *'Development* is one of the more slippery terms in our tongue. It suggests an evolutionary process, it has positive connotations, in at least some of its meanings it suggests an *unfolding from within.'* Much of the ambiguity over the use of the term 'development', arises because it refers to both a process and a state, with the state of development deriving from the economic, social, political, and cultural processes which have caused it (Pearce, 1989).

development is always of something, a human being, a society, a nation, a skill . . . It is often associated with words such as *under* or *over* or *balanced*: too little, too much, or just right . . . which suggests that development has a structure, and that the speaker has some idea about how this structure *ought* to be developed. We also tend to think of development as a process of change or as a complex of such processes which is in some degree lawful or at least sufficiently regular so that we can make intelligent statements about it. (Friedmann, 1980, p.4)

Pearce (1989, pp.7–10), drawing on the work of Mabogunje (1980), has identified five different ways in which the concept of development is used:

- economic growth
- modernisation
- distributive justice
- socio-economic transformation
- spatial reorganisation

Pearce (1989) noted that 'development' is a dynamic concept, interpretations of which have changed over time. From a primarily economic orientation, 'development' has also come to reflect broader social, political and cultural values, and attributes such as self-reliance and regional development. For example, according to Hall (D., 1991b, pp.11–12) in the former state socialist countries of Eastern Europe, tourism development has a multi-faceted role in the 'long-term and painful process' of the transformation of the region's economies, acting as:

1. A means of gaining hard currency and improving balance of payments/indebtedness problems, through admitting much larger numbers of Western tourists.
2. A catalyst of social change, by permitting greater and closer interaction between host populations and those from the outside world, particularly as constraints on tourist accommodation and itineraries are eased.
3. A symbol of new found freedoms by permitting the region's citizens to travel freely both within and outside of their own countries, albeit initially constrained by financial considerations.
4. A means of improving local infrastructures by upgrading tourist facilities, with or without foreign assistance.
5. An integral part of economic restructuring, with the freeing of

service industries through privatisation, exposure to national and international market forces, Western transnational corporations' expansion within the region's tourism industry, and through the elimination of centralisation, subsidy and bureaucratisation.

6. A complement to commercial development through the growth of business and conference tourism, reflecting the region's entry/return into the essentially capitalist world economic system.

Given the changing nature of our understanding of development it should therefore be no surprise that from a tourism studies perspective, tourism development has also acquired two additional meanings in the way in which it is applied: first, the analysis of the impacts of tourism; second, the idea that tourism development may be made sustainable (Hall, C., 1991; Bramwell and Lane, 1993). 'Tourist development might be narrowly defined as the provision or enhancement of facilities and services to meet the needs of tourists. Tourism, however, might also be seen as a means of development in a much broader sense, the path to achieve some end state or condition' (Pearce, 1989, p.15).

Tourism development is an essentially political concept. The pursuit by governments around the world of various states of tourist development, and the perceived benefits of such development, raise questions about the economic, social and political dimensions of the development process and the directly political manner in which overt and covert development objectives are pursued at the expense of other objectives. Political philosophy and ideology will have a substantial impact on tourism development processes. For example, 'flexibility, market-response and changing fashions were not concepts which sat easily within the Stalinist model' within which tourism was perceived as an 'utterly inessential diversion from the major socio-economic priorities of state socialism' (Hall, D., 1991d, p.83). To return to one of the key points of Chapter 2, the selection of particular tourism development objectives represents the selection of a set of overt and covert values. Both the selection and implementation of these values will depend on the relative power of 'winners' and 'losers' in the political processes surrounding tourism development. Furthermore, not only is the development process political but so is its analysis. The selection of a particular theory or approach to development by the researcher or policy analyst will set the boundaries within which research is conducted, conclusions are reached and recommendations made. For many years students of tourism tended to concentrate on the economic dimensions of tourism development. More recently greater attention has been given to environmental, socio-cultural and political considerations, but the economic imperative of tourism development studies still predominates. This is perhaps because tourism studies cannot easily transcend the capitalistic nature of most travel and tourism consumption and production on which most researchers are dependent (Britton, 1991). (See the final chapter for a further discussion of this argument.)

Identification of the elements of the political process which surrounds tourism development will vary according to the level of analysis and the range of actors, interests and values operating within the policy environment. Although interrelated, the focus of studies at the national and international level will clearly be different to that of those examining tourism politics in the local state. Clearly, there is a relationship between the actions and policies of the state at the national and local level and actions of significant actors in the policy-making process and the individual. The manner in which policy pronouncements at the national level become distorted and reinterpreted as they channel through the local level and then affect the individual is testimony to this interrelationship. Nevertheless, different sets of problems present themselves to the researcher at each level of analysis.

This chapter examines tourism development policies at the national level and the stress placed on the perceived economic benefits of tourism, such as employment and regional development. As Roche (1992, p.567) noted, 'probably the main political and social stimuli and motivations for developing a tourism industry at all derive from its assumed potential to generate *employment*.' Given the significant role that tourism has in the economies of many developing countries, the chapter focuses on issues of dependency in relation to tourism development in the less developed countries. However, it is also argued that issues of dependency and core–periphery relations may be applied to the developed countries, in which the development of tourism in economically marginal areas may still be controlled by metropolitan centres. A case study of tourism development in the Solomon Islands is used to indicate the interrelationship between the various elements acting on the tourism policy environment in the less developed countries. The case study also serves to illustrate the relationship between the analysis of the politics of national and local tourism development and highlights the significance of local élites, the allocation of power, institutional arrangements and significant individuals in the tourism development process, an issue which is returned to in the following chapter.

NATIONAL TOURISM DEVELOPMENT: THE POLICY AGENDA

The advent of tourism, either at the community or national level, occurs almost invariably during periods of rapid change or precipitates local change. Elements within national governments may make policy commitments to the promotion and development of tourism as a quick expedient to shore up a quaking economy, and a local community may be 'discovered' overnight as one of the 'last' unspoiled tourist meccas. (Nuñez, 1989, p.268)

As noted in Chapter 2, national tourism policies tend to be geared to the generation of economic growth. The concept of tourism development for governments is therefore almost synonymous with *economic* development. In particular, politicians and many members of national tourist organisations focus on the potential employment generation and regional development aspects of tourism. In addition, pleas from the tourism industry for government support typically reflect such arguments along with balance of payments benefits and the industry's growth potential (Hughes, 1984; Ashworth and Bergsma, 1987; Cater, 1987; Martin and Mason, 1988; Williams and Shaw, 1988a; Dieke, 1989; Pearce, 1989; Hall, C., 1991; Hall, D., 1991a). As Airey (1983, p.236) commented in respect to the European situation, it is 'likely to be tourism's role in creating employment, in earning and spending foreign exchange and in regional distribution of wealth, that attracts the most attention' from governments. Similarly, in the case of Thailand, government attitudes towards tourism changed rapidly when tourism became the top foreign currency earner in 1982, replacing rice exports. 'As the Deputy Industry Minister stated, "Thailand should try to get more tourists to compensate for the shortfall from tin exports; there is a need for real support to increase this type of industry". There was also a feeling that tourism could help cut unemployment and provide jobs for the increased number wanting to join the work force' (Elliot, 1987, p.223).

Undoubtedly, government tourism policy is not solely concentrated on the economic dimension of tourism. For example, in Australia national tourism policy is directed towards the achievement of four principal goals:

- Economic—to improve the competitiveness of the tourism industry and minimise constraints on growth, so as to stimulate increased national income, employment growth and an improved balance of payments.
- Social—to encourage a range of opportunities for increased tourism participation and the appropriate operation of tourism activity in the public interest.
- Environmental—to develop the tourism potential of our natural resources and cultural heritage, consistent with their long-term conservation, through sensitive, balanced and responsible management.
- Support—to ensure that the necessary planning, co-ordination, research and statistical support for policy formulation is provided in accordance with the previous goals.
  (Department of the Arts, Sport, the Environment, Tourism and Territories, 1988, p.2)

A relatively broad set of development goals also exists in Portugal's national tourism policy. The *Plano Nacional de Turismo* 1986–1989 set out four major objectives for the industry:

1. To increase tourism so as to contribute to the balance of payments by
   (a) increasing external receipts;
   (b) increasing earnings, and
   (c) increasing foreign investment.
2. To contribute to regional development by
   (a) creating priority zones for tourism development;
   (b) developing spa towns; and
   (c) implementing measures which favour regional development.
3. To contribute to the quality of life in Portugal by
   (a) increasing domestic tourism;
   (b) increasing agritourism;
   (c) increasing *turismo de habitação*; and
   (d) supporting social tourism.
4. To contribute to conservation of the natural and cultural heritage by
   (a) organising a more balanced use of space between tourism and other needs;

   (b) protecting the natural environment, especially flora, in the
        littoral;
   (c) defining the optimum numbers of tourists in particular areas;
   (d) protecting regional and urban traditional architecture;
   (e) preserving monuments; and
   (f) developing artisanal crafts and supporting folklore
   (in Lewis and Williams, 1988, pp.120–121)

However, in both of the above cases it is not just the range of
objectives that needs to be considered but the relative priority
attached to objectives as they are implemented. While policy and
implementation are two sides of the same coin, it is essential to
note that policy needs to be turned into action. For example, in the
case of the Portuguese national tourism policy, Lewis and Williams
(1988, p.121) noted that 'it is difficult not to believe that the
greatest weight will tend to be given to the first objective—if only
because of national economic necessity.' Similarly, in the case of
Australian tourism policy, several commentators have argued that
economic goals are given a far higher priority than social and
environmental concerns in state and national governments' tourism
policy agenda (Craik, 1990, 1991; Hall, C., 1991).

Tourism is often given a major role by government in regional
development strategies for economically marginal areas and is a
major force for modernisation in less developed countries, but also
in marginal areas of the developed world. As Roche (1992, p.566)
observed,

> whether for good or ill, the development of tourism has long been
> seen as both a vehicle and a symbol at least of westernisation, but
> also, more importantly, of 'progress' and 'modernisation'. This has
> particularly been the case in Third World countries. But this role as
> both a symbol and vehicle of economic and socio-cultural change
> and 'modernisation' is potentially just as significant for the advanced
> industrial countries.

In the case of the Netherlands, Ashworth and Bergsma (1987,
p.154) observed that 'The central government has identified specific
local areas where tourist development could profitably be
concentrated . . . There has also on the regional and local scales
long been the hope expressed that tourist development in the
peripheral regions is well suited to support the economic goals of
regional development policy.' Regions which have been affected by
economic restructuring, such as rural and former industrial areas,
frequently perceive tourism as a mechanism to bring employment

and income back to the region. In the case of the European Community, tourism's role in regional development is the element most frequently referred to in Community members' tourism policies (Airey, 1983; refer to Table 2.1).

The European Community has long attempted to encourage development in economically peripheral regions, but tourism is a more recent mechanism to achieve economic and social objectives. The European Regional Development Fund was established in 1975 as a means of implementing EC regional policy. The purpose of the ERDF is 'to contribute to the correction of the principal regional imbalances within the Community by participating in the development and structural adjustment of regions whose development is lagging behind and in the conversion of declining industrial regions' (European Economic Community, 1984, in Pearce, 1988, p.14). According to the EC:

> In the past, development and job creation in regions experiencing difficulties often relied on large-scale investment projects decided on outside the region. With the onset and continuation of the economic crisis, such investment projects are encountered much less frequently. As a result, greater emphasis has nowadays to be placed on harnessing local resources and the potential for internally generated development potential, involving small and medium-sized firms, craft industries, alternative sources of energy, the environment, etc. (European Economic Community, 1985, in Pearce, 1988, p.15)

Tourism has become an essential part of the shift in EC development strategies because it is perceived as being highly labour intensive. According to the EC, 'it is generally agreed that tourism can be particularly beneficial in the present difficult employment situation. It is a labour-intensive industry, and its continuing expansion offers a valuable counterbalance to the unemployment which is devastating other sectors and the less favoured regions' (EEC, 1984, in Pearce, 1988, p.15). Such thinking will clearly have substantial implications for the allocation of resources to regional development projects and the use of tourism as an economic development mechanism. Decision makers tend to think of tourism as labour intensive and a relatively cheap employment generator. For example, the comments below by Brown (1985, p.8) can be regarded as typical of this perspective:

> One of the most important characteristics of the [tourism] industry is its relative labour intensity in an age of great technological

advancement and declining relative demand for labour. The industry and those industries closely aligned with it (which also tend to be labour intensive) provide many jobs both for the unskilled and highly skilled, and it has the potential to provide many further jobs, a large number of which can be introduced with minimum delay.

Nevertheless, such statements tend to obscure the somewhat problematic success of tourism as a tool for regional development. For example, while globally there has been a general growth in employment in service sector industries such as tourism, many of these positions are part time. In the case of Britain's hotel and catering sector, Robinson and Wallace (1984) noted that, while there had been extensive growth in part-time female employment, such workers were badly paid and earned about 4 per cent less than the average for part-time female workers in all industries. The highly seasonal nature of many tourist destinations may also serve to mitigate some of the potential economic goals of regional tourist development strategies. Indeed, Urry (1987, p.23) has observed that 'the more exclusively an area specialises in tourism the more depressed its general wage levels will be,' a situation that, if it holds true, has substantial implications for the use of tourism as a development mechanism. In the case of tourism development policies in the European Alps, for instance, Dorfmann (1983, p.20, in Pearce, 1989, p.204) noted that:

> these policies may have permitted mountain regions to experience a certain quantitative growth (an improvement in the demographic situation and a per capita increase in revenue) but they have not triggered off a veritable process of economic, social and cultural development. In other words, the policies for mountain regions have prevented them from falling into the vicious circle of poverty but they have not generated autogenous growth.

The potential for tourism to contribute to regional development will depend on a broad range of economic, social and political factors, including the degree of linkage among the various sectors within the regional economy, the pattern of visitor expenditure, and the extent of leakage from the regional economic system. Where substantial imports of goods and services are necessary to maintain the tourism industry, the relative worth of the industry may be somewhat doubtful from the perspective of national economic and social policy. The question of 'who benefits?' should be fundamental to the assessment of development policies. In the case of many peripheral economic regions, primary control of the flow of tourists to the destination region may lie with companies based in the tourism-generating metropoles. The economic pattern of development may therefore replicate a situation which is often ascribed to Third World or developing nations.

Perhaps in many economically peripheral areas the creation of some jobs is better than no jobs at all, but given the substantial amounts of money that governments place in regional development schemes a closer examination of the redistributive effects of tourism development within a region is warranted. For example, while tourism may be relatively labour intensive compared to some other industries, it is that labour input which is most vulnerable to minimisation by owners in order to restrict costs, therefore creating the situation in which employment is often casual, part time, under labour award rates and, at least in many Western countries, heavily centred on women because of the possibility of paying lower wages. In the situation in which tourism is promoted as an alternative to other economic activities, such as marginal agricultural or forestry operations or the mining industry, the ability of employees to transfer from those sectors to the tourism industry is somewhat limited unless there is both massive investment in retraining schemes and dramatic shifts in traditional gender roles. Therefore, in many situations, the ability for tourism to provide an employment alternative is extremely limited. At a gross level the same or even a greater number of jobs may exist in a region, but employment patterns may dramatically shift by gender, with a corresponding potential for the development of social problems because of breakdowns in traditional roles.

At a micro level, regional development schemes may also reinforce existing disparities. For example, farm or rural tourism is often promoted as a mechanism to support regional agricultural communities (e.g. Council of Europe, 1988; United States Travel and Tourism Administration, 1989). 'Rural tourism ... is concerned with using tourism to help the economic base of rural areas. In particular it involves schemes to encourage or assist farmers to supplement their earnings with incomes from tourism' (Airey, 1983, p.240). According to Hall (C., 1991, p.182):

> The growth of farm tourism has been most encouraged and is most evident in marginal agricultural regions. The conventional wisdom which surrounds farm tourism is that it has potential for growth because of the increased demand for simple, inexpensive vacations

by tourists and the need for income supplementation for farmers in a time of agricultural restructuring.

However, there is a substantial body of evidence which suggests that while farm tourism may bring visitation and income into a region, it is the farmers with surplus capital or at least enough capital to reallocate from agricultural activities into touristic activities which have the most to gain from rural tourism strategies. The most economically marginal farms, and the ones for whom such policies are often supposedly developed, are those with the least flexibility to participate in tourism enterprises because of their lack of capital. Rural tourism strategies may therefore reinforce existing income disparities for households within a region, although on a per capita or household level incomes may be maintained or rise (Bouquet and Winter, 1987).

Tourism is clearly of significance to many governments as a mechanism to promote national and regional development. However, the analysis of the economic impacts of tourism indicates that our understanding of its effects is incomplete, not only in terms of macro- and micro-economic impacts but also in terms of its social consequences. Policies do not always lead to desired outcomes. As Shaw and Williams (1990, p.240) observed, 'there is still no clear consensus as to tourism's role in economic development. The picture is clouded not only by the different assessments of economic development, but also by its socio-cultural and environmental implications.'

The question 'who benefits?' is increasingly being asked with respect to development policies, particularly in economically peripheral regions which paradoxically, by virtue of their lack of development, may have a range of resources that are most attractive to tourists. While jobs may be created they are often not taken up by those at which tourism development policies were targeted. Furthermore, unless there is a substantial amount of local entrepreneurial skills and available capital, local communities will be disadvantaged in competition against companies from metro-politan centres. The situation within developed countries may therefore parallel that which exists in the developing nations in terms of the economic and political relationship between the core and periphery. As Goodall (1987, p.72) has observed:

> significant decisions as to which destination regions are to be favoured with tourism developments are frequently exercised by

travel intermediaries based, not in destination regions, but in the tourist generating countries. Given such external control over the fortunes of the tourism industry in destination regions it must be concluded that tourism is too fragile and unpredictable an industry on which to base the total economic development of destination regions.

This point will be examined in closer detail in the following discussion of tourism development in the less developed countries and the nature of dependency.

THE POLITICS OF TOURISM DEVELOPMENT IN THE LESS DEVELOPED COUNTRIES

There are good reasons for focusing on tourism to LDCs . . . Their governments are anxious to promote economic growth and tourism—especially *international* tourism—is one means to this end. However, it necessarily involves visitors from rich countries visiting the poor—but not necessarily the poorest—thus highlighting disparities in wealth and raising their expectations. In such circumstances, the welcome to tourists may become ambivalent and tourism becomes a political as well as a social, economic and moral issue. (Harrison, 1992b, p.2)

Considerable attention has been given to tourism issues in developing countries (e.g. de Kadt, 1979; Lea, 1988; Harrison, 1992a). As Pearce (1989, p.87) noted, 'tourism in such countries is generally portrayed as distinctive.' However, there are few attempts to identify why in fact they should be regarded as such in terms of the economic, socio-cultural and political processes of tourism development. Indeed, the changes which have taken place in the former state socialist countries of Eastern Europe (the old 'Second World') have meant that 'those features that distinguished it from the "Third World", always a problematic concept . . . become increasingly less marked' (Harrison, 1992b, p.1). Therefore, 'when discussing issues of development, it is no longer possible to regard Albania, Romania and Bulgaria, for example, as obviously different from Egypt, Zambia or Pakistan. The whiff of convergence is in the air' (Harrison, 1992b, p.1).

The less developed countries, the old 'Third World' or low income countries, are primarily defined as such by virtue of their per capita incomes. Other factors which such countries may have in common include dependence on subsistence and primary production, a corresponding lack of secondary and tertiary production, and a history of colonialism. It may be noted, of course, that the nations of Eastern Europe are only recently starting to emerge from the yoke of Soviet colonialism and could also be described as 'developing'. Geographically the less developed countries may be regarded as being concentrated in central and South America, Africa, south Asia and the South Pacific, with the countries of eastern Asia being regarded as newly industrialised countries because of their rapid growth rates over the past two decades. Therefore, the notion of less developed nation status is heavily Eurocentric and economically focused.

The processes by which development occurs are extremely problematic. Competing theories, modernisation and under-development exist in Western economic and political thought to explain the nature of development. Modernisation theory primarily focuses on the process of Westernisation and assumes that developing countries seek to emulate Western patterns of production and consumption. In contrast, underdevelopment theory regards development and underdevelopment to be a part of the same global process: '"underdevelopment" is explained by reference to the structurally subordinate position of under-developed countries within the world system, rather than by the dead hand of tradition, the lack of an educated élite, or the absence of values conducive to capitalist development' (Harrison, 1992b, p.9). Academic research on tourism development processes in developing countries has tended to utilise an underdevelopment framework in their analysis. Governments and local élites in developing countries, usually Western educated, tend to utilise modernisation theory, or what might be described as the 'World Bank approach', in attempting to understand and alter their nation's economic circumstances.

Governments in developing countries utilise tourism for the same reasons as politicians in developed countries (see Chapter 3) (Jafari, 1974; Jenkins, 1980; Jenkins and Henry, 1982; Richter, 1989; Harrison, 1992b). Governments are wanting to promote economic growth and obtain the benefits of modernisation: tourism, particu-larly international tourism, is a means to this end. International tourism is seen as bringing foreign exchange into the country, improving the level of foreign debt, attracting foreign investment and creating employment. As Richter (1989, p.104) observed with respect to tourism development policies in Asia:

In many respects, the countries of south Asia share with the rest of the Third World some of the same motivations towards tourism development and some of the same problems and doubts concerning the cultural impacts of foreign guests. The earning of foreign exchange is most frequently cited as a justification for investment in tourism . . . The desperate need to find some 20 million jobs a year for the region's unemployed also encourages South Asian governments to consider tourism development, a reputedly labour-intensive sector.

The search for the benefits of modernisation through tourism development may also have its undesired effects, with the political wish for the economic benefits also serving to reinforce other political, economic, social and gender-based inequalities. For example, the authoritarian nature of successive South Korean governments through the 1970s and 1980s, in which individual freedoms were limited, has played a major role in the commoditisation of people through 'kisaeng' tourism. Kisaeng originally referred to females who were hired as companions and served a similar social function as the geisha in Japan; however, the word is now synonymous with prostitution (Hall, C., 1992c). A survey of kisaeng girls in 1978 by Korea Church Women United estimated that 'no less than 100,000' tourist service girls were operating in 1978, mainly serving Japanese male tourists (1983, p.2). However, this figure excluded the large number of unregistered sex workers. For instance, Gay (1985) estimated that some 260 000 prostitutes were operating in South Korea. Prospective kisaeng endured lectures by male university professors on the crucial role of tourism in the South Korean economy before obtaining their prostitution licences. However, more telling is the attitude of the South Korean Minister for Education who stated that 'the sincerity of girls who have contributed with their cunts to their fatherland's economic development is indeed praiseworthy' (Witness 2, 1976 International Tribunal on Crimes against Women, p.178, in Symanski, 1981, p.99). Nevertheless, while some readers may be shocked at what, to many Westerners, is an outright abuse of power and gender relationships, it should also be noted that some benefits clearly did accrue to Korea at a macro level and perhaps also at the level of the individual. Western notions of human rights and the position and responsibilities of the individual within a society should not be regarded as universally applicable. As noted in the quote from Harrison (1992, p.10) at the beginning of this chapter, 'ultimately tourism in less developed countries, *or anywhere else*, is justified by its many participants, "host" or "guest", according to the alleged benefits it brings.' Harrison, for example, goes on to use the example of Boracay Island in the Philippines (Smith, V., 1988) which has been invaded by 'drifter' tourists which has increased the amount of pollution, depleted coral resources and imported narcotics and prostitution onto the island:

> Yet the people of Boracay, like all rural Filipinos, would enjoy having the infra-structure that is needed to support tourism, because it would make their lives easier, pleasanter and safer. And they certainly want the income generated by tourism, in the form of cash with which to buy goods and services including better education for their children. They appreciate the employment that is enabling their young people to stay on the island, or to return home to Boracay from the squalor of big cities, and be with their families. In the eyes of most villagers, tourism has been very positive—and the sins of the 'drifter' tourists can be temporarily overlooked in the face of their largesse. (Smith, V., 1988, pp.15–16)

For many developing countries there are currently few if any viable alternatives to tourism if those nations are wanting to create employment and economic development opportunities. 'If communities wish to gain the benefits of modernisation in the full knowledge of the potential difficulties it may create, then why should outsiders, often academics, aid agencies and conservation organisations, be in a position to criticise or prevent them gaining their tourism development goals?' (Hall, 1994a). The issue should therefore perhaps be more one of control over the development process rather than the process itself, and it is here that theories of dependency are at their most powerful.

TOURISM AND DEPENDENCY: LEISURE IMPERIALISM AND THE NEW PLANTATION ECONOMY?

> Tourism may add to the numbers of jobs available and it may increase the trappings of modernity with modern buildings and new services, but if it does not contribute to the development of local resources, then it differs little from the traditional agricultural plantation. (Matthews, 1978, p.80)

According to several commentators, many developing countries are characterised by forms of 'dependent development' (e.g. Hills and Lundgren, 1977; Hivik and Heiberg, 1980; Britton, 1982b; Francisco,

1983). Dependency can be conceptualised as a historical process which alters the internal functioning of economic and social subsystems within a developing country. This conditioning causes the simultaneous disintegration of an indigenous economy and its reorientation to serve the needs of exogenous markets. This internal transformation determines the specific roles and articulation of various modes of production within a developing country, and thereby creates specialised commodity export enclaves, such as tourism or primary agricultural production (cocoa, copra, sugar) and structural inequality between social groups (Britton, 1982b, pp.333–334). Santos (1968, in Erisman, 1983, p.341) has observed:

> By dependence we mean a situation in which the economy of certain countries is conditioned by the development and expansion of another economy to which the former is subjected. The relation of inter-dependence between two or more economies, and between these and world trade, assumes the form of dependence when some countries (the dominant ones) can expand and be self-sustaining, while other countries (the dependent ones) can do this only as a reflection of that expansion, which can have either a positive or negative effect on their immediate development.

The clear concern in most studies of dependency is that the locus of control over the development process shifts from the people that are most affected by development, the host community, to the tourism-generating regions. However, fears of the effects of dependency are not just isolated to economic considerations. As Erisman (1983, p.339) observed, 'beyond economics lies the deeper and generally unarticulated fear that the industry's impact is even more pervasive and insidious, that it will somehow shape and affect in adverse ways the entire fabric of . . . society.' Concerns over dependency are also expressed in terms of former colonial relationships. Indeed, to several commentators, dependency is the former imperialism of Western nations by another name:

> The travel industry in the Caribbean may very well represent the latest development in the historical evolution of the neocolonial context of the West Indian socio-economic experience. Through tourism, developed metropolitan centers . . . in collaboration with West Indian élites, have delivered the Caribbean archipelago to another regimen of monoculture. As an industry based on the appropriation of West Indian human and natural resources for the ephemeral pleasure of foreigners, tourism offers the Antilles less

opportunity and less immediate likelihood of modifying the basic constellation of dependent relationships established first in the sixteenth century. (Perez, 1975, p.1, in Erisman, 1983, p.339)

Undoubtedly, for many developing countries, the manner in which the tourism industry is planned and shaped 'will recreate the fabric of the colonial situation' (Crick, 1989, p.322). Indeed, Crick went on to argue that tourism was a form of 'leisure imperialism' and represented 'the hedonistic face of neocolonialism' (1989, p.322). Although elements of the core–periphery relationship between tourist-generating developed Western nations and the developing nations which host tourism are reflective of former colonial relationships, the range of foreign economic and tourist interests in developing countries is usually greater than that which existed during the colonial period. Nevertheless, ideas of 'neocolonialism' or 'imperialism' act as powerful metaphors with which to describe the relationship between core and periphery areas, and serve to illustrate the potential loss of control which the host community may have in the face of foreign tourism interests and the actions of local élites.

Nash (1989), in one of the better known statements concerning tourism as a form of imperialism, perceived the concept quite broadly: 'At the most general level, theories of imperialism refer to the expansion of a society's interests abroad. These interests—whether economic, political, military, religious, or some other—are imposed on or adopted by an alien society, and evolving intersocietal transactions, marked by the ebb and flow of power, are established' (1989, p.38). Clearly, such an approach to ideas of imperialism is far too wide, otherwise every expansion of state interest overseas would be seen as a form of imperialism. Instead, imperialism should be conceived of as a particular kind of reality: 'What it denotes is a relationship: specifically, the relationship of a ruling or controlling power to those under its dominion . . . What we mean when we speak of empire or imperialism is the relationship of a hegemonial state to peoples or nations under its control' (Lichtheim, 1974, p.10). Nash (1989, p.39) correctly identified the importance of the relationship between the metropolitan centre and the periphery:

Metropolitan centers have varying degrees of control over the nature of tourism and its development, but they exercise it—at least at the beginning of their relationship with tourist areas—in alien regions. It is this power over touristic and related developments abroad that makes a metropolitan center imperialistic and tourism a form of imperialism.

However, the extent to which power is able to be exercised and hence development controlled in any nation or destination is somewhat problematic. As noted above, in many destination areas both the range of foreign investors and the sources of tourists are too wide for one country to exercise a degree of control that could be accurately described as 'imperialistic' or 'neocolonial'. Nevertheless, there are major exceptions, particular with respect to island microstates in the Pacific or the Caribbean who are often dependent on foreign-controlled aviation routes tied to a specific tourist-generating area such as Australia, Japan or the United States. As Connell (1988, p.6) observed, 'Island microstates are . . . unusually dependent on external relations, of trade, aid, migration, loans and investment, yet are largely unable to influence those international events which affect them most critically.'

Therefore, perhaps the crucial determinant of whether tourism is a form of imperialism or whether it is a form of economic dependency is the extent to which the relationship between the metropolitan area and the periphery can be described as hegemonic. The concept of hegemony derives from the writings of the Italian Communist Antonio Gramsci (see Gramsci, 1975):

> hegemony is nothing more than a conceptualization of the observation that the supremacy of one class over others relies on a tight net of intellectual and moral relations that involve a capacity for determined leadership on the one hand and more or less spontaneous acceptance of this leadership on the other. In short, the social order is an essentially cultural phenomenon. It is the institutionalization of a certain model of collective life—its norms, values, and collective aims—achieved through the assimilation by the subordinate classes of the ideology of the hegemonic class. (Pellicani, 1981, p.3)

The relationship of ruling class to ruling culture, explicit in the idea of hegemony, signals the fears of some commentators that the potential economic dependency of touristic relationships between the developed and developing worlds will enter into the social and cultural spheres. That tourist destinations need to serve the interests of metropolitan tourist-generating regions is implicit in the notion of tourism as a service industry (Urry, 1987). 'The touristic process involves the generation of the touristic impulse in productive centers, the selection or creation of tourist areas to serve their needs, and the development of transactions between the productive centers and tourist areas' (Nash, 1989, p.40). Despite fears over the social and cultural impacts of tourism, particularly in terms of the Westernisation, 'internationalisation' or 'sanitation' of indigenous culture (e.g. O'Grady, 1981; Hong, 1985), international tourism is as responsible for the revitalisation of indigenous culture as it is for its demise. Clearly, there is no simple relationship between international tourism and cultural imperialism. Although the gaze of the tourist on host culture and landscape does potentially signal the incorporation of those features within the culture of the tourist (Urry, 1990a, 1992), the implications of the relationship between host and guest for global and regional capital and culture are still being considered (see Chapters 7 and 8).

The notion of dependency is also closely tied to the role of élite vested interests and their close relationship with former colonial powers, with the élite determining the objectives of development in conjunction with foreign interests. According to Britton (1982b, p.334) '"dependency" involves the subordination of national economic autonomy to meet the interests of foreign pressure groups and privileged local classes rather than those development priorities arising from a broader political consensus.' Similarly, Crick (1989, p.323) has identified the significance of 'indigenous collaborative élites' in tourism in developing countries, who:

> in tourism, as in other imperialist situations, are linchpins by means of which foreign interests maintain their hold in poor countries. Those with political sway, able to hand out contracts and the like, are the beneficiaries. Local élites may well identify with the consumerist life-style of international tourists rather than with the aspirations of their own people

Local élites are of particular importance in determining the nature and pattern of tourism development. 'In a neo-colonial context, it is usually members of the ruling classes who have the power to bargain with foreign industry or government representatives, and to implement policies consistent with these interests' (Britton, 1982b, p.334). For example, the development of international tourism in Fiji, as with many other developing countries, was based on the interaction of foreign and local élites in pursuit of their own interests and mutual benefit (Britton, 1983).

The relationship of foreign and local élites, and the pursuit of development objectives by local élites which are exogenously derived, has led to some commentators noting that tourism in some developing countries may exhibit the characteristics of a colonial plantation economy in which 'Metropolitan capitalistic countries try to dominate the foreign tourism market, especially in those areas where their own citizens travel most frequently' (Matthews, 1978, p.79). Similarly, Nash (1989, p.50) noted that 'a tourist system, once established, must meet the touristic needs of one or more metropolitan centers, it will inevitably reflect the development of such needs.' Air services, bus companies, hotels, resort developments, recreational facilities such as golf courses, and food and beverage are all potential markets related directly to tourism which may become owned by foreign interests.

The elements of a plantation tourism economy (Best, 1968) are that:

1. tourism is structurally a part of an overseas economy;
2. it is held together by law and order directed by the local élites; and
3. there is little or no way to calculate the flow of values.

In the case of many microstates, it has been argued that tourism development, along with foreign financial services such as tax havens, demonstrates elements of a plantation economy (Britton, 1982a, b, 1983; Connell, 1988), in which nations are nothing more than the place of production in a system of trade and production in which control lies with the demand for produce in the developed countries and with the merchants (Girvan, 1973, p.17).

Within the plantation economy overseas interests are the determining factor in the creation of both the demand and supply of the tourist product. In the absence of a domestic tourism market, many developing countries are clearly dependent on foreign interests to keep the industry going. For example, in a study of tourism development in South Pacific microstates, Britton (1987, p.131) argued that 'without the involvement of foreign and commercial interests, Tonga has not evolved the essential ties with metropolitan markets and their tourism companies. It would seem that Tonga's tourist industry has paradoxically suffered because the country was not exploited as a fully-fledged colony.'

The potential implications of dependence on overseas interests for tourism development in island microstates (IMS) has been highlighted by Connell (1988, p.63):

The goods (especially food and drinks) consumed by tourists are often imported, hence the most positive role of tourism is in employment in the services, handicraft and construction industries, rather than in direct income benefits. Even payments made within the IMS are exported; sources of leakage include foreign ownership, employment of foreigners (hence repatriated incomes) and imported materials. The high energy costs of modern tourism are also a significant cost factor, and a possible constraint to future development in more remote states.

The dependence of island microstates on tourism in the Caribbean and the Pacific is often regarded as having numerous negative economic and social impacts. For example, several authors have questioned the employment benefits of tourism in microstates and other small developing countries (e.g. Finney and Watson, 1977; Britton, 1983, 1987a; Bastin, 1984; Cater, 1987; Connell, 1988; Lea, 1988; Hall, C., 1994a). In a recent study of tourism development in the Pacific, Hall (C., 1994a) noted that employment in the tourism industry in the region is often marked by low payment levels, a low skills base and seasonal unemployment, although greater indigenous involvement in tourism management does appear to occur over time. However, in the case of many Pacific nations there are few or no other employment alternatives in a situation where populations and expectations are rapidly increasing. Therefore, the labour-intensive nature of many hotel and resort developments is seen by island governments as an important employment generator and, hopefully, a mechanism for improving the business skills of the indigenous population. Furthermore, indirect employment is also provided in the construction of hotel and tourism facilities and through improvements in linkages with other sectors in the economy such as agriculture and fisheries. Undoubtedly, several microstates in the Pacific area are highly dependent on one or two tourism-generating regions. For example, the Cook Islands, Fiji, the Solomon Islands and Vanuatu are all highly dependent on Australia and New Zealand tourist arrivals. From these countries also come the greatest amounts of investment in tourism development and aid for infrastructure development.

In recent years the increase in Japanese tourism investment and aid projects in the region and a corresponding rise in visitor arrivals have lessened the dependence of the South Pacific on Australia and New Zealand. Therefore, rather than exhibiting dependency on one tourism-generating region, the countries of the

South Pacific appear to be attempting to spread their sources of foreign investment and arrivals in order to minimise potential downfalls in any one market and play off metropolitan regions against one another. Similarly, in discussing tourism development in south-east Asia, Hivik and Heiberg (1980) argued that because of the diversity of sources of international tourists, the region was less prone to develop the sort of centre–periphery dependency relationship that affects many other developing countries. Nevertheless, in a broad sense such countries still demonstrate aspects of economic dependency because of their inability to generate substantial amounts of domestic investment in the tourism sector.

Perceived foreign control of national or regional economies, and subsequent loss of local economic and political control, may give rise to substantial resistance from indigenous communities. Even in one of the international meccas of tourism and, supposedly, one of the great success stories of international tourism, Hawaii, increasing dissatisfaction with foreign (non-Hawaiian) control of tourism and the island's cultural and natural resources is leading to a backlash against tourism development from native Hawaiians.

Opposition to large-scale tourism development in Hawaii has existed for a number of years. For example, in describing tourism in Hawaii, Farrell (1974, p.206) posed the question, 'Do a few persons in corporate boardrooms have the right to engineer major migrations from the mainland when need, beyond providing reasonable growth and shoring up agriculture, cannot be established?' In the past decade, substantial opposition to further tourism growth and tourism *per se* has begun to develop in Hawaii, particularly with indigenous Hawaiians seeking to receive greater economic benefit from tourism, greater political control over tourism development, a larger say in the use of their traditional lands, and greater control over the presentation of indigenous culture to tourists. As has happened throughout much of the Pacific Rim, indigenous Hawaiians have protested about golf course and hotel development, often associated with Japanese investment, and their effect on agriculture, fisheries, and environmental quality (Hall, C., 1994a). In Hawaii, 'many resort communities imposed on local communities have run into oppositions at zoning and at shoreline management permit hearings, run into delays of years and have been stalled by law suits in the courts' (Minerbi, 1992, p.9). Resentment towards the effects of tourism on indigenous culture has reinforced the growing political power of native Hawaiians. Trask, an indigenous Hawaiian, has gone so far as to state, 'If you are thinking of visiting my homeland, please don't. We don't want or need any more tourists, and we certainly don't like them. If you want to help our cause, pass this message on to your friends' (1991, p.14).

The perceived disproportionate spread of the economic benefits of tourism in Hawaii has led to widespread dissatisfaction among many indigenous Hawaiians, who increasingly feel that they are strangers in their own land. According to Kent (1977, p.182), 'for the working people of Hawaii, the widely acclaimed "age of abundance" has never materialised, tourism has only brought the same kinds of low-paying, menial, dead-end jobs that have always been the lot of the local workers.' Indeed, in a manner reflecting the above concerns over the potential for tourism to become a plantation economy, Kent described tourism as 'a new kind of sugar' in which the industry was dominated by large corporations (then from the United States' mainland, now also from Japan) which utilise a vertically integrated economic structure to maximise their returns from the tourism dollar, thereby leaving little economic prospects for secondary businesses run by local people:

> The wheel of history spins full circle. In the same way that the old plantation aristocracy held workers in a state of feudal dependency through ownership of the houses they lived in, modern resorts will be able to threaten rebellious workers with outright eviction from their company-owned homes. (Kent, 1977, p.193)

In one respect the picture painted by Kent is not quite as gloomy as it seems (Hall, C., 1994a). Indigenous Hawaiians have been able to seek sole political and legal redress for the damage that tourism development and tourists have caused to sacred sites and the loss of traditional access and use of resources. For example, a native Hawaiian group, the Hui Alanui o Makena, filed six lawsuits against a Japanese resort developer, Seibu Hawai'i, because it had cut public access to the coast at a section of a traditional trail which had been built around the island of Maui in the sixteenth century. After three years a settlement was reached which bound the corporation and its successors to keep the trail open and restore, at its own expense, public access. 'In addition Seibu contributed half a million dollars for a community based corporation to perpetuate Hawaiian culture and dedicated three acres of land for a living cultural center' (Minerbi, 1992, p.52). Nevertheless, despite the success of some indigenous Hawaiian groups in curbing some of the excesses of tourism development, the extent to which they have lost control over their own land to non-Hawaiians serves as a potential warning to other microstates and tourism destination regions in developing countries and illustrates some of the more severe consequences of dependency.

According to Minerbi (1992, p.51), 'tourism is associated with loss of self-reliance skills and the diminishment of traditional ties to land and sea when people shift to hotel employment or when the resort cuts access to those resources.' However, the growth of culturally based tourism would tend to indicate that this need not be the case (Hall, C. and Zeppel, 1990; Zeppel and Hall, 1992). (See Chapter 7 for a more detailed discussion of the politics of cultural representation.) For example, the safeguarding of traditional values and norms, cultural activities and folklore is now a central tenet of the tourism strategies for a number of Pacific states, although the effective implementation of such policies is still to be assessed. Nevertheless, according to the Fiji Ministry of Tourism (1992, p.8):

> attention is now being turned to the notion of 'controlled tourism' [which] would enhance and definitely preserve and enrich authentic culture and tradition . . . a cautious approach to tourism would . . . advocate the preservation and enrichment of authentic culture and tradition.

Although the domination of aviation links by foreign carriers and hotel and resort development by foreign corporations will continue to be unavoidable concerns for many microstates, the development of special interest travel opportunities would appear to be a potentially valuable alternative to mass tourism. However, while superficially attractive, the concept of 'controlled tourism' begs the question, controlled by whom? To be made effective 'controlled tourism' necessitates that the concerns of traditional landholders and local communities be addressed. Tourism must be appropriate to indigenous communities rather than local élites or foreign investors. In the case of Hawaii many problems emerged because the indigenous community lost control of their land and the political process. As Britton (1983, p.2) observed, 'because of the importance of foreign capital within island states, the introduction of new economic sectors such as tourism have usually occurred through initiatives shown by foreign capital, or through local political and commercial élites in close liaison with foreign capital.' Controlled tourism therefore means control by local landowners and discussion at the village level, rather than the implementation of schemes by 'big men' who are members of the local élite, overseas corporations, or Western aid agencies and conservation organisations, without due approval by traditional landholders.

The issue of the control of tourism development and the role of local élites and foreign interests in determining the direction of the tourism development process is discussed in more detail in the following case study of tourism development in the South Pacific.

The politics of ecotourism development in the Solomon Islands

Ecotourism has become one of the buzzwords of the tourism industry. The development of nature-based or ecotourism products is a response by the tourism industry to perceived value shifts in Western society which favour environmental conservation, and which may translate into greater active tourist participation, interest and concern for the environment and hence consumption (Hall, C., 1992d). Ecotourism is generally regarded as a positive dimension of tourism, particularly as it implies the potentially symbiotic relationship between tourism and conservation fore-shadowed by Budowski (1976) in his seminal work on tourism and the environment. The concept of a form of income and employment generator which helps preserve the environment clearly has substantial appeal to many authorities, particularly in Third World nations where alternative development mechanisms may be in short supply (Hall, C., 1994a). However, substantial concerns over the actual benefits of ecotourism to host communities are increasingly being voiced. For example, Helu-Thaman (1992, p.26) argued:

> Ecotourism is fast becoming the modern marketing manager's source of inspiration for the new sale. It's got a lot going for it: it gives great pictures; it offers pretty much what people want when they wish to escape from pressured polluted urban living, and it offers a sort of moral expiation of guilt for our contribution to the degradation of our own planet.

Concern over the impacts of inappropriate forms of ecotourism has concentrated on the effects of ecotourists on the physical environment. After all, the footprint of an ecotourist is the same as that of a 'mass' tourist. Indeed, several writers have argued that it is essential for conservation to be an integral component of our understanding of ecotourism (e.g. Bragg, 1990; Valentine, 1992). More often than not ecotourism has come to be regarded as tourist visitation to national parks and reserves. However, such a notion of ecotourism provides an extremely limited approach to understanding ideas surrounding environment, ecology and the maintenance of biodiversity.

Ecotourism often appears inherently biased toward Western ideas of environmental conservation which separate humankind from nature, in contrast to a concept of environment which treats nature as a cultural resource. Indeed, the concept of the environment in the search for sustainable forms of tourism development, such as ecotourism, must include social and political dimensions as well as physical features (Hall, C., 1994d). As Brookfield (1991, p.42) argued, environmental sustainability not only refers to environmental regeneration and the maintenance of biodiversity but must also 'be measured by progress along a vector made up of attributes that include improvement in income and its distribution, in health, in education, freedoms, and access to resources.' Within this context the potential of ecotourism to contribute to sustainable tourism development may be somewhat problematic. Any analysis of ecotourism development must therefore detail the political and social dimensions of tourism as well as the potential contribution of nature-based tourism to conserving biodiversity. However, as the following study of ecotourism on the Weather Coast in the Solomon Islands (Hall, C. and Rudkin, 1993; Rudkin and Hall, 1994a) indicates, the full implications of ecotourism development may be either neglected or deliberately ignored in order to serve political and economic interests separate from those directly affected by the tourism development process.

The Solomon Islands: the development context

The Solomon Islands comprise the third largest archipelago in the South Pacific and collectively have a land area of nearly 30 000 km^2 distributed over 1.28 million km^2 of ocean. The islands are mainly volcanic in origin and are subject to frequent earthquakes, which often cause substantial ecological destruction and social dislocation. Most of the islands have lagoons and considerable lengths of coral reef, many formed around eroded volcanic cones. Subsequent growth of the coral has formed spectacular terraces of coral reef which provide the habitat for numerous varieties of fish and other marine life, which in turn attract diving and marine enthusiasts from around the world. Almost 80 per cent of the Solomon Islands is still covered in dense tropical rainforest which contains many endemic species of flora and fauna (Lees, 1991, p.9). The forest cover also serves to restrict soil erosion and the subsequent sedimentation of streams and reefs (Lees, 1991).

In 1987 the population of the Solomons was 292 000 people. More than 80 per cent of the population remain engaged in agricultural and fishing activities, many still at a subsistence level. The GDP of the Solomon Islands was US$144.6 million in 1987, with a GDP per capita of US$485. The main sources of foreign exchange are fishing, logging, cocoa beans, copra and tourism. Foreign aid is also a significant contributor to the Solomon's economy, with US$35 million being received in 1988 (Siwatibau, 1991). The major sources of foreign aid are Australia, New Zealand, Japan and the European Union.

Traditional Solomon Islands society was underpinned by a structure based on the role of 'big men' and customary land tenure. Big men achieved status through the accumulation of wealth, although their power was kept in check by various socially sanctioned mechanisms which stressed the importance of clan consensus, while land was collectively held by the clan. Nevertheless, the advent of Christianity, colonialism and the monetised economy has meant that the desire for individual benefits is increasingly gaining ground over collective benefits, even in the traditionally oriented communities throughout the islands. 'Often individual rights will be pursued over clan rights as exploitative practices accelerate access to consumer goods, creating inter-clan conflict' (Sofield, 1992, p.91). 'Big men' still remain very important in Solomon Islands politics and society, but their role has changed with the onset of modernisation and they have become part of the local élite, their interests being achieved through both modern and traditional political methods.

The modernisation of a society has substantial implications for the nature of the political process and the allocation of power. The increase of state power is typically at the cost of local control through traditional power structures. As Narokobi (1989, p.80) observed:

> All Melanesian states, on becoming independent, acquire all the colonial apparatus of power and 'constitutionalise' most former colonial acts or omissions. Traditional institutions and norms are swept beneath the carpets of power or neglected to an idyllic future when 'custom' or 'tradition' will be incorporated into state practices and law. Whilst state power increases, implying an increase of power for the 'law men' and a limited number of 'law women', the power of the villages, the clans and the people withers.

'Big men' or 'law men' are therefore key actors in the political process surrounding development in the Solomon Islands and set the 'rules of the game' by which decisions are made (see Chapter 2). The role of traditional bases of power, the clan, the village, the tribe or the chief, is not clearly defined in the new postcolonial political order which is derived from Western rather than traditional political traditions. Therefore, traditional 'Melanesian social orders exist within an imposed state order, and yet operate outside it . . . Neither a village nor a clan nor any chief, as such, exists as a legal entity within the state legal order unless a process of incorporation into state law takes place (Narokobi, 1989, pp.80–81). This means that there is considerable tension between those who have utilised the Western-style governance structures to gain power and those who adhere to a more traditional clan model, although it would appear true to say that the traditional model is on the decline or at the very least is being modified to suit the interests of the Western-educated élite (Rudkin and Hall, 1994a). As Narokobi (1989, p.84) commented in contrasting the conflict between Western-oriented and *kustom* (customary or traditional) law and governance, 'For most of the time, the people are without power even to rule their own clans, tribes and villages.'

Solomon Islands politics and elections are carried out under a *wantok* system in which people vote for candidates on the basis of performance and achievement in their own areas (Alasia, 1989, p.137). The *wantok* system reflects the predominance of big men in Solomon Islands politics and therefore must influence the nature and characteristics of tourism development in the country. Indeed, Sofield (1992, p.94) has argued that for tourism ventures to be successful they should 'inter alia support traditional leadership roles' in order to help ensure 'an equitable and acceptable system for distribution of rewards among the communities involved.'

However, given the decline of broader collective restraints on the pursuit of individual wealth by big men, the desired distribution of the benefits of tourism may be somewhat problematic. The integration of the big man system within a monetarised society leads to the development of a new, often urban, élite with a set of personal interests substantially different from that sought by 'big men' in traditional society (Hau'ofa, 1987).

Most of the land and its resources is customarily owned by the indigenous people living in scattered rural communities. The opportunity to stay overnight in a 'leaf hut' and partake in village cuisine is regarded as an essential experience for the more adventurous tourist (Harcombe, 1988). Nevertheless, the majority of the population is still dependent on subsistence fishing and gardening. Forest resources provide food, traditional medicines, housing and canoe building materials. Forests also retain social and cultural significance, but increasingly traditional economic value is giving way to monetary value for village residents and the national economy. 'Many land owners have agreed to logging of their forest resources in order to have access to desired goods, education for their children, and other development opportunities. In addition, forest is being cleared to provide new gardening land and for plantation agriculture to feed a rapidly growing population' (Lees, 1991, p.1). However, some landowners, as well as sections of the Solomon's government, have also recognised the importance of preserving the natural environment and local culture for attracting tourists to the country.

The European Community funded Tourism Council of the South Pacific (TCSP) (1987, 1988) has argued that 'ecotourism' based on protected natural areas could provide greater long-term returns than logging. Consultant Annette Lees, of the New Zealand conservation group the Maruia Society, has argued the classic case for ecotourism, which 'functions as a vehicle for preservation, not only bringing considerable revenue to the country and to local landowners, but also preserving valuable resources intact for the enjoyment and utilisation by future generations of visitors and Solomon Islanders' (1991, p.75). Nevertheless, members of many villages remain opposed to tourism development because of fears as to its cultural impacts and doubts as to its economic benefits; leading to substantial conflict between the opposing values of the various groups engaged in the decision-making processes surrounding tourism development.

Tourism in the Solomon Islands

Unlike other South Pacific Islands such as Fiji and Tahiti, the Solomon Islands have only recently begun to develop a tourism industry. Regular air service routes to the Solomons suitable for tourist visitation were only established in the mid-1970s (De Burlo, 1989). Although only a small number of tourists visit the Solomons, tourism is one of the major sources of foreign exchange for the country and, like many countries in the Pacific, is increasingly seen as a mechanism for economic development and employment generation.

Tourist visitation to the Solomon Islands remained static from 1985 to 1991 with an average of approximately 11 000 visitors a year. In 1992 visitation was down substantially for the first half of the year, although tourist numbers recovered in the second half with the celebrations surrounding the 50th anniversary of the Battle of Guadacanal (Government of the Solomons, 1993). The major attractions for tourists are scuba diving, rainforest treks, and the opportunity for war veterans to return to the battlefields of the Second World War (De Burlo, 1989). The actual proportion of visitors to the Solomons who can be categorised as recreational tourists is uncertain. According to the Solomon Islands 1985–1989 Tourism Development Plan, approximately 70 per cent of air arrivals were classified as leisure travellers (Tourism Council of the South Pacific, 1990). In contrast, a survey carried out by the Tourism Council of the South Pacific in 1987 identified only 32 per cent of visitors as holidaymakers, with the remainder being business people, convention attendees, visiting friends and relatives and transit passengers (Economist Intelligence Unit, 1989, p.87). As with a number of South Pacific destinations Australia is the dominant source of tourist arrivals, representing approximately 40 per cent of total arrivals. The other significant markets for tourist visitation to the Solomons are New Zealand, Japan and the United States.

Since the mid-1980s the Solomon Islands government, along with other South Pacific nations, has given high priority to tourism development as it is perceived as a growth industry with the potential to earn foreign exchange for a country which has traditionally been reliant on the export of primary produce. Furthermore, tourism development is regarded as a means to offset a growing national debt and scarcity of foreign funds, and to slow the high rate of inflation and the rising cost of living due to the high price of importing basic commodities (McKinnon, 1990).

One of the major directions identified in the Solomon Islands National Tourism Policy is the development and promotion of ecotourism projects which are culturally sensitive. According to the Solomon Islands Government (1989, p.17):

> a relatively moderate rate of development will be followed to minimise disruptive and harmful socio-economic, cultural and environmental impacts . . . The development of tourism should be based on the inherent natural, cultural, and historical features of the country so as to achieve domestic cultural and environmental conservation and to facilitate international . . . interaction.

The TCSP has invested a substantial proportion of funds in the development of ecotourism in the Solomon Islands in recent years, promoting it as an environmentally sensitive, economic alternative to rainforest cutting. As the Solomon Islands tourism development plan states:

> In those areas where environmental protection is needed, tourism can provide the custom owner with the needed cash, the area is left undisturbed, and the cash return is ongoing.
> Tourism, therefore, allows for cash to be received for the privilege of visiting the land, but with no resource depletion. Economic benefits are thus gained with future land use options being retained. (Tourism Council of the South Pacific, 1990, p.42)

Nevertheless, many traditional landowners remain uneasy at the social and economic effects of tourism development. As Kudu (1992, p.158) noted, 'the TCSP is cognisant about the problems in getting communal landowners convinced that their land often serves better unexploited than exploited, in particular as the latter often provide the landowners with immediate and visible economic benefits.' The TCSP primarily perceives the difficulties in establishing nature reserves supported by ecotourism development as being a failure of the indigenous people to see the economic returns that would accrue to them from ecotourism. From the TCSP's perspective the problem lies with the indigenous communities and 'not the TCSP, the consultants, conservation groups, or the tourism industry' which are seeking to promote tourism development (Hall, C., 1994d).

Although potentially beneficial for the conservation of rainforests, visitation from foreign tourists could have its social costs while the economic benefits may not accrue to the host community (Isaccson, 1991). If local people are excluded from the decision-making process and from their customary lands and resources, then their way of life will undoubtedly change, possibly resulting in resentment and negative social and environmental impacts. For example, following a change of ownership at the Anuha Island Resort in the Solomon Islands and a consequent series of actions which angered the customary landholders (Sofield, 1990), 'The angered islanders dug holes in the airstrip, sent painted warriors to force guests off the islands, and closed down the resort in spite of a court ruling against them' (Minerbi, 1992, p.19). Therefore some commentators, such as Sofield (1992), part-owner of the Vulelua Resort and former chairman of the TCSP Management Committee, have suggested that it becomes imperative that local big men be used to ensure that tourism projects are successful and conservation goals are met. However, given the nature of big men in postcolonial society as discussed above, the focus on big men may mean that local community concerns surrounding tourism development may not be addressed. The rules of the tourism development game are set by the big men and the tourism industry rather than by the communities who will be directly affected by tourism development. By making economic and conservation objectives the prime consideration in tourism projects, the social and political dimensions of tourism can be ignored to the detriment of broader development goals.

Tourism development at the central Weather Coast, South Guadacanal

Guadacanal is the largest island in the Solomon Islands with an area of just over 5300 km^2. The southern 'Weather' Coast is dominated by a volcanic mountain range which runs the length of the island. The mountains are extremely rugged and contain tropical rainforest of high conservation value. However, the rainforest is also under pressure from commercial logging interests. The coastal area of the Weather Coast has only poor quality agricultural land, is highly earthquake and cyclone prone, and has one of the highest rates of malarial infection in the world (Rudkin and Hall, 1994b). During field research it was noted that the people of two of the villages closest to Lauvi Lagoon in the south of the island were having to sleep on the stony beach because the villages were so infected with mosquitoes (Rudkin, forthcoming).

On most of the Weather Coast the village lands and the forest are under customary ownership and not under registered titles, as ownership by title would mean exclusion to many traditional landowners. The likelihood of multiple claimants for land therefore makes the development process somewhat problematic. 'Proof' of ownership would give legitimisation to land claims and improve access to aid and commercial loans for those named on the title, a prerequisite of lending institutions and many aid organisations. Not only would that result in financial and material benefits for the 'owners' and their *wantok*, it would also exacerbate existing disparities in income distribution and ownership of scarce capital resources and limit or restrict access to land and waterways (Rudkin, forthcoming).

In October 1988 a proposal for a rainforest trail traversing Guadacanal 'under the control of an indigenous company of customary landowners' (Sofield, 1992, p.96) was proposed from within the Prime Minister's Office by Trevor Sofield, the former Australian High Commissioner, as an alternative to commercial rainforest logging. The proposed trail would start at Aola on the north coast of Guadacanal and end at Lauvi Lagoon on the south coast, where a light airstrip was available at the village of Avu Avu. According to Sofield (1992, p.96) 'a central feature of the design objective was to provide a magnitude of income equal to that to be obtained from logging so that it could counter offers of logging companies.' Overseas conservation organisations, such as the Australian Conservation Foundation, have tried to introduce environmental education programmes in the Solomons, but according to Ezekiel Alebua (1991, p.38), a former Prime Minister, they 'offered idealism without cash, and the resource owners decided to stick with the logging companies'. Sofield (1992, p.96) noted that the proposed rainforest trail would 'also achieve another key feature lacking in educative efforts of some conservationists: it would make a cultural "fit" with the pursuit of "big man" status.'

In November 1988, at the meeting of the local area council, it was reported that the council had applied for funding for a Lauvi Tourist Resort which had been proposed by Ezekiel Alebua, the local national parliamentary member (Rudkin, forthcoming). It was stated at the meeting that there was no objection to supporting the application, but if the landowners had any concerns it was not the problem of the council. The acquisition of land for the resort was to be undertaken by a form of public notice to be placed in villages with interests in the land on which the resort would be built. It was noted that the proposed project would generate income for the council and provide employment. However, the resort proposal was not debated at village level by those traditional landusers who would be directly affected by the proposal (Rudkin, forthcoming).

In August 1990 the Solomon Islands government and the TCSP were seeking consultants to develop a tourist plan for the Lauvi Lagoon. According to the proposed terms of reference for the environmental planning specialist, the project consultant would undertake a number of activities including (in Rudkin, forthcoming):

- a preliminary look at management options with discussions with traditional landowners
- an 'awareness phase' in which landowners must be identified and any disputes resolved before proceeding further
- a resource inventory in which development options would be evaluated
- a draft plan which would outline all aspects of the operation and which would be widely distributed for general comments prior to adoption of a final plan
- the establishment and maintenance of initial meetings and the flow of regular information to the relevant government and area councils

The Guadacanal Provincial Government welcomed the terms of reference for the proposed tourism development at Lauvi Lagoon, its only comment being that the Ministry should liaise directly with the appropriate area councils and landowners when the specialist consultant embarked on his initial work. On 18 March 1991, the Dangroup environmental consultant for the TCSP inspected and evaluated the natural attractions of the Lauvi Lagoon for their tourism potential. However, he was confronted by a group of angry traditional landowners who claimed they had never been consulted about the proposed Lauvi resort project. Strong objections were made to the Guadacanal Province regarding the fact that Ezekiel Alebua, the local member of parliament, and officials from the Ministry of Tourism and Aviation had never discussed the project with this group of customary landowners. The landowners objected to any form of tourism development, primarily on the basis that the resort had the potential to displace them from their traditional use of the lagoon, and maintained their approval should be gained before carrying out project-related studies (Rudkin, forthcoming). Despite the forthcoming concerns surrounding the Lauvi Lagoon tourism resort project, the TCSP (1991) highlighted the potential of the area for ecotourism development, while the *Solomon Islands Tourism Development Plan, 1991–2000*, also produced by the TCSP, stated that the Lauvi Lagoon:

> has potential for development of a small scale nature-oriented attraction with associated visitor accommodation and other services. There appears to be scope for developing and managing the crocodile populations for tourist viewing, this being the major attraction. Other attractions which should be developed are trails in the surrounding forest, and trips to the outlying reef. It may also be possible to integrate custom and traditional villages with tourism depending on the wishes of the people. (TCSP, 1990, p.359)

The proposed development of marine tourism activities such as scuba diving in the lagoon and on the outlying reef was somewhat surprising given that local people avoid swimming in those areas because of the fear of shark attack. The TCSP (1990) proposed that a market study and demand forecast be carried out and that a detailed inventory of natural resources of the area be undertaken. Little consideration was given to the local people's attitude towards the development, except in relation to land ownership. The scope of the resource inventory was also rather restricted as it perceived resources purely in terms of tourist consumption rather than of the effects of tourism development on the traditional owners' use of the lagoon and forest resources (Hall, C. and Rudkin, 1993).

In May 1992, following increased concern of traditional landowners at the likelihood of the resort development going ahead, the debate over the resort proposal at Lauvi Lagoon became an issue in the national media. On 5 May the people of an affected village wrote to the Guadacanal provincial government, noting that as traditional landowners and users of the Lauvi Lagoon area they had not been consulted about the resort proposal:

> We are concerned that the site indicated is our main fishing ground. Our ancestors were using the land as we are and our generation will be using it. We will fish for food, collect shells, crabs, cabbages and gardening etc etc without fear because we own it rather than foreigners restricting rules over the area we roam freely . . . we have been negated of our rights in our land by not having knowledge of the Agreement, because we did not sign it. Proper negotiations must be done to our satisfaction. (in Rudkin, forthcoming)

On 8 May a press release was sent to the Solomon Islands Broadcasting Commission (SIBC) and the national newspaper, the *Solomon Star*, on behalf of some of the traditional landowners regarding the 'continuing saga of non-consultation with community involved tourist development Lauvi Lagoon.' The press release was not published (Rudkin, forthcoming).

On 11 May, two news stories were read by the SIBC regarding the project. The first story, carried in the early news bulletins, stated that the Ministry of Tourism and Aviation was helping the landowners of South East Guadacanal to start a small-scale tourism project at Lauvi Lagoon and that a representative of the Ministry would accompany the local member of parliament, Ezekiel Alebua, to the area for 'further discussions with the landowners'. The broadcast also reported that the director of the Guadacanal Province's Cultural Centre, Victor Tutu, had stated that the people of the area had not been consulted about the project and sought to know more about the advantages and disadvantages of tourism. In stark contrast, the evening news bulletin reported that:

> Lauvi Lagoon on the Weather Coast could be developed into a tourist resort. It is one of a number of sites recommended for tourism development by the TCSP.
> Funding for such tourism development has been secured from the EEC under its Pacific Regional Tourism Development Program.
> Initially, the villagers were concerned about the prospect of tourism finding its way to the village, now they realise [they] could derive benefit from the industry.

The Ministry of Tourism and Aviation and Ezekiel Alebua received further criticism about non-consultation with some traditional landholders over their concerns regarding tourism development in the lagoon area. The landholders felt that with no other avenue available to them to participate in the tourism development process, they had little option but to try and use the SIBC as an outlet for their objections. In opposition to the arguments of the customary landholders, Alebua stated that he had widely discussed the resort project with people in the Lauvi region, but that land issues were not important given that he was also the leader of a tribe that used the lagoon. Members of several tribes represented within the villages of the Lauvi area strongly disputed Alebua's position on the Lagoon project and stated that as landowners of the development site they had never wanted the proposed resort project for several reasons, including retention of the customary ownership of the land, concerns over the effects of tourism on lifestyles, and the use of the lagoon as a food source (Rudkin, forthcoming).

The sentiments of village representatives were also repeated in a press release to the SIBC on 12 June, which stated that the resort project did not have widespread local support because of the lack of consultation and concern over the potential effects of tourism. In representations to the Ministry of Tourism and Aviation it was also argued that Alebua was serving his own interests under the guise of gaining funds for his own tribe:

> The people strongly oppose the project proposal for Lauvi Lagoon resort, and that they urge your Ministry to withdraw the whole proposal, which means any further moves would lead to destruction . . . The people denies Alebua's ownership to the lagoon and request that any further doubts on his behalf would be best solved through legal procedures. (correspondence quoted in Rudkin, forthcoming)

In response, Iumi Together Holdings Ltd, of which Ezekiel Alebua was chairman, stated that if funds could not be released by government for the resort project then they would secure their own funding. Alebua claimed that he was not a landowner. Instead, he argued that he was a member of a tribe that owns land in and around the lagoon area and that therefore gives him a right to use such land. According to Alebua, there was nothing to indicate or imply that he had any personal interest in the proposal of the Lauvi Lagoon Resort, and instead he was seeking to initiate a development project for the people of the region. Given the opposition to the resort project he therefore concluded that it may be appropriate to divert TCSP funding into an alternative ecotourism project (Rudkin, forthcoming). In January 1993 cyclone Nina devastated many of the villages in the study area.

In the village nearest to the lagoon not a single house was left standing. The airstrip was covered with logs and other debris. It took several days of clearing by the local people before flights could resume. Health, sanitation, water supply and agricultural development remain major issues for the local people.

Setting the tourism development agenda

The above case study of a proposed ecotourism project on the Lauvi area of the Weather Coast indicates the political complexities of tourism development in developing countries. Local élites, who clearly have much to gain financially, the tourism industry and overseas aid and conservation organisations, may well have a different set of objectives in promoting tourism development than local communities. In the above case study, the 'rules of the game' were established by the local élite and it was only when several traditional landholders were able to gain access to institutions within the decision-making process that they were able to promote their interests. The rules of the game also met the needs of overseas interests, and it is from this perspective that elements of tourism as a plantation economy (see above) could be seen in the Lauvi example, as the development framework was held together by law, order and political institutions directed by the local élite (Best, 1968).

In the above case study power generally did not lie within the traditional decision-making structures of the village but instead was mediated within the state institutions of the postcolonial era. Power is never evenly allocated within a society but, at least in many Western societies, there is usually at least some attempt to provide equitable access to the decision-making process. In the case of the Solomons, imported Western political institutions provide a thin veneer for the activities of the local élite who still retain vestiges of the big-man system in order to gain access to culturally sourced political power. For example, in the case of the electoral system, Crocombe (1992, p.14) noted that 'where there are many candidates for a single electorate, as often happens in . . . [the] Solomon Islands . . . a first-past-the-post system, which elects the person with most votes, can be very unrepresentative.' During the 1993 Solomon Islands national elections, Ezekiel Alebua, standing against five other candidates, was re-elected with 28 per cent of the vote.

In the Solomon Islands, as elsewhere in many developing countries, local power arrangements are transformed by processes of modernisation of which tourism development is only one component. Significant individuals in traditional power structures may either be bypassed by new institutional arrangements or they may become members of the new élite, thereby utilising particular traditional roles and relationships to reinforce their own interests. As Hau'ofa (1987, p.9) recognised, in many South Pacific societies which are undergoing political transformation 'it is the privileged who can afford to tell the poor to preserve their positions. But their perceptions of [what] to preserve [is] increasingly divergent from those of the poor.' A more passionate perspective on the interaction of international tourism development, the process of modernisation and political outcome is provided by Minerbi (1992, p.68):

> Tourism is not an indigenous practice, but a way for large corporations to make as much profit as possible in manners usually incompatible with balanced island development. Its profit maximization orientation conflicts with the giving and sharing ethics of the island kinship system. Tourism planning tends to bypass the local people.

'Conventional tourism is a vehicle for "metropolitanization" of islanders either through "Westernization" or "Japanization", which may be quite different from a "Pacific way" to "modernization" more in tune with local culture and needs' (Minerbi, 1992, p.1). In the case of the Solomon Islands it is the members of the ruling élite, the big men, who are in a position to select what should be preserved and what should be changed with respect to traditional practices such as customary land ownership:

> the very sections in island communities which preach against adherence to what they think are outmoded traditions, are the very groups that simultaneously try to force the dead weight of other traditions on the poor . . . increasingly the privileged and the poor observe different traditions, each adhering to those that serve their interest best. The difference is that the poor merely live by their preferred traditions while the privileged often try to force certain other traditions on the poor in order to maintain social stability, that is in order to secure the privileges that they have gained, not so much from their involvement in traditional activities, as from their privileged access to resources in the regional economy. In such a situation, traditions are used by the ruling classes to enforce the new order. (Hau'ofa, 1987, p.12)

The political processes witnessed in the above case study are not restricted to the Solomon Islands. While actors, interests and cultural practices change, the interaction of values, interests and power is universal to any situation in which tourism development is occurring. Unfortunately, this is often ignored by many researchers.

Within many economically peripheral regions the central issue at the heart of the Lauvi Lagoon example is being repeated: who controls the tourism development process? Control in this sense refers not only to the political ability of local people to exercise their interests over tourist developments, but also to the direction of broader economic, social, cultural and political processes that operate at the level of the society. The notion of dependency implies that such processes are controlled in metropolitan regions rather than in the destination region or host country. Furthermore, it can be safely assumed that if such dependency occurs at the macro-political level then it will have ramifications for the tourism development process as it operates at the micro-political level, as in the case of the Solomon Islands.

The Solomon Islands, as with many other microstates, does exhibit several of the characteristics of dependency. In the case of the Solomons the tourism industry is heavily dependent on Australian visitation and hence Australian tour operators. The government is largely dependent on foreign aid. Indeed, much of the support for ecotourism development comes from Australian and New Zealand conservation agencies and organisations who are seeking to promote their approach to conservation practice within the South Pacific, an approach described by Hall (C., 1994d) as a form of 'ecological imperialism'. Finally, the approach of the local élite to tourism development is reinforced by the European Community funded TCSP which is extremely active in its promotion of tourism as a means to achieve economic development. Many of the forces which therefore determine the pattern and process of tourism development in the Solomons are external to the country. While some individuals in the Solomons may reap the benefits of modernisation available through present tourism development policies, the majority of the population still seek the broader social, economic and health benefits potentially available through tourism.

THE POLITICS OF TOURISM DEVELOPMENT

> Tourism does offer economic benefits, but the total market for tourism is still limited, if expanding. Most communities, therefore, can only hope for small-scale economic advantages and in such areas tourism can be no more than one element in a wider development strategy. (Williams and Shaw, 1988b, p. 239)

This chapter has provided a discussion of the concept of tourism development and some of its political aspects. Tourism development is political in terms of the issue of control of the development process and also in terms of its outcomes, e.g. who are the winners and losers in terms of the goals of government development policies? The politics of tourism development can also be examined at the macro level, in terms of concepts such as dependency, and at the micro level, through examination of the interests, values and power of significant individuals and groups within the development process. At the micro level the notion of the 'rules of the game' was regarded as being significant in terms of equity of access of individuals and communities to the decision-making process. In addition, it was also noted that the processes occurring at the macro and micro political level should not be regarded in isolation and instead should be seen as being entwined within broader global patterns of tourism development.

Despite there often being a number of economic, social, cultural and environmental objectives within national and regional governments' tourism policies, economic objectives lie at the top of the policy agenda. The effectiveness and success of tourism policy are invariably set according to the number of tourists that arrive at particular destinations rather than the nett benefit that tourism brings to the destination. As Williams and Shaw (1988b, p.230) observed, 'In essence . . . the aim of policy has to be to influence the number of visitors that are attracted and to modify their quality (spending capacity and range of activities), the timing of their visits and their special destinations or, indeed, some combination of these.'

Tourism does not automatically lead to economic prosperity, as Gilg (1988, p.132) noted with respect to tourism in Switzerland, 'there have been growing doubts about its overbearing importance and fears have been expressed about the dangers of a mono-structural economy.' The economic costs and benefits of tourism development may also be unevenly spread in the destination area. As Greenwood (1989, p.171, 172) observed:

> tourism provides a considerable stimulus to the local and national economy, but it also results in an increasingly uneven distribution of wealth. Tourism thus seems to exacerbate existing cleavages within the community. It is not, therefore, the development panacea that a few hasty planners proclaimed . . . The conclusion that tourism-related development tends to produce inequalities takes on added significance because it seems to parallel the inequalities produced by other development strategies, like enclave factories, capital formation schemes, and the 'Green Revolution'. This serves as a needed corrective to overly exuberant dreams of an El Dorado paved with tourism receipts.

Tourism development is not necessarily superior to other forms of economic development. However, for many regions, it does appear to be an attractive development option despite the potential for negative economic, social and environmental impacts. Why is this so? Three reasons can be provided. First, the economic effects of tourism appear at face value to provide substantial benefits to the host region. Such superficial analysis is common among many government agencies and is also promoted by those interests, especially the tourism industry, which will benefit from government policies which are in favour of tourism development. Secondly, the socio-cultural and environmental effects of tourism, while well understood by students of tourism (e.g. Mathieson and Wall, 1982; Pearce, 1989), are poorly recognised by those in government or by many national tourism organisations whose primary responsibility is promotion rather than protection. Furthermore, national tourist organisations' client group is the tourism industry, whose *raison d'être* is to increase tourism, not communities who seek nett benefit from tourism. Thirdly, the very nature of international tourism is such that core metropolitan economic dominance will occur over tourist destinations which are located at the economic periphery. Such dominance may well also be translated into hegemonic effects in relation to culture and society. As Lundgren (1973, p.14) concluded:

> It seems quite evident by looking back over the different eras of tourist travel that international tourism in its present form can only be metropolitan-generated in terms of flows and metropolitan-based in terms of tourist demanded supply inputs. With present scale economies for different supply inputs, transport, services, investment, modern management, the centre–periphery syndrome exemplified by the international tourist flows will be difficult to alter. The present travel system is too committed to itself, functionally, and too specialized an institution to be able to reverse its raison d'être. It will continue to operate until drastic changes in traveller behaviour and preferences, or among other elements in the system, occur.

Fourthly, and possibly an inevitable consequence of the previous observation, tourism development may well induce its own particular political dynamics in destination regions by which control of development processes lie with the local élite in conjunction with external interests. As Matthews (1975, p.200) enquired, 'What is perhaps most intriguing to the political scientist are the effects of tourism growth upon political power arrangements in small developing states. Does the growth of tourism produce new bases of power?'

Greenwood's (1972, 1976, 1989) study of tourism in a Basque village noted that as tourism grew political power became increasingly concentrated among those involved with tourism and their outside investors. However, this study is one of the few to examine in detail the issue of control in tourism development. Nevertheless, as this chapter has indicated, local élites and external interests may have a greater influence in directing tourism development processes than many of the people who will be most affected by such development, a point which we will examine in further detail in the next chapter.

6

Tourism and the Local State: Development, Image and Interests at the Community Level

As a major, yet typically unappreciated and unacknowledged, avenue of accumulation in the late twentieth century, tourism is one of the most important elements in the shaping of popular consciousness of places and in determining the creation of social images of those places. (Britton, 1991, p.475)

The local state is an essential but often neglected aspect of tourism policy. The local state comprises 'local authorities as well as the local/regional representatives of various national-level bodies, including tourist boards' (Urry, 1990a, p.112). Tourism development typically occurs within the context of the local planning framework and community interest groups. Therefore, in order 'to further our understanding of tourism policy, greater focus is required at the levels of the individual enterprises and the smaller implementing organizations (rather than the higher levels), for this is where a large part of tourism policy is made' (Greenwood, Williams and Shaw, 1990, p.55).

As at the national and regional level, tourism has come to be seen as a panacea for many economic and social needs in contrasting types of local environments (Williams and Shaw, 1988c,

1988d; Greenwood, Williams and Shaw, 1990; see also Chapter 5). However, the perceived value of tourism development for employment and economic growth has substantial implications for the allocation of state resources at the local level. In particular, given the increasingly scarce resources available to the local state, questions need to be asked about the manner in which the provision of resources for tourism-related development and promotion may represent a switch from more traditional welfare functions. Furthermore, the potential of the growth of service industries, such as tourism, for employment generation 'in which the final product of the enterprise is a commodity which is, in some sense, at least partly intangible or immaterial, but which contains a labour force made up of both service and non-service occupations' (Urry, 1987, p.5), also needs to be examined in greater detail. As Urry later noted, tourism services 'are inherently labour-intensive and hence employers will seek to minimise labour costs' (1990a, p.41), a position in stark contrast to the employment-generating objectives of many national and regional government tourism policies (see Chapter 5).

Despite doubts about the economic benefits of tourism on the part of some researchers, the attitude of local government to tourism generally appears to be quite positive. Local governments seek many of the same employment and economic development goals as national governments in their tourism policies. For example, in a survey about opinions of local councillors of three districts in Surrey, United Kingdom, towards tourism, Wanhill (1987) reported that councillors had a generally positive attitude towards tourism regardless of which political party they belonged to (Table 6.1). Although evidence is often sketchy, the results of the Wanhill study would seem to be representative of many local government bodies which are seeking to reap the perceived economic benefits of tourism development. Indeed, studies such as that of Jones (1986) on Australia's Gold Coast tourist destination would tend to indicate that the values of many local government bodies may be more reflective of that of the local élite than broader community interests.

Despite the significance of the local state for tourism development, the role of local government tourism policies has not received the attention it merits. As Wanhill (1987, p.54) recognised, 'at the end of the day, the implementation of any tourism strategy on the ground rests with the tiers of local government.' National

Table 6.1. Local councillor attitudes towards tourism

Attribute	Number of respondents	Strongly agree (%)	Slightly agree (%)	Neither agree nor disagree (%)	Slightly disagree (%)	Strongly disagree (%)	Don't know (%)
Positive							
Provides local jobs	93	34	53	9	2	2	–
Brings money to the area	94	59	36	3	2	–	–
Buildings, parks, attractions better preserved	94	11	48	26	10	6	–
More shops and local facilities	93	8	37	26	18	11	1
Better roads and car parks	93	4	22	27	16	30	1
Adds atmosphere	94	16	31	23	18	11	1
Negative							
Burden on the rates	92	1	21	12	24	42	–
Damages the environment	93	7	33	18	16	25	1
Raises prices	93	3	16	36	24	17	4
Crowding on streets and in shops	93	11	47	22	12	9	–
Crowding on local transport	93	1	10	28	25	32	4
Tourists are rude/ insensitive	92	1	10	26	12	48	3

Source: Wanhill, 1987, p.56. Reproduced by permission of Butterworth-Heinemann, Oxford, UK

tourism policies and the effectiveness of national tourist organisations, on which the majority of tourism policy research has been focused (e.g. Richter, 1989; Pearce, 1992), cannot be understood in terms of either their formulation or implementation in isolation from the local scene. In nearly all political systems, and especially in federal systems (see Chapter 2), there are overlapping levels of policy formulation and implementation. Such a situation can often lead to problems in translating tourism policies from the national to the local level and vice versa (Greenwood, Williams and Shaw, 1990).

This chapter focuses on the politics of tourism at the level of the local state. Specific attention is paid to the changing function of tourism within the local state and in urban centres in particular. The revitalisation of downtown areas through the creation of new tourism and leisure precincts is regarded by some commentators (e.g. Henry and Bramham, 1986) as being indicative of a crisis of the local state in which the importance of traditional welfare functions is lessened. However, in a broader context the current use of tourism to re-image the city may also be seen as a response by urban élites to the globalisation of capital and the changing nature of the role of the state in society. Regardless, 'it looks as though major shifts are taking place in the political and economic context of city development, leading to new social and spatial segregation and new private and public cultures' (Mommaas and van der Poel, 1989, p.255).

The creation of urban leisure spaces and the hosting of hallmark events in order to establish new images for cities and attract international capital have substantial implications for the interests of groups within urban areas, especially in the inner city areas which are most susceptible to re-imaging strategies. Urban imaging strategies can change a community's relationship to place and may also affect and reflect the ability of community interest groups to influence tourism policies and the nature of tourism development. The chapter concludes with a brief discussion of the nature of community participation in the tourism development process and argues that many models of community planning only focus on the visible dimensions of power in decision making. Such a pluralist notion of power is regarded as inadequate to explain the broader political dimensions of tourism development and fails to account for how certain groups may be excluded from decision-making processes or how non-decisions occur.

THE NEW URBAN TOURISM: THE CITY AS PRODUCT

> the question arises as to whether or not there should be some form
> of public life or culture, accessible to all local citizens of the city; and
> if so, how this can be stimulated by local policies. This last question
> is particularly relevant in local politics. Is the city a product to be
> sold on the tourism market and/or as a location in which to invest
> money? Or is a city a place to live, where people can express
> themselves, even if it is in terms of resistance to, rather than rejoicing
> in, the dominant culture? (Bramham *et al.*, 1989b, p.4)

Although urban centres have long served to attract tourists, it is
only in recent years that cities have consciously sought to develop,
image and promote themselves in order to increase the influx of
tourists. Following the deindustrialisation of many industrial and
waterfront areas in the 1970s and 1980s, tourism has been
perceived as a mechanism to regenerate urban areas through the
creation of urban leisure and tourism space. This process appears
almost universal in North America, Western Europe, Australia and
New Zealand (e.g. see Law, 1985; Houston, 1986; Fondersmith,
1988; Cameron, 1989; Frieden and Sagalyn, 1989; Hall, C., 1989a,
1992a; Judd and Parkinson, 1990; Watson, 1991; Bianchini and
Parkinson, 1993; Page, 1993; see Table 6.2 for examples of urban
imaging strategies). Such a situation led Harvey (1988, cited in
Urry, 1990a, p.128) to ask 'How many museums, cultural centres,
convention and exhibition halls, hotels, marinas, shopping malls,
waterfront developments can we stand?' For example, events and
inner city renewal projects have been used to revitalise Rotterdam
by attracting tourists and new investment (Rijpma and Meiburg,
1989). Similarly, Urry (1990a, p.119) observed that 'in recent years
almost every town and city in Britain has been producing mixed
development waterfront schemes in which tourist appeal is one
element.' However, according to Mommaas and van der Poel
(1989, p.263) the development of a more economically oriented city
development policy style, aimed at the revitalisation of the city, has
led to 'projects, developed in public–private partnerships, [which]
are meant not for the integration of disadvantaged groups within
society, but for servicing the pleasures of the well-to-do.'

The primary justification for the redevelopment of inner city
areas for tourism is the perceived economic benefits of tourism.
The nature of the urban core is changing. Although the commercial
function of central business districts is still important, leisure and

Table 6.2. Examples of urban imaging strategies in Australia, Canada, New Zealand and the United Kingdom

City	Components of Urban Imaging Strategies
Australia	
Adelaide	Adelaide Grand Prix, cultural tourism, bid for 1996 Commonwealth Games
Brisbane	1982 Commonwealth Games, 1988 Expo, South Bank Development, bid for 1992 Summer Olympic Games
Hobart	Waterfront redevelopment, cultural tourism
Melbourne	Bid for 1996 Summer Olympic Games, proposed dockland redevelopment, development of the South Bank cultural precinct, host of Australian Grand Prix from 1997
Sydney	Darling Harbour redevelopment, cultural tourism, special events, winning bid for 2000 Summer Olympic Games
Canada	
Calgary	1988 Winter Olympic Games, cultural tourism
Toronto	Bid for 1996 Summer Olympics, large-scale waterfront redevelopment, cultural tourism, including Indy Grand Prix
Vancouver	1986 Expo, large-scale waterfront redevelopment, cultural tourism and special events, including Indy Grand Prix
Victoria	1998 Commonwealth Games, cultural tourism strategy
New Zealand	
Auckland	1990 Commonwealth Games, cultural and regional tourism strategy, special events, maritime museum
Dunedin	Cultural tourism, waterfront redevelopment, special events, marketing campaign 'It's All Right Here'
Wellington	Cultural tourism, waterfront redevelopment, construction of new Museum of New Zealand, special events, marketing campaign 'Absolutely Wellington', street car racing
United Kingdom	
Bradford	Museum development, heritage attractions
Bristol	Dockland redevelopment, museums, exhibition areas
Gateshead	Garden festival
Glasgow	Exhibition and conference centre, art gallery, cultural promotion, garden festival
Liverpool	Dockland redevelopment, maritime museum
London	Dockland redevelopment, redevelopment of Battersea Power Station
Manchester	Exhibition centre, museums, heritage walks
Sheffield	World Student Games, bid for 2002 Commonwealth Games

Sources: Martin and Mason, 1988; Hall, C., 1992a

tourist functions are increasing in their significance. According to Jansen-Verbeke (1989, p.233) 'The entire urban core is presently looked upon as a recreational environment and as a tourism resource.' The ramifications of such an approach are far reaching, particularly in the way in which cities are now perceived as products to be sold. As Bramham *et al.* (1989b, p.9) observed, 'it is no longer unusual to see the city as a tourist product, although on the level of local policy this may still be more an expression of certain political ideas than a coherent policy with practical consequences.'

Urban imaging processes are clearly significant for urban governance, planning and tourism development. Contemporary urban imaging strategies are important elements in policy responses to the social and economic problems associated with deindustrialisation and economic restructuring, urban renewal, multi-culturalism, social integration and control (Roche, 1992, 1993a). Indeed, according to Mommaas and van der Poel (1989, p.264) the imaging of the city in order to attract the middle class employment market and the associated focus on the economic benefits of tourism has 'reinforced the idea of the city as a kind of commodity to be marketed.

The principal aims of urban imaging strategies are to attract tourism expenditure, to generate employment in the tourist industry, to foster positive images for potential investors in the region, often by 're-imaging' previous negative perceptions (e.g. the attempted transformation of the image of Sheffield from an 'industrial' to a 'modern' city through the hosting of the World Student games), and to provide an urban environment which will attract and retain the interest of professionals and white-collar workers, particularly in 'clean' service industries such as tourism and communications. Urban imaging processes are characterised by some or all of the following: the development of a critical mass of visitor attractions and facilities, including new buildings/ prestige centres (e.g. the Inner Harbor development in Baltimore and Darling Harbour in Sydney); hallmark events (e.g. Olympic Games, World Fairs and the hosting of Grand Prix); development of urban tourism strategies and policies often associated with new or renewed organisation and development of city marketing (e.g. in New Zealand the Wellington City Council's 'Absolutely Wellington' or Dunedin's 'Its All Right Here' promotional campaigns); and development of leisure and cultural services and projects to support the marketing and tourism effort (e.g. the creation and renewal of museums and art galleries and the hosting of art festivals, often as part of a comprehensive cultural tourism strategy for a region or city).

According to Harvey (1989a, 1989b) imaging a city through the organisation of spectacular urban space is a mechanism for attracting capital and people (of the right sort) in a period of intense inter-urban competition and urban entrepreneurialism:

> the modernist penchant for monumentality . . . has been challenged by an 'official' post-modernist style that explores the architecture of festival and spectacle, with its sense of the ephemeral, of display, and of transitory but participatory pleasure. The display of the commodity became a central part of the spectacle, as crowds flock to gaze at them and at each other in intimate and secure places like Baltimore's Harbor Place, Boston's Faneuil Hall and a host of enclosed shopping malls that sprung up all over America. Even whole built environments became centrepieces of urban spectacle and display (Harvey, 1987, pp.275–276).

In the case of the redevelopment of the inner harbour in Baltimore Harvey (1990, pp.421–422) commented:

> The present carnival mask of the Inner Harbor redevelopment conceals the long history of struggle over this space. The urban renewal . . . effort was stymied by the unrest of the 1960s . . . The inner city was a space of disaffection and social disruption. But in the wake of the violence that rocked the city after Martin Luther King's assassination in 1968, a coalition sprang to life to try and restore a sense of unity and belonging to the city . . . One idea that emerged from that effort was to create a city fair in the inner city that would celebrate 'otherness' . . . but which would also celebrate the theme of civic unity within that diversity . . . By 1973, nearly two million came [to the Fair] and the inner harbor was reoccupied by the common populace in ways which it had been impossible to envisage in the 1960s . . . During the 1970s, in spite of considerable public opposition, the forces of commercialism and property development recaptured the space . . . The inner city space became a space of conspicuous consumption, celebrating commodities rather than civic values.

The new inner city space of leisure consumption is reflective not only of particular values but also of particular interests. As noted in Chapter 2, values and interests are inextricably linked: the 'new' civic values reflect those of the local élites which influence urban redevelopment and planning processes. As Mommaas and van der Poel (1989, p.267) observed, 'local policy has increasingly sought to stimulate the mixture of economic enterprise, culture and leisure, attempting in this manner to attract the new economic élite to the city.' However, in focusing on one set of economic and social interests other community interests, particularly those of traditional inner-city residents of lower socio-economic status, are increasingly neglected:

> because urban policy has adopted and legitimated the profiles and potentials of the lifestyle of this new economic élite, thereby also legitimating the economic dimensions involved (the acceptance of making leisure, culture, and welfare strategies and criteria), the interests of those not having the opportunity to emulate the new economic élite in its pleasures fail to be considered. (Mommaas and van der Poel, 1989, p.267)

The creation of a 'bourgeois playground' (Mommaas and van der Poel, 1989, p.263) in the name of economic progress may create considerable tension in the urban policy-making environment. For example, the integration of tourism functions in the inner city may contest with traditionally different functions such as residential areas. The redevelopment of the inner city in terms of visitor attractiveness can lead to the transformation of the community-based organisation of local spaces and populations into an individual, or family-based organisation, or what Castells (1983) has characterised as the 'disconnection of people from spatial forms'. The implications of the transformation of the core of many cities for lower socio-economic groups is amplified by the reallocation of local state resources from social welfare to imaging functions, because at the same time as the inner city is being promoted and developed as a leisure resource public spending on social programmes has also been decreasing (Mommaas and van der Poel, 1989).

According to some commentators, such a situation has led to a crisis of the local state in Western Europe and North America. The crisis of the local state is bound up in a crisis of legitimacy in which certain groups in society, particularly the powerless and disadvantaged in the inner cities, have become disenchanted with the existing political arrangements which have failed to deliver needed social, economic and infrastructural improvements in inner-city areas. In addition, it may be asked whether city centres, the focal point of the new urban tourism, are gaining resources at the expense of the interests of those in the suburbs. A second crisis is what may be termed a 'fiscal crisis' in which:

> The central state is attempting to revitalize private industry by reducing expenditure on social consumption, and therefore reducing grant aid to local government which is responsible for many such services, while local government, deprived of such income and with a declining tax base (as the local economy suffers), is faced with increasing demands both for welfare services and for local economic development. (Henry and Bramham, 1986, p.190)

The two crises are intimately related and may be regarded as two sides of the same coin, with the reallocation of scarce financial resources only serving to exacerbate the frustration of certain groups in society to achieve desired social and welfare ends. However, while many civic governments claim that by encouraging the development of visitor attractions they will also be creating new employment, it should be recognised that many of the jobs do not go to those who were most affected by such developments in the first place because they often do not have the requisite skills or, if they do gain employment, it will often be at the most unskilled and menial levels.

The widely held justification of many local government authorities of the economic and social benefits of using large-scale redevelopment projects or tourist events as a component of urban imaging programmes is presented by Hillman (1986, p.4): 'As center city revitalization continues to be viewed as a major ingredient of economic development, the questions of enlivening public spaces and extending usage of downtowns after 5 o'clock have become critical issues ... Events are a proven animator capable of turning barren spaces into bustling places.' Nevertheless, according to Dovey (1989, pp.79–80), large-scale tourist developments also 'create a political and economic context within which the hallmark event is used as an excuse to overrule planning legislation and participatory planning processes, and to sacrifice local places along the way.' Despite the potential for negative economic and social impacts on certain sections of the community, hallmark events are almost invariably seen by urban élites, politicians and governments as beneficial at both collective and individual levels because of their ability to promote appropriate images of places and attract investment and tourism (Hall, C., 1992a). Events may therefore act to strengthen dominant ideologies or further individual interests, legitimise hegemonic relationships and change the meaning and structure of place. Furthermore, events can even be used to legitimise what would otherwise be unpopular decisions, particularly in the area of urban development because of the climate of urgency they can create within the planning and development process.

Perception by some groups, such as conservation, ratepayers or resident action organisations, of the prospect of unwanted impacts, such as resident displacement and architectural pollution, may give rise to interest group politics and a call for greater public participation in the planning process. However, the importance and prestige attached to hallmark events by government often means a commitment to 'fast track' planning practices which ignore community resistance to either the hosting of the event or the construction of associated infrastructure (Hall, C., 1989a, b, 1992a; Roche, 1991). For example, in the case of Sydney's massive Darling Harbour redevelopment project which was undertaken as part of New South Wales' celebrations of the Australian bicentenary in 1988, Thorne, Munro-Clark and Boers (1987) observed:

> National 'hallmark' events . . . are prone to generate (at least in prospect) a heady atmosphere. In some government quarters in particular, time comes to be experienced as a count-down interval, in which everything must be made ready for the day the show begins, and any call for deliberation amounts to sabotage. In the excitement of putting a good face on things, more sober, long-term commitments are apt to be lost sight of or denied, and normal legal safeguards are set aside, in the spirit of a state-of-emergency.

In the case of the Darling Harbour Redevelopment Project, 'the focal point of the bicentenary celebrations for New South Wales' (Unsworth, 1984, p.1485), there was an absence of consultation and community participation in the decision-making process. All this taking 'place under a government whose own recent legislation explicitly enshrined community participation and provided for the dissemination of information through the publication of environmental impact statements' (Thorne and Munro-Clark, 1989, p.156). As Premier Unsworth commented 'It means we are determined to have this done—to see it finished—and we're not going to be frustrated by legal technicalities . . . This is a national project, it's something for Australia, and we cannot have government aldermen or anyone else frustrating our intentions to achieve one of the great features of 1988' (*The Australian*, 2 May 1984, p.13).

In 1993 Sydney and New South Wales won the right to host the 2000 Olympic Games. Despite a new state government which had promised greater participation in the development planning process, the Sydney bid and the impacts of associated infra-structure were not open to public debate. Media scrutiny of the costs of hosting the event or the voicing of negative opinions of the Games were subject to harsh criticism from the government and from members of the bidding team. People who were against the Games were regarded as 'unpatriotic' and 'unAustralian', while the only community consultation was in the form of opinion polls.

The creation of the urban leisure environment associated with contemporary imaging strategies often has a major impact on the socio-economic groups that occupy the inner-city areas which are designated for 'renewal'. The creation of a 'desirable' middle-class environment invariably leads to increased rates and rents, and is accompanied by a corresponding breakdown in community structure, including ethnicity, as families and individuals are forced to relocate (Hall, C., 1992a). Moreover, the people who are often most affected by hallmark events are those who are least able to form community groups and protect their interests. This tends to lead to a situation in which residents are forced to relocate because of their economic circumstances. Inner-city community structures may be severely eroded by the effects of hallmark events on real estate values and rents (Olds, 1988, 1989; Hall, C., 1989a, 1992a). For example, in the case of the 1986 Vancouver Expo, 600 tenants were evicted including long-term, low-income residents from hotels near the Expo site (Olds, 1988). Similarly, the 1987 America's Cup in Fremantle, Australia, and the 1988 Brisbane Expo also led to resident dislocation (Hall, C., 1991).

Since the 1850s World Fairs have been major expressions of urban spectacle and capitalist accumulation which are concerned not only with goods and services but also notions of idealised social structures and relationships (Benedict, 1983; Ley and Olds, 1988; Mills, 1990, 1991; Britton, 1991). According to MacAloon (1984, p.273), 'Spectacle . . . is full of events that make us notice and heed moral and social boundaries that have become blurred and banal in daily life.' World Fairs may well broaden the potential scope of political hegemony by presenting particular expressions of values and interests and giving shape to élite notions of political and social reality (Susman, 1980; Ley and Olds, 1988). World Fairs, as with all large-scale hallmark events or city imaging strategies, are the product of urban élites. The fairs are built in the élite's image 'and thus present a dominant ideology' to those who consume the experience of the Fair (Ley and Olds, 1988). As evidenced in both the 1986 Vancouver and the 1988 Brisbane Expos, public consciousness becomes riveted on the 'bread and circuses' that the event has to offer, thereby providing both the élites and the state with an opportunity to expand patterns of formal and informal social control (Craik, 1989; Hall, C., 1992a). Formal social control is evidenced in the laws and regulations established to ensure the success of hallmark events and development projects, while élite and state influence on political socialisation occurs through the presentation of images and history in large-scale spectacles such as World Fairs or Olympic Games.

In the 'party atmosphere' which hallmark events often create, élite hegemony and state interests may be enhanced through the promotion of politically dominant values (Hall, C., 1992a). Moreover, as noted above, the minority who represent the oppositional forces to the conduct of hallmark events are often held to be negative, 'unpatriotic', or downright 'evil'. As one Vancouver city priest noted prior to the hosting of the 1986 World Fair: 'if one did resist Expo, boycott it, or tell the negative sides of this expensive party, you're a bad B.C.'er' (in Ley and Olds, 1988). In the creation of spectacle through either the hosting of a large-scale event or the establishment of permanent visitor attractions in urban tourism developments, the focus is on 'fun'. Conflict over place is concealed by the spectacle, with the problems of lower socio-economic groups typically being hidden by the presentation of 'positive' images of a clean, modern urban environment and happy, smiling faces. As Huxley (1991, p.141) argued in the case of Sydney's Darling Harbour redevelopment:

> The logo of Merlin International, developers and managers of Darling Harbour's Festival marketplace, displays a merlin falcon picked out in stars. It is a clever play on the name, invoking the freedom and beauty of a bird in flight and making reference to merlin the magician. The accompanying motto is 'Making Cities Fun'. The whole concept of the city as 'fun' is redolent with the post-modernist approach to playful spectacle, display and ironical references to other eras. It is the essence of the 'yuppy' lifestyle and yet our cities contain increasing numbers of unemployed, homeless, disadvantaged people: urban infrastructure is inadequate or non-existent at the fringe and outdated and overloaded at the centre. What sort of 'fun' can Merlin bring to the city?

The imaging and redevelopment strategies that are associated with the hosting of hallmark events do not just have an impact for the duration of the event. The 'improvements' to the physical appearance of urban locations and the conduct of 'renewal projects' will linger for a number of years. Indeed, the effect of imaging strategies on the political and social environment of the local state and community power structures may take a number of years to be revealed.

The hosting of the 1987 America's Cup in Fremantle, Western Australia provided further impetus to the processes of gentrification that had already been operating within the city (Hall, C. and Selwood, 1989, 1993). As Jones and Selwood (1991, p.6) reported: 'Fremantle's trajectory from working class port to world class resort was immensely accelerated by the arrival and departure of the America's Cup and the speed of this change has inevitably been disorienting for many local residents and businesses.'

The America's Cup provided a major impetus to the social and economic trends which had been influencing the character of Fremantle since the early 1970s. However, the influx of middle-class, well educated and politically able people, concerned with lifestyle, environment and heritage issues, is creating tension with some of the longer-term residents and business people. For example, resident groups have been active in resisting the granting of new liquor licences because of perceived problems of social disturbance and vandalism. However, as the co-owner of the Tarantella nightclub stated: 'I support inner-city living, but if residents are going to oppose every project that comes up they might find themselves living in a ghost town' (Jones and Selwood, 1991, p.6). In contrast, local retailers have criticised a trial art and crafts market in the Town Square because they regarded it as unfair trading, while a major study on road planning, port access and traffic calming (Sinclair Knight, Buchanan, 1991) has received two starkly opposed responses which reflect the social divide that now runs through the city: most local residents favour the traffic calming measure, probably because it would raise the value of houses on existing major roads, while local businesses fear the loss of the car-borne customer. Indeed, now the issue for Fremantle is whether its future lies as a working port with tourism as the add-on, or as a postindustrial leisure space in which the port is presented as an historical artefact. The extent of social change in Fremantle is best indicated in the comments of Fremantle Society spokesperson, Les Lauder: 'Twenty years on from the Council's publication of *Fremantle: Preservation and Change*, the Fremantle Society now contends that further port development is unacceptable because it "threatens the residential quality of the city . . . it lies in its people and its past"' (*Fremantle Herald*, 24 June 1991, p.1).

In the case of Fremantle the transformation of the physical landscape from a port city to a historic-tourist city in which the built environment has become a centrepiece of urban spectacle and display (Harvey, 1987), has been accelerated by the hosting of a hallmark event. Imaging strategies employed since the event have only served to reinforce the creation of a middle-class environment and leisure space, which coincides with the values of members of the local élite and serves to attract visitors. The post-America's Cup Fremantle reflects the shifts in regimes of capital accumulation which have occurred in recent years and which are paramount in the goals of contemporary urban imaging strategies. As Page (1993, pp.218–219) observed, 'Local government policy, especially in tourism and leisure provision, has responded to the changing regime of capital accumulation with an emphasis on an economic rationale for tourism and leisure policy in the public sector compared to the former concern with the public good.'

Although the longer-term impacts of the hosting of the 1991 World Student Games in Sheffield are still to be identified, the Sheffield experience has many elements in common with that of Fremantle and Vancouver. The World Student Games was the key vehicle and symbol of Sheffield's urban regeneration strategy and provided the impetus for major capital expenditure (Foley, 1991; Roche, 1991, 1993a). 'Sheffield's new civic leadership deployed a political discourse of modernisation and the future, a discourse of "visions" of a regenerated city' (Roche, 1993a). However, the Games became 'political, 'controversial' and failed to win wide-spread community support because 'the fundamental problem as far as the political legitimacy of the Games goes is that the Labour leadership never asked the people of Sheffield directly (e.g. by a referendum) whether or not they actually wanted to stage a sporting mega-event or to build a new generation of prestige sport facilities, nor what they would be prepared to pay for them' (Roche, 1991, p.18). An indication of the need for legitimacy is to be found in the words of councillor Peter Duff who resigned from the city council in part at protest at the Games:

> The council has been dragged into the Thatcher myth that the future lies in tourism, leisure and recreation. We should be playing to the traditional strengths of a working class city not to the false future that Sheffield is a sports centre. We have partnerships with the private sector which need properly defining, because at the moment we have politicians playing at being businessmen and businessmen playing at being politicians. The World Student Games sums it all up. (*Sheffield Star*, 18 January 1990, in Roche, 1991, p.20)

The purpose of hosting the hallmark event was defined by the local élite, even though the supposed outcomes were often couched in terms, e.g. employment and economic growth, considered favourable by disadvantaged groups in the city. 'In this essentially paternalistic and charismatic . . . discourse, democracy and rationality were not themes which were strongly represented.' Instead, there was a basic political disempowerment of some sections of society, with the focus by boosters on potential gross benefits, while minimising or ignoring the event's probable and possible risks and costs which would be spread throughout the community rather than on those who initially pushed to host the event (Roche, 1993a). Indeed, 'Sheffield citizens will be contributing to the repayment of capital and debt interest charges on the Games facilities through taxation until at least the year 2010' (Roche, 1993a). However, the proponents of urban imaging strategies remain strong in their ability to influence decision-making processes, and given that Sheffield has new sporting facilities, the city is currently seeking to host the 2002 Commonwealth Games.

The situation in Sheffield is not untypical. The development of urban imaging strategies has substantial implications for our understanding of the local state and contemporary political and economic processes. Hallmark events, the creation of urban leisure and tourism space and the development of visitor attractions is political at both the micro and macro political levels. At the micro level we can see the interaction of actors and interest groups in influencing urban policy and the allocation of resources by the local state; at the macro level we can see the related shifts in political process. Connecting them is the manner in which events, spectacles and the creation of new urban environments serve to influence the nature of political socialisation and the presentation of ideology. As Roche (1993a) has observed:

> Citizenship in modern Western capitalist democracies is usually understood to involve state organised policies and systems to

provide to offer civil and political rights to all on an equal basis, together with equal access to some agreed optimal or minimal 'welfare state' packages of social rights (to such things as health, education, employment, social services, leisure, etc). Mega-event policy makers and researchers have tended to assume that such events are beneficial to local citizens in terms of some of their *social rights* (i.e. employment and leisure services, and also social integration and political identity), and also in terms of some of their *political rights* (i.e. to democratic control and character of government, (via such things as community participation in planning; openness; and accountability) and to rational (non-arbitrary/ comprehensible, competent and efficient) government).

Unfortunately, the reality of urban re-imaging strategies is that they are not universally positive in their impacts, although clearly some sections of the urban élite do benefit as well as some elements of the broader community. As Roche (1993a) observed, 'In the debate about the character of mega-events, their planning and effects the "citizen disempowerment" view would appear to be more grounded in the realities of urban life and politics than the "citizen empowerment" view.'

COMMUNITY ORIENTED TOURISM AND CITIZEN EMPOWERMENT

It has long been recognised that tourism development is often accompanied by conflict in decision making, particularly in relation to the social and physical impacts of tourism (e.g. Forster, 1964). Geographical space is a strictly limited resource. Locational conflict represents an 'overt public debate over some actual or proposed land use or property development' (Dear, 1977, p.157). Tourism land use and the location of tourism infrastructure can lead to substantial opposition from some interests in the destination region (Roehl and Fesenmaier, 1987). In an effort to improve the planning of tourism developments and to reduce the perceived negative social and physical impacts of tourism on host communities, greater attention has been given by researchers to improving the nature of the planning process (Cook, 1982; D'Amore, 1983). For example, although Gunn (1979) emphasised a *laissez-faire* perspective in the first two of his three goals of tourism planning in the form of satisfactions to users and rewards to owners, the third goal, that of the protected utilisation of environmental resources, did signify a new appreciation of the renewable nature of tourism resources. Similarly, McIntosh and Goeldner (1986, pp.308, 310) highlighted the need for community control in their five goals of tourism development in which they argued that tourism development should aim to:

1. provide a framework for raising the living standard of local people through the economic benefits of tourism;
2. develop an infrastructure and provide recreation facilities for both residents and visitors;
3. ensure that the types of development within visitor centres and resorts are appropriate to the purposes of these areas;
4. establish a development programme that is consistent with the cultural, social and economic philosophy of the government and the people of the host area; and
5. optimise visitor satisfaction.

One of the clearest statements of the community approach to tourism development is to be found in Murphy's (1985) book *Tourism: A Community Approach*. Murphy (1985) advocated the use of an ecological approach to tourism planning which emphasised the need for local control over the development process. One of the key components of the approach is the notion that in satisfying local needs it may also be possible to satisfy the needs of the tourist. Nevertheless, despite the undoubted conceptual attraction to many destinations of the establishment of a community approach to tourism planning, substantial problems remain in the way such a process may operate and how it may be implemented (Haywood, 1988; Murphy, 1988).

A community approach to tourism planning is a 'bottom-up' form of planning, which emphasises development *in* the community rather than development *of* the community (Hall, C., 1991). As Blank (1989, p.4) recognised, '*Communities* are the destination of most travellers. Therefore *it is in communities that tourism happens*. Because of this, *tourism industry development and management must be brought effectively to bear in communities*.' Under this approach, residents are regarded as the focal point of the tourism-planning exercise, not the tourists, and the community, which is often equated with a region of local government, is regarded as the basic planning unit. Nevertheless, substantial difficulties arise in attempting to implement the concept of community planning in tourist destinations.

One of the main difficulties in implementing a community approach to tourism planning is the political nature of the planning process. Community planning implies a high degree of public participation in the planning process (Haywood, 1988). As Arnstein (1969) argued, public participation implies that the local community will have a degree of control over the planning and decision-making process. Therefore, a community approach to tourism planning implies that there will be community control of the tourism development process. However, such a community approach has generally not been adopted by government authorities; instead the level of public involvement in tourism planning can be more accurately described as a form of tokenism in which decisions or the direction of decisions has already been prescribed by government. As noted above, communities rarely have the opportunity to say no.

Attempts to formulate community approaches to planning (e.g. Murphy, 1985, 1988; Haywood, 1988; Ritchie, 1988; Blank, 1989; Getz, 1991) are valuable contributions encouraging wider participation in tourism planning. However, by focusing on overt aspects of decision making and by concentrating on existing interest groups within communities, such an approach may inadvertently ignore broader issues of power and the inability of some interests to effectively participate in decision making. The 'rationality' of the community approach may therefore be at odds with the 'irrational' nature of policy formulation and decision making. As Simmons *et al.* (1974, p.466) observed, 'the concept of policy as a conclusion derived from a relatively rational consideration of alternatives is insufficient.'

Community-oriented approaches to tourism planning (e.g. Murphy, 1985; 1988; Blank, 1989; Getz, 1991) posit a pluralistic approach to tourism development. In the pluralist view of power and decision making, 'power is totally embodied and fully reflected in "concrete decisions" or in activity bearing directly upon their making' (Bachrach and Baratz, 1970, p.7). Furthermore, the pluralistic basis of community tourism planning assumes that all parties have an equal opportunity to participate in the political process. Under a pluralistic approach power is relatively evenly distributed within the community and will shift according to issues and the range of interests and values involved. However, community-oriented tourism planning still creates a set of 'rules of the game' by which certain interests can be excluded from the decision-making process. For example, the blockage of certain policies within the decision-making process, as in the case of giving communities a veto on the hosting of events, may be regarded as a form of non-decision making, As Bachrach (1969–70, p.160) has observed, non-decisions are 'instrumental in preventing an issue potentially threatening to the interests or values of a decision-maker from reaching the agenda of a decision-making body of the political system.'

In the above discussion of urban tourism, the cases of the World Student Games in Sheffield, Darling Harbour in Sydney, the Inner Harbor in Baltimore and the 1986 Expo in Vancouver all indicate the manner in which non-decision making and the rules of the game can be utilised by urban élites to meet their own ends. As Bachrach and Baratz (1970, p.7) observed:

> Of course power is exercised when A participates in the making of decisions that affect B. Power is also exercised when A devotes his energies to creating or reinforcing social and political values and institutional practices that limit the scope of the political process to public consideration of only those issues which are comparatively innocuous to A. To the extent that A succeeds in doing this, B is prevented, for all practical purposes, from bringing to fore any issues that might in their resolution be seriously detrimental to A's set of preferences.

The absence of the 'citizen empowerment' promised by the new urban tourism (Roche, 1993a) should encourage students of tourism to give closer attention to the relationship of power and interests to the tourism development process. Fundamental questions about the spread of the costs and benefits of tourism development are typically not debated in the local state. However, 'to the extent that a person or group—consciously or unconsciously—creates or reinforces barriers to the public airing of policy conflicts, that person or group has power' (Bachrach and Baratz, 1970, p.8). In this way, 'local political institutions and political leaders may . . . exercise considerable control over what people choose to care about and how forcefully they articulate their cases' (Crenson, 1971, p.27).

Pluralists study 'actual behaviour, stressed operational definitions, and turned up evidence' (Merelman, 1968, p.451). However, by only studying the 'important, concrete decisions within the community, they were simply taking over and reproducing the bias of the system they were studying' (Lukes, 1974, p.36). Such a situation now exists in much of the discussion of the applicability of community approaches to tourism planning and prescriptive approaches to tourism policy formulation (e.g. Ritchie, 1988; Edgell, 1990). As Crenson (1971) suggested, a policy that is pluralist in its decision making can be unified in its non-decision making.

The study of non-decision making was anathema to the pluralists. Polsby (1963, pp.96–97) believed that an attempt to study non-decisions 'is likely to prejudice the outcomes of the research', and Wolfinger (1971) observed that the idea of non-decisions is adaptable to various ideological perspectives. However, all research is prejudiced or ideological as the researcher is trapped within the assumptions of his or her analytical framework (see Chapter 1). Polsby and Wolfinger moved 'from a methodological difficulty to a substantive assertion' (Lukes, 1974, p.39).

For power to have been exercised it must be both operative and effective:

> An attribution of the exercise of power involves, among other things, the double claim that A acts (or fails to act) in a certain way and that B does what he would otherwise do. In the case of an effective use of power, A gets B to do what he would not otherwise do; in the case of an operative exercise of power, A, together with another or other sufficient conditions, gets B to do what he would not otherwise do. Hence, in general any attribution of the exercise of power always implies a relevant counterfactual, to the effect that (but for A, or but for A together with any other sufficient conditions) B would otherwise have done, let us say, b. (Lukes, 1974, p.40–41)

As noted in Chapter 1, politics is concerned with power. The study of tourism has neglected the role that power, interests and values play in the pattern and processes of tourism development. Crenson (1971, p.vii) believed that one should study the way 'things do not happen . . . The proper object of investigation is not political activity but political inactivity.' Such investigation is almost non-existent in the field of tourism studies. However, it should be readily apparent that the exercise of both decisions and non-decisions serves to cut interests out of the formal tourism decision-making process. In the urban situation in particular, the rules of the tourism game have been dominated by those who uphold the ideology of development (Roche, 1992). As Gottdeiner (1987, p.18) observed:

> Despite the costs of growth the ideology of development possesses great appeal as the universal panacea for the ailments of society and

is most often pursued with only minor concessions to those asked to pay for its local burdens. A narrow fix on pursuing growth chains local governments to the unquestioned acquisition of development projects, often of a spectacular nature such as football stadiums or world fairs, with limited payoffs to local areas.

THE LOCAL STATE AND THE POLITICS OF TOURISM

This chapter has been concerned with the politics of tourism at the level of the local state, and with the urban situation in particular. The presentation of the city as product is a new development in tourist imaging and is related to a political and financial crisis at the local state level. The discussion and examples used in this chapter indicate that the production, exchange and consumption of goods, services and space is not simply an economic phenomenon but also has political implications. Urban policies designed to provide economic growth and employment cannot be divorced from the interests, values and power of those who formulate them.

In the case of the urban imaging strategies utilised in the Western world, only limited attention has been given by students of tourism to the political implications of the creation of desirable middle-class leisured environments (e.g. Ley and Olds, 1988; Hall, C., 1992a; Roche, 1992). Given the marginalisation of certain community interests that the contemporary transformation of the urban core represents, it is apparent that the crisis of the local state demands greater attention.

The growth of interest in community-based tourism planning represents one response, albeit limited, to the excesses of some tourism development. However, while the approach does have some value, empowerment of the affected citizenry may not necessarily be forthcoming. The pluralistic basis of much community-oriented planning fails to account for how certain values and interests are excluded from the tourism decision-making process. Restrictions on the scope of decision making may 'stunt the political consciousness of the local public' by limiting the range of opinions and denying 'minorities the opportunity to grow to majorities' (Crenson, 1971, pp.180–181). Such has been the case with opposition to urban imaging strategies such as hallmark events and large-scale tourism developments which create cities of fun and spectacle. The next chapter continues the focus on the significance of power for the politics of tourism development and the manner in which values and interests may serve to influence not only decision making but also culture, ideology, political socialisation and the presentation of heritage.

7

Tourism, Culture and the Presentation of Social Reality

Tourism is seen as an avenue, along with others, depending on the country's resources, toward development and modernization. This situation indicates an interesting irony: in order to survive and perpetuate their cultural identity and integrity, emerging new nations or quite traditional cultures caught up in a competitive world economy encourage and invite the most successful agents of change (short of political or military agents) active in the contemporary world. This kind of initiative on the part of a host culture introduces a novel variable into the traditional equation of acculturation. (Nuñez, 1989, p. 267)

This chapter discusses the nature of the politics of tourism in terms of culture, values and the individual. It expressly concentrates on the role of ideology and contemporary discourse in tourism and the manner in which tourism provides a political dimension to the representation of culture and heritage. 'Ideology is not the exclusive domain of political science, but any study of the politics of tourism surely must include it' (Matthews, 1975, p.200). However, with a few notable exceptions (e.g. Matthews, 1978; Papson, 1981; Thurot and Thurot, 1983; Urry, 1990a), questions over the relationship between tourism and ideology have not been addressed in the mainstream of tourism studies research. Nevertheless, ideology, values and the vision or gaze of the tourist play a critical role in influencing the nature of tourist development and the formulation of tourism policy.

TOURISM, IDEOLOGY AND VALUES

One of the difficulties in examining the relationship between tourism, ideology and values is that the concept of ideology, like power (see Chapter 1), is a contested concept. Recreational tourism is typically perceived as a leisure activity which is undertaken voluntarily, without constraint or sense of obligation. On the other hand, politics denotes the struggle over scarce resources, the domination of one group over another and the potential exercise of state control. The two would therefore seem to be completely different social realms or spheres. Nevertheless, as Wilson (1988, p.9) noted in discussing the positioning of leisure activities, such as tourism, in either a private or public sphere:

> The liberals and conservatives both locate leisure firmly within the private sphere, a region of life in which the individual can engage in those integral and significant social relationships that are the building blocks of personal identity. The private sphere connotes freedom and autonomy, while the public sphere means constraint and alienation. In the private sphere the individual is in control; in the public sphere the individual is under control.

The problematic positioning of tourism within either the public or the private sphere reflects the importance of understanding the social context within which tourism is both defined and occurs as an activity. The notion of the contextuality of tourism as a form of leisure implies the recognition that there is no such thing as absolute freedom. 'Social and material resources and the prevailing figurations of legitimating and signifying rules to which the individual or group has access will mediate freedom to choose as well as to constrain leisure activities' (Bramham *et al.*, 1989b, p.9). Each state sets the framework and rules by which tourism activities can be pursued. Even within the 'free' countries of the West, certain tourist behaviours may be prohibited. 'Freedom is hedged by the prevailing distribution of resources and by rules which qualify activities as admissible or inadmissible pleasures, and which define those activities which may be legitimately pursued in their own right rather than for instrumental purposes, and which specifies by whom they may be pursued' (Bramham *et al.*, 1989b, p.11). For example, in totalitarian states the private sphere does not exist: 'the boundary between the public and private sectors or that between bureaucratic and political authorities [is] no longer recognised' (Alford and Friedland, 1985, p.418). In the case of the former state socialist countries of Eastern Europe, the nature of tourism activity was a substantial political concern of the state and was geared to serve the political and ideological goals of the state with benefits to the individual being a secondary consideration (Hall, D., 1991a). Therefore, tourism can play a major role in socialising certain values in individuals and reinforcing dominant ideologies.

The role that tourism plays in the socialisation process need not be as blatant as that which occurred in the state socialist countries. Socialisation can take place in a directive or non-directive manner. In the case of concerns over the role that dependency can play in the transfer of social and cultural values (see Chapter 5), Erisman (1983) argued that when social orientation is primarily determined by the metropole, cultural dependency exists. It exists because the main stimuli for cultural development are coming from outside. Tourism is clearly not the only economic field in which dependency exists. However, the potential for wholesale contact between peoples of different cultures and values that tourism represents clearly has the potential for greater value change than industries which primarily deal with physical product, such as agriculture, manufacturing or mining.

The role that tourism can play in transforming collective and individual values is inherent in ideas of commoditisation (Cohen, 1977), which implies that what were once personal 'cultural displays' of living traditions or a 'cultural text' of lived authenticity become a 'cultural product' which meets the needs of commercial tourism. 'We already have a changed language in which we talk about the arts. We no longer discuss them as expressions of imagination or creativity, we talk about "product"; we are no longer moved by the experiences the arts have to offer, we "consume" them. Culture has become a commodity' (Hewison, 1988, p.240). For example, according to Dawson (1991, pp.42–43):

> ethnic and multicultural festivals may be seen as cultural products to be exploited for tourism ends. Individual ethnic cultures and multiculturalism itself are to be 'sold' using 'professional business practices', through the medium of festivals and other special events. Marketing initiatives and advertizing campaigns are the means by which ethnic and multicultural festivals can promote themselves as 'sales packages' to tourists ... When ... an archaic revival of necrotic cultural practices takes place in order to satisfy the tastes of tourists, this deliberate, specialized revival renders ethnicity a commodity. It is valued for the profit it accrues through its exchange in the commercial tourism market and little more.

In recent years Australian Aboriginal art forms, such as bark paintings, have become much sought after in the art world. However, in becoming a marketable commodity, Aboriginal art may become removed from its traditional social and cultural context. For example, art forms, such as the Papunya Tula paintings of Central Australia, are now being produced in large quantities to meet tourist demand. This has led to reduced quality, sameness, and the potential denigration of meaning in the artwork through the commercialisation and trivialisation of important events from the Aboriginal creation period or 'Dreamtime' (Hollinshead, 1988). Culture and heritage, as expressed through the arts, can be either stimulated or degraded by the impact of tourism (Hughes, H., 1987, 1989). With the advent of the tourist gaze and its attendant market impact, the materials, form and content of much Aboriginal art have become adapted to meeting external tourist demands. However, the demands of the tourism industry are such that a universal return to traditional Aboriginal art and cultural forms would be almost impossible and, perhaps from an economic perspective, undesirable (Hall, C., 1991).

The value change associated with tourism does not just occur through the transformation of social activities into products. In a comparative study of Vent and Obergurgl, two Alpine villages in Austria, Meleghy, Preglau and Tafertshofer (1985) noted that changes in the value orientations of each village appear to go hand in hand with structural changes initiated by tourism. Undoubtedly, the introduction of other new forms of economic activity would also probably have certain value and structural effects. Tourism is often blamed for every value transformation under the sun (Crick, 1989). Nevertheless, the very nature of the tourism industry may well create processes of acculturation and value change which are peculiar to tourism. For example, the imaging and marketing of destinations in tourism *must* commodify visitors' and community notions of place. As Papson (1981, p.225) commented:

> Tourism depends on preconceived definitions of place and people. These definitions are created by the marketing arm of government and of private enterprise in order to induce the tourist to visit a specific area ... government and private enterprise not only re-define social reality but also recreate it to fit those definitions. This process is both interactive and dialectical. To the extent that this process takes place, the category of everyday life is annihilated.

Tourism redefines social realities. Advertising creates images of place which then also create expectations on the part of the visitor, which in turn may lead the destination to adapt to such expectations. Destinations may therefore become caught in a tourist gaze from which they cannot readily escape unless they are willing to abandon their status as a destination. 'Policies which are used to attract tourists, lengthen their stay, and increase their expenditures also function to redefine social realities. As definitions are imposed from without, the socio-cultural reality which arises out of everyday life becomes further consumed' (Papson, 1981, p.233). Tourist marketing, routing and zoning transform the image of place, the creation of community events for the tourist and the organisation of history in tourist settings transform the cultural and historical life of communities and hence transform place itself.

Two of the key elements in the commodification of place by tourism identified by Papson (1981) are the creation of community events and the turning of history into a marketable commodity. In the case of the latter, Papson argued that history becomes sensual rather than something which is conceptual and is to be experienced. Two Australian examples of the transformation of social reality for the tourist are provided below. The first is a brochure for Tumbalong Park, Darling Harbour, Sydney, entitled 'Face to Face' and featuring a male Aboriginal with an ochred face (Darling Harbour, n.d.). The pamphlet explains that the name Tumbalong Park comes from the Wanegal word *tuom-b-long* meaning 'many shellfish'. 'The Early Years' are described as follows:

> Prior to European settlement. Darling Harbour was the home and meeting place of members of the Wanegal clan—a sub-group of the Aboriginal EORA Nation, occupiers of the Darling Harbour and Glebe Island regions.
>
> Wanegal elders were responsible for the farming of shellfish such as cockles, pippies, oysters, crabs and mussels—their role integral to the hunting, agricultural and spiritual practices of the EORA community.
>
> Soon after European settlers arrived, the local people moved on, making way for more than a century of industrial development which continued until 1980.

The contemporary environment is described under the heading 'Today':

In 1984 Darling Harbour was returned to the people of Sydney, a 60 hectare leisure and business development with Tumbalong Park at its centre. This round 'village green' is the place where Sydney-siders gather for free concerts and entertainment, where children enjoy fun school holiday activities, where people can just sit on the grass and relax and where visitors can experience Aboriginal culture face to face.

Traditional Aboriginal Culture Shows
Tumbalong Park
Gather by the stage at 12 noon from Monday to Friday for a free 15 minute show of music, dance and boomerang throwing.

The brochure concludes with the slogan 'Darling Harbour where Sydney celebrates' (see Chapter 6 for the comments by Huxley, 1991, on the 'fun' nature of the Darling Harbour redevelopment). The significance of the brochure is that it glosses over the forced displacement of the local Aboriginal people through the colonis-ation of New South Wales by the British. The use of the phrase 'the local people moved on' almost implies that they did so willingly! The second section of the brochure connects the return of the land to the people of New South Wales with the departure of the previous Aboriginal inhabitants. However, the land is not Aboriginal land, instead Aboriginality is found in a 15-minute presentation of aspects of Aboriginal culture most accessible to the visitor. Issues of land rights, displacement and the marginal positions of Aboriginals in Australian society are sanitised for the benefit of the visitor into a 'safe' social and political reality which does not lead the tourist to question.

The second example of the transformation of social reality comes from a heritage park called Old Sydney Town. The headings in the brochure describe Old Sydney Town as 'Re-creating the birth of a nation 1788–1810', 'The greatest adventure in living history', and 'One hour north of Sydney—200 years back in time'. According to the brochure, 'Old Sydney Town is more than an authentic re-creation of Sydney as it was in 1788; it's a living adventure where you will feel the charm of the past mixed with the harsh realities of colonial life.' However, the next line states 'Relax and enjoy our fine places to wine and dine. A-la-Carte Restaurant, Bistro, Kiosk and Tea Shop. Barbecue facilities.' According to the pamphlet 'Unique experiences you'll always remember' include:

- See soldiers on parade and hear the thunder of the daily cannon salute.

- Thrill to the excitement of a pistol duel or boxing match.
- Be part of a typical trial of the day as colonial justice takes it's course in the Magistrate's Court. See convicts tried and punished.
- Take a leisurely ride around 'Sydney Cove' to the animal park on a bullock. Hand feed the kangaroos and emus.
- Chat with the townspeople as they go about their business.
- Browse through authentic stores of the period and choose from a wide range of craft products.

Undoubtedly, the curious juxtaposition of the past and the present is typical of many theme parks throughout the world. For example, Horne (1992, p.117) describes the Jorvik Viking Centre in York as a 'cult tourism trap . . . which tuned the enticements of realism to a new pitch by offering authentic Viking sounds, authentic Viking sights—and authentic Viking *smells*.' What is significant about both the Old Sydney Town heritage park and the brochure is the manner in which, again, the past is sanitised for consumption and particular representations of history provided for the tourist. The claim to authenticity comes as an affirmation for tourists that they are being provided with the real thing. While Aboriginal history is ignored, the 'typical day' of the convict past serves to perpetuate the myths surrounding Australia's convict history (see Hughes, R., 1987). The representation of history by the heritage park is that of entertainment rather than education, although clearly the representation of social reality by the park will influence visitors' notions of heritage. As Thomas (1951, p.81) commented, 'if men [sic] define situations as real, they are real in their consequences'.

Throughout the world heritage and tourism have become inextricably linked. Tourism is used as an economic justification for the preservation of heritage, although tourism also serves to preserve artifacts and folklife in the gaze of the tourist (Hewison, 1987; Urry, 1990a; Boniface and Fowler, 1993). The representation of heritage will have substantial implications for both collective and individual identity and hence for the creation of social realities. In some cases, as in some of the state socialist nations, the political nature of heritage is overt in its attempts to use heritage as a source of political legitimacy. For example, according to Nallbani (1989, in Hall, D., 1991f, p.270), 'Any visit to [Albania's] museums is . . . still prefaced/justified by quotations from Enver Hoxha emphasising the need to treasure and learn from past Albanian material culture. Onufri [a sixteenth-century icon painter], for example, is linked with the "anti-Ottoman resistance of the Albanian people".' Heritage may therefore serve a direct ideological function. For example, the former Soviet Union's most popular tourist attraction was the embalmed remains of Lenin in Red Square, while the hundredth anniversary of Mao's birth provided a focal point for celebrations which aimed to reinforce the legitimacy of the current Chinese leadership.

In the former state socialist nations, heritage has played an important part in the formulation of post communist identities. As Hall (D., 1991e, p.284) observed, 'The immediate past state-socialist period has quickly become the source of a new heritage industry.' The relics of the communist period have become relegated to the foundries or to the backs of museums or have become political curiosities. History is being rewritten and represented in order both to attract foreign tourists and forge new national identities by reference to a precommunist past. Heritage and tourism are therefore important components of the new politics of Eastern Europe, the definition of political and social reality, and the repositioning of recreational tourism within the private sphere.

THE POLITICS OF CULTURAL TOURISM

> Culture is being packaged, priced, and sold like building lots, rights-of-way, fast food, and room service, as the tourism industry promises that the world is his/hers to use. All the 'natural resources', including cultural traditions, have their price, and if you have the money in hand, it is your right to see whatever you wish. (Greenwood, 1989, p.179)

One of the most often cited examples of the expropriation or commodification of local culture is that of Greenwood's (1972, 1976, 1989) study of the transformation of the *Alarde* in Fuenterrabia, Spain, from a community celebration to an event performed for tourists. According to Greenwood (1989, p.179), when a cultural activity is made into a public event that becomes an asset to be sold and promoted in the tourist marketplace, the meaning of the ritual can be directly violated, 'definitely destroying its authenticity and its power for the people.' In the case of the *Alarde* in Fuenterrabia, 'it was not a performance for pay, but an affirmation of their belief in their own culture. It was Fuenterrabia commenting on itself for its own purposes' (Greenwood, 1989, p.178). The municipal government's declaration that the *Alarde* should become part of the tourist package for the town meant that the local people 'can still perform the outward forms of the ritual for money, but they cannot subscribe to the meanings it once held because it is no longer being performed by them for themselves' (Greenwood, 1989, p.179). However, despite the loss of original meaning attached to the initial transformation of the event into a tourist product, Greenwood noted that over time the event has had a new set of meanings attached to it and the social reality presented by the event has become transformed yet again: 'it has now become a much more political event and is imbued now with contemporary political significance as part of the contest over regional political rights in Spain' (1989, p.181).

The transformation of cultural meaning and presentation described by Greenwood indicates the difficulties inherent in discussing the political implications of cultural change brought about by tourism. Social change is a problematic concept which involves the values of both the viewer and the viewed. MacCannell's (1984, p.368) comment that 'touristified ethnic groups are often weakened by a history of exploitation, limited in resources and power' does have an element of truth. However, 'the objectification of local culture via tourism does not always destroy it; on occasion it transforms and even stimulates its further proliferation' (Greenwood, 1989, p.183). Change is an inevitable part of social process. 'To argue globally against cultural change is a startling position; to accept all change as good is mindless and cruel. The challenge, as yet unmet, is to conceptualize communities as a complex process of stability and change, and then to factor in the changes tourism brings' (Greenwood, 1989, p.182).

The growth of cultural tourism has substantial implications for the representation and status of indigenous peoples. 'In our contemporary, and perhaps postmodern age, there has been a centrifugal pull of interest away from centred cultures towards previously marginal peoples' (Hollinshead, 1992, p.44). The current tourist interest in indigenous societies is perhaps reflective of a desire for authenticity in Western society and of the role that heritage plays in establishing identity. The desire for authenticity and the implications that this has for the presentation of certain social realities for the tourist gaze has significant political consequences. As Greenwood (1989, p.183) observed, 'The concept of cultural authenticity is part of a much broader polemic about the meaning of history, long important in the Western world. We vacillate between allocating political rights on the basis of authentic racial and ethnic claims, and trying to convert all members of the population to political equals.' The allocation of political rights on cultural grounds may lead to the invention of cultural traditions for the purpose of acquiring such rights; although the allocation of a more universal set of rights which cross cultural boundaries may also lead to the dilution of uniqueness. 'Tourism necessarily operates within this conflictive arena' (Greenwood, 1989, p.184):

> those groups seeking to establish or expand political rights by the reinforcement of their cultural traditions and ethnic identity see tourism as a double-edged sword. The ability to attract tourists to their locations is itself a ratification of cultural claims about uniqueness. The aesthetic dimensions of tourism that emphasize native architecture, art, and performances offer opportunities for cultural advertisements and consolidation. Yet the very process of packaging and merchandising ethnicity for tourism alters local culture in important ways, creating internal divisions that may be politically destructive or diluting local culture in ways that make it unconvincing to the natives. (Greenwood, 1989, p.184)

The relationship between tourism and North American Indians provides a valuable example of the problematic situation in which indigenous peoples often find themselves when it comes to tourism development. The vision and the communication of North American Indians, as with other indigenous peoples, are often conducted solely within the dominant mainstream discourse which stereotypes indigenous peoples in a Eurocentric gaze. As Hollinshead (1992, p.44) argued:

> Beneath that enquiring and incessant gaze the contemporary descendants of the First Americans find themselves in a sort of tourized confinement in the suffocating straightjacket of enslaving external conceptions. They are caught under the objectifying slant of 'Whites', 'Westerners' and 'Wanderers-from-afar' in an anonymous but continuing process of subjugation. It constitutes the Foucaultian vision of the hidden and unsuspected structures of knowledge and disciplinary power in society.

The dominant Eurocentric vision has important implications for the manner in which indigenous peoples are perceived. For example, there is a fear among many Australian Aboriginal groups that contact with tourists may devalue Aboriginal culture and lead to further social breakdown in some communities. Mr S. Brennan from the Bureau of the Northern Land Council commented that the

Gagudju people in the Kakadu region of the Northern Territory 'do not like the idea of being a bit like a zoo, feeling that they are on display for tourists to come and see what an Aboriginal person looks like in his environment, to see whether he still walks around with a spear. They certainly do not like that concept of tourism' (in Senate Standing Committee on Environment, Recreation and the Arts, 1988, pp.28–29).

In New Zealand, the focus on the indigenous people, the Maori, as a component of the country's tourist product has been longstanding. Representations of Maori in tourist brochures have existed since the 1870s while destinations, such as Rotorua, have long used aspects of Maori culture as a mechanism to attract overseas tourists. Nevertheless, with a few notable exceptions, the images provided by the tourism industry have been *Pakeha* (European or outsider) dominated. As Barber (1992, p.19) commented:

> Pakeha New Zealanders have never been slow to exploit this indigenous culture in promotion and advertising—often in ways that drew Maori disapproval. There was a time when foreigners could have been excused for thinking, by the posters and videos they saw, that New Zealand existed solely of flax-skirted Maori jumping in and out of steaming pools.

The inappropriate use of Maori images in tourist promotion and the transformation of Maori culture to provide a suitable product for tourists have had substantial impacts on Maori attitudes towards tourism (Hall, C., Mitchell and Keelan, 1992; Hall, C., Keelan, and Mitchell, 1993). According to the Maori Tourism Task Force (1986, p.25):

> It has been of deep concern to the Maori that the Maori image has been used as a marketing tool in the promotion of the tourist industry for over a hundred years . . . Maori are also critical of the way they are stereotyped into guides, entertainers, carvers, and as components of the natural scenery. This has been without consultation and with little commercial benefit to the Maori people. There is a notable undercurrent of bitterness about this which could easily turn to anger. This means the industry must rethink its present tendency to stereotype the Maori role in tourism and the goods and services the Maori are attempting to provide.
>
> It is clear that the Maori image has commercial value. The expressed desire of the Maori people is that they should control their image so they can build a Maori dimension within the tourist industry.

Control is an important issue in the presentation of indigenous culture. However, indigenous peoples who seek to assert their rights, particularly over land, are typically stereotyped as 'troublemakers', while Europeans who were seeking the same level of access to land would be regarded as protecting their rights. In New Zealand many *Pakeha* are concerned that Maori land claims will prohibit access to recreational and tourist areas. For example, the Ngai Tahu claim amounts to more than 70 per cent of the South Island of the country and included substantial portions of national parks, high country areas, and lakes and waterways (Waitangi Tribunal, 1991). Aspirations of the Ngai Tahu in respect to some of the Crown lands which they claim include joint title to all or some national parks in the claim area; some responsibility for management of some or all of the parks; sole responsibility to control tourism and possibly other concessions in parks (the Ngai Tahu have said they will give preference to Maoris and to concessions 'with the right culture'); and outright legal title to natural features of special cultural value (Barr, 1992; Hall, C., 1994b).

The country's peak outdoor recreation body, the Federated Mountain Clubs (FMC), in its submission to the Waitangi Tribunal on the Ngai Tahu claim, expressed concern about transferring areas of Crown land which have recreation and conservation value into Maori title. They argued that privatisation of any Crown land will reduce freedom of access for the general public to enjoy such lands (by banning access or charging entrance fees). The FMC did not question the validity of the Maori claims. Nevertheless, the FMC is providing substantial opposition to the claim, for example, with reference to the possibility of national park land being transferred to Maori control the FMC argues:

> But even if the Ngai Tahu were the greenest group in the nation, they shouldn't be granted control, because whoever manages these lands must be answerable to the people, and private owners are not . . .
> Maori claims cover almost all of our country. If private land is excluded, then most of the land left is conservation land. If the Ngai Tahu claims are successful they will have set an unstoppable precedent that other tribes will want to follow. (Barr, 1992, p.9)

The New Zealand situation has parallels in Australia, Canada and the United States with respect to indigenous claims to land and the relationship of those claims to the Eurocentric gaze of the tourist. As Hollinshead (1992, p.58) observed, 'North American Indians are not appreciated by many Westerners, through the White gaze, because they differ from what they *ought* to be.'

> Traditional and mythical constructions by Westerners of what indigenous peoples should be, can blind external perception to an indigenous group or native community's present day needs. Non-Indians too frequently impose their own concepts of legitimate traditional upon particular Indian tribes: Westerners cannot accord 'Indian-ity', and ought not attempt to approve or deny change. Each Indian group must be encouraged to have its own right to convert and substitute as it sees fit. (Hollinshead, 1992, p.56)

Hollinshead's (1992) discussion of the North American Indian situation has parallels throughout the world. Given Papson's (1981) identification of the role of marketing, promotion and government tourism policies in shaping social reality, discussed above, it clearly becomes vital that lead agencies and players which orchestrate the gaze of tourism carefully monitor the cultural product that is under their stewardship (Hollinshead, 1992; Lea, 1993). The goal of responsible agencies should be to transform the stereotyped and commodified image into what has been rightfully deemed to be 'the historically specific' and 'the culturally unique' (Albers and James, 1983). Therefore, the cultural and heritage resources of any country should not be seen as existing solely to serve the needs of the tourism industry (Cossons, 1989; Hall, C. and Zeppel, 1990).

POLITICS, POSTMODERNISM AND THE TOURIST GAZE

> We now live in a post-Marxian world of the 'political economy of the sign'; the emphasis has shifted away from production itself to image, advertising and consumption. We are now interested in what Baudrillard has termed the 'mirror of production', and tourism, being so much a matter of leisure, consumption, and image, is an essentially (post-) modern activity. (Crick, 1989, p.333)

Through the effect of the visions or gaze of the tourist on hosts and destinations, tourism is visually consuming the environment. According to Urry (1992, p.5), 'People continuously seek ever-new images and hence ever-new places to visit and to capture.' However, the semantics and politics of the industry image-makers alter tourists' experiences of space and time (Crick, 1989), leading to what Harvey (1989a) described as 'time–space compression'.

According to Urry (1992, p.6), time–space compression 'refers to the way in which changes in the organization of capitalist labour-time have transformed space, suppressing all sorts of differences between places. Events and processes are increasingly inter-dependent. Simple narratives are implausible'. For example, nostalgia and heritage have become components of the tourist experience with local government playing a major role in reconstructing and representing whole places as heritage objects for the tourist gaze. Five effects of time–space compression are identified by Urry (1992): volatility and the ephemeral nature of products, instantaneity and disposability, the encouragement of short-termism, the development of certain signs and images, and the production of simulcra.

Time–space compression and the development of 'the present day image economy' (Sharrat, 1989, p.38) are regarded as central elements of postmodernity. Postmodernism 'is a regime of signification whose fundamental structuring trait is "de-differen-tiation"' (Lash, 1990, p.11) and 'refers to a system of signs or symbols, which is specific in both time and space. Such a system is characterisable in terms of a specific regime of signification in which particular cultural objects are produced, circulated and received. Such objects involve a particular set of relations between the signifier, the signified and the referent' (Urry, 1990a, pp.83–84). Whereas modernism involved structured 'differentiation' between cultural forms, postmodernism is a process of 'de-differentiation' which involves a dissolving of cultural boundaries, not only between high and low cultures, but also between various cultural forms, such as art, architecture, education, heritage, shopping, sport and tourism. For example, we now talk of art tourism, educational tourism, heritage tourism and sport tourism as forms of special interest tourism (Weiler and Hall, 1992). What now is tourism and what now is culture are relatively unclear. The tourist gaze is therefore 'intrinsically part of contemporary experience, of postmodernism, but the tourist practices to which it gives rise are experiencing rapid and significant change. Such change cannot be separated from these more wide-ranging structural and cultural developments in contemporary society' (Urry, 1990a, p.82).

'Postmodernism problematises the distinction between repre-sentations and reality ... what we increasingly consume are signs or representations. Social identities are constructed through the exchange of sign-values (Urry, 1990a, p.85). For example, Hewison

(1987, p.135) observed that there is a loss of the historical sense of meaning in the postmodernist stage of heritage tourism, which creates 'a shallow screen that intervenes between our present lives, our history. We have no understanding of history in depth, but instead are offered a contemporary creation, more costume drama and re-enactment than critical discourse.' Spectacle and display, through the hosting of hallmark events or urban redevelopment projects, become sought after community symbols. 'This world of symbol is one in which there is nothing which is original, no real meaning, everything is a copy, or text upon a text. It is a depthless world of networks and information and communication in which information has no end-purpose or meaning' (Urry, 1988, p.39).

In the postmodern society the commercialisation of leisure has meant that tourism is often treated purely as a commodity to be sold through the established rules of marketing. 'Postmodernism . . . signals nothing more than a logical extension of the power of the market over the whole range of cultural production' (Harvey, 1989a, p.62). Krippendorf (1987, p.20) has admirably illustrated the issue:

> The techniques are the same as in selling cars, vacuum cleaners, detergent or other consumer goods. But because they deal in desires and dreams, landscapes, people and cultures, travel sellers, one would presume, carry a much greater responsibility. However, they don't seem to be aware of it—or else they simply do not want to realize it. The 'producers' of the item called travel are not charitable institutions but commercial undertakings, a fact that they admit quite openly. Why a journey is undertaken is of no consequence to them—what matters is that it is undertaken. Their primary interest is the short-term growth of their own business and not the long-term development of a well-balanced tourist trade. It would be naive to censure them for it, because they act in accordance with established principles of the free-market economy. But today we must try to see where the limits of this freedom lie.

The commoditisation of tourism experiences has been a significant theme in this chapter. The transformation of social and cultural experiences into a product to be bought and sold has tremendous implications for social reality, the significance of which we are only now beginning to appreciate. 'Because of the importance of the visual, of the gaze, tourism has always been concerned with spectacle and with cultural practices which partly implode into each other' (Urry, 1990a, p.86). Tourism colours our belief systems. The transformation of social reality has substantial political implications: for example, in terms of the presentation of culture and heritage and perhaps, particularly, to the extent that Eurocentrism is the dominant discourse within the tourism industry. As noted above, the presentation of social reality influences perceptions of collective and individual identity and the socialisation process. However, our understanding of the political dimensions of tourist phenomena at both the macro and micro political levels is still sparse.

Perhaps the most fundamental political question surrounding tourism which has been raised in this and the previous two chapters is that of control. As Krippendorf (1987, p.55) has asked, 'Why has the loss of local autonomy—certainly the most negative long-term effect of tourism—been practically ignored? Why does the local population tolerate it?' Chapter 6 highlighted the role of local élites in controlling the pattern and process of tourism development, while the present chapter has noted the role of broader socio-economic process within the contemporary capitalist system in determining the presentation of tourist reality. The intersection of values and interests which these two focal points for research on the politics of tourism represent will clearly provide a potential direction for understanding the who gets what, where, how and why of tourism. It is to this and other questions surrounding the politics of tourism that the final chapter will now turn.

8

Situating Tourism in Capitalist Society: Towards an Understanding of Tourism Politics, Policy and Place

International tourism is a major, fast-growing industry in its own right, which momentarily brings people from different cultures face-to-face on a scale unknown in previous migratory areas. It has some aspects of showbiz, some of international trade in commodities; it is part innocent fun, part a devastating modernising (or corrupting) force. Being all these things simultaneously, it tends to induce partial analysis only. (Turner, 1974, p.181)

Tourism has been rarely studied in terms of its political importance. (Matthews and Richter, 1991, p.122)

SITUATING TOURISM IN CAPITALIST SOCIETY

This book has provided a discussion of the relationship between tourism and politics, both in terms of how tourism may serve to change power arrangements and values in destination areas and how, in turn, tourism patterns and processes are a response to different contested values and interests. Despite an overall growth in tourism studies as a field of interest in the social sciences, most research is still economically or market oriented. Given the primary roles that economic growth and employment play in government tourism policy, such a concentration should hardly be surprising. Nevertheless, 'as tourism emerges from the shadows of economic policy to a centre-stage position, it has become imperative to evaluate its role in economic development' (Williams and Shaw, 1988c, p.1) in a more detailed manner than has hitherto been the case.

Unfortunately, the 'dominant approaches to understanding tourism and its effects tend to be narrowly economic, implicitly functionalist or (economic) system-reproducing, and de-contextualising' (Roche, 1992, pp.564–565). For example, while research may consider gross or even nett economic impacts within the supply and demand of tourism product, the issue of distribution of available employment and income and leisure time in the destination and generating regions is little discussed. In other words, many of the key questions of who gets what, where, how and why remain unasked. All forms of tourism development involve the dominance of one set of values over alternative values through the exercise of power. For example, in the case of international tourism between destination and generating regions, Crick (1989, p.321) has argued:

> Many of the specific relationships between 'hosts' and 'guests' in tourism are only comprehensible in the context of these wider international relations between the developing world and the affluent West . . . Indeed, for some critics of standard international tourism . . . the piecemeal analysis of tourism without the political-economic overview is typical of bourgeois social science and is a strategy often used to avoid real social issues.

Tourism policy cannot be separated from the milieu in which it evolves. According to Simmons and Dvorin (1977, p.406), 'Analysis of a specific policy environment would center upon identifying the component features and dynamic characteristics of such an environment, particularly those which have a bearing upon policy itself.' Similarly, Majone (1989, p.118) noted that consideration of the context is crucial in undertaking policy analysis:

> A practical problem is not solved by offering a theoretical solution that does not take into consideration the limitations upon which the context imposes. Thus, it is quite misleading to employ ideal standards in evaluating or comparing alternative policy instruments; the standards must relate to the particular context in which the instruments are used. And because the context in which public policy is made includes values, norms, perceptions, and ideologies, technical considerations are insufficient as a criteria of choice.

Unfortunately, much tourism research does not provide a basis for the contextualisation of tourism. In other words, it does not deal with 'the obvious', but critical social fact that tourism needs to be situated in capitalist society (Rojek, 1985; Britton, 1991). 'The consumption of tourist-services cannot be separated off from the social relations within which they are embedded' (Urry, 1990b, p.23). As Wilson (1988, pp.5–6) noted, to consider the 'political factor' in leisure, including recreational tourism, 'is to acknowledge that people's use of their free time is not simply the result of social and economic forces but is the outcome also of political struggle.'

Tourism grew out of the changing politics of space and time as the social and economic impacts of industrial revolution took place in the nineteenth century. As capitalism has changed its form and structures so has mass tourism. Tourism is a product of capitalist society and cannot be understood without reference to it.

'Mass tourism and travel is a quintessentially modern (late twentieth-century) capitalist industry and socio-cultural phenomenon' (Roche, 1992, p.565). Western industrial capitalism has undergone profound structural changes during the 1980s with regional, national and international shifts in opportunities for capital accumulation and employment (Bramham *et al.*, 1989a). Tourism is an essential component of these shifts which may be described as 'postindustrial' or 'post-Fordist', referring to the shift from an industrial to an information technology/service base. In addition, tourism is part of the globalisation of the international economy, in which economic production is transnational, interdependent and multipolar with less and less dependence on the nation-state as the primary unit of international economic organisation. Linked to these dramatic economic changes have been dramatic cultural shifts. As noted in the previous chapter, the term 'postmodernism' has been used to describe contemporary cultural relativism and fragmentation in which image, spectacle, the power of the market and the gaze of the tourist dominate the tourist experience (Jameson, 1984; Harvey, 1989a; Urry, 1990a; Roche, 1992).

Leisure, including tourism, is not just the 'free time' remaining once work is over. 'Not only does this notion miss the point of why and how leisure occurs in the socially prescribed activities that it does, and the social relations and functions embedded in them, but it is insufficient even in its own terms' (Britton, 1991, p.452). Leisure and tourism activities have become increasingly commodified. In capitalist society, people's leisure is shaped most directly by what the 'culture industry' is offering, and only to the extent that the state sees itself as regulating or subsidising this industry do people feel the impress of political actions (Held, 1980; Wilson, 1988). The dominant ideology of leisure and tourism in Western capitalist societies, which is increasingly being exported throughout the world through the modernisation dynamic, portrays leisure and tourism as essentially a private and individual choice. Such an ideology only serves to legitimise the relationship between the culture industry and dominant ideology. Somewhat paradoxically, 'this process complements, yet subverts, the trend towards individuation of leisure, with the personalisation and differentiation of leisure products expressed in market niching, cosmetic design variations, and advertising disguising the industrialisation and mass production of such products' (Britton, 1991, p.453). Tourism and leisure are therefore something to be 'consumed', selected from an array of offerings produced and distributed by a highly competitive and enterprising tourism industry. This ideology, and the dynamism and volatility of the leisure and tourism market, help 'perpetuate the notion that "having fun" and "being entertained" are entirely free of political consequences' (Wilson, 1988, p.51).

> The ideology of 'consumer sovereignty' encourages us to regard leisure choice as an exercise in individual freedom; and it lends support to the notion that politics, which connote domination and control, should be kept out of leisure ... A market or consumer model of leisure planning dominates the recreation profession as well as government bureaucrats; leisure services ... must be developed to meet 'preferences'. The market model competes vigorously with the much more feeble idea that leisure services must compensate for deprivations or disadvantages, and the equally unpopular idea that leisure services should uplift or educate. (Wilson, 1988, p. 52)

Commercial tourism largely consists of activities which require passive yet uncritical participation in patterned cultural products. The ideology of 'consumer sovereignty' disguises the extent to which capital controls leisure. 'Modern leisure corporations may follow consumer demand, but they can also create it, and their ability to do so increases with their growing domination of leisure production' (Clarke and Critcher, 1985, p.200). The extent of this domination is in no way affected by the high turnover rate experienced among leisure and tourism enterprises. Specific markets may be difficult to control, but there is no question about capital's collective control over the production and distribution of leisure and tourism (Rojek, 1985; Wilson, 1988). The tourism industry sells experiences, which are the outcomes of what Urry (1990a, b) referred to as 'the tourist's gaze'. Tourists are 'armies of semiotics' for whom the identification and collection of signs—represents/something/to someone (MacCannell, 1989)—are 'proof' that experiences have been realised (Culler, 1981; Britton, 1991). The 'culture industry' of which tourism is a part,

> reproduces and reinforces dominant interpretations of reality, while including sufficient degrees of novelty to capture audience (market) attention, by classifying and coding the entertainment, and predisposing consumers of how to interpret it through suitable cues (commentaries, brochures, reviews, advertisements) for eliciting the intended response. (Britton, 1991, p.454)

As the previous chapter has indicated, one of the key aspects of the politics of contemporary tourism is the manner in which place has become commodified. The notion of the 'globalisation' of the leisure and tourism marketplace implies its increasing capitalisation or commodification (Wilson, 1988). The tourist production system simultaneously 'sells' places in order to attract tourists, the means to the end (travel and accommodation) and the end itself (the tourist experience). Therefore, tourism finds itself at the forefront of an important recent dynamic within capitalist accumulation in terms of the creation and marketing of experiences. Tourists 'are purchasing the intangible qualities of restoration, status, life-style signifier, release from the constraints of everyday life, or conveniently packaged novelty' (Britton, 1991, p.465). Within this setting place is commodified and reduced to an experience and images for consumption.

The production of 'leisure spaces' (Lefebvre, 1976), which are discrete and categorised landscapes that actively maintain and consolidate prevailing production relations, is 'a functional necessity given the subsumption of the individual to capital in the workplace (a holiday to enable the reconstitution of "human capital")' (Britton, 1991, p.462). An example is the inner city tourism and leisure redevelopments discussed in Chapter 6. 'There is a distinct hierarchy of holiday spaces in terms of the nature of the reconstitution they are designed to provide, and the social classes which use them' (Britton, 1989), ranging as a continuum in terms of physical, cultural and monetary accessibility from overseas holiday resorts to local parks, or from local camp grounds to exclusive hotels, or from amusement parks to wilderness areas. Indeed, much of the overt conflict over leisure and tourism reflects patterns of domination and subordination in the cultural hierarchy: 'just as different groups and classes are unequally ranked in relation to one another, in terms of their productive relations, wealth and power, so cultures are differently ranked, and stand in opposition to one another, in relations of domination and subordination, along the scale of "cultural power"' (Clarke, 1981, p.54). However, to concentrate just on one aspect of overt conflict in the public sphere may be to ignore the broader effects of processes of restructuring and territorial accumulation within contemporary capitalism with which they are intimately related. Leisure and tourist spaces must therefore be seen as a significant 'element of the sociospatial division of labour in modern capitalist society' (Britton, 1991, p.463).

As Chapter 6 noted, many urban centres are re-imaging themselves in order to attract capital. Such strategies are an essential element of the new territorial competition in which both the local and nation-state find themselves involved in order to rejuvenate and restructure national and regional economies. The governance of urban centres is increasingly motivated by an entrepreneurial rather than a welfare ideology and is geared toward creating a 'favourable environment' within which to attract capital, investment, white-collar workers and, of course, tourism which comprises a substantial element in the new urban service economy.

Urban centres are attempting to position themselves as centres of consumption within the increasingly globalised capitalist system. The creation of 'symbolic' (Harvey, 1989a) or 'cultural capital' (Zukin, 1990) in the form of cultural industries, such as tourism and leisure, serves as the basis with which to create new or rejuvenate existing regional and international investment poles (Britton, 1991); for example, through the hosting of 'events of heroic consumption' such as World Expos and the Olympic Games (Ley and Olds, 1988, p.191). Tourism is therefore very much part of the competition for and consumption of scarce resources, the seeking of which *must* surely lead one to the essential elements of the politics of tourism: *politics is about power, who gets what, where, how and why*. It is time that students of tourism placed tourism within capitalist society and examined the stark implications of Crick's (1989, p.334) observation:

> Tourism is the conspicuous consumption of resources accumulated in secular time; its very possibility, in other words, is securely rooted in the real world of gross political and economic inequalities between nations and classes. In fact . . . tourism is doubly imperialistic; not only does it make a spectacle of the Other, making cultures into consumer items, tourism is also an opiate of the masses in the affluent countries themselves. (Crick, 1989)

TOWARDS AN UNDERSTANDING OF THE POLITICS OF TOURISM?

In 1975 Matthews stated that 'the literature of tourism is grossly lacking of political research' (1975, p.195). Some 20 years later the situation has not changed markedly. Studies of the political dimension of tourism have tended to be incidental to social, economic or environmental considerations in tourism research, rather than a main focus. Indeed, much of the work on tourism policy has really been about what *should* be in terms of a set of objectives rather than what *is* and how it was arrived at.

As this book has demonstrated, an examination of the relationship between politics and tourism can be dealt with at a number of levels: international, national, regional, local and the individual. Each of these levels presents its own structural and analytical dynamic to the researcher. However, all of these levels of analysis should be incorporated by the student of tourism within the increasingly globalised capitalist system in order to contextualise tourism phenomena. 'Tourism assists us in recognising how the social meaning and materiality of space and place is created through the practice of tourism itself, and how these representations are then incorporated into the accumulation process' (Britton, 1991, p.478). Tourism, as with all leisure phenomena, is therefore part of the struggle for the control of space and time in which social groups are continually engaged, a struggle in which the dominant group seeks to legitimate, through statute and administrative fiat, its understanding of the appropriate use of space and time, and the subordinate groups resist this control through individual rebellion and collective action (Wilson, 1988, p.12).

The study of tourism is also caught up with debates over ideology and values. Most tourism research, particularly with respect to policy analysis, is caught up in 'the intellectualist bias of decisionism, with its emphasis on "knowing that" rather than "knowing how"', and a corresponding neglect of the craft aspects of policy analysis. 'In turn, this bias is related to the positivistic tradition in the philosophy of science. Being mainly concerned with the logical and epistemological problems of achieved knowledge, this school has paid very little attention to the actual processes of the production of scientific knowledge' (Majone, 1989, p.50). However, tourism research is not value free. There is no objective or value-free social science. Subject and object are inextricably linked. The researcher, student of tourism or tourism policy analyst must therefore consider carefully the underlying assumptions of analytical frameworks, their explanatory power, and the contribution that they make to any policy debate. Nevertheless, as noted in Chapter 1, most tourism studies have tended to assume a conservative, non-critical, value-free approach to their subject matter (see also the comments by Roche, 1992). Such an approach is also to be found in many policy statements, as Richter (1989, p.103) noted:

> In most countries, the industry's health is assumed to be the best indicator of a successful policy. This is not so. A tourism policy in a developing nation, particularly, should be judged by its net impact on the economic, social, and political life of the people. Since net economic benefits, as opposed to overall receipts, and social and political factors are seldom considered quantifiable, in many countries they are simply left out of the policy equation.

'Value-free' tourism research, akin to that which often emerges from economics and marketing, is not a sufficient approach to the study of tourism. Undoubtedly, the socio-cultural and environmental effects of tourism are increasingly being considered, although even in these cases the political context of tourism development is typically ignored. Tourism is a central element of some of the critical economic and political issues of the contemporary era: the internationalisation of capital; industrial and regional restructuring; urban redevelopment; and the growth of the service economy (Britton, 1989), but from a reading of the mainstream tourism literature you would never know it. Critical and political economy perspectives, with a few important exceptions (e.g. Urry, 1990a; Hollinshead, 1992; Roche, 1992), have been largely ignored in contemporary tourism research. For example, within the current debate on the politics of sustainable tourism, the focus is primarily on ecological and, narrowly defined, economic processes, rather than the cultural and political framework within which policy choices are made (Hall, C., 1994c). As Friedmann (1980, p.8) commented, 'the *limits to growth* are both environmental (external) and *psycho-social* (internal).' To ignore the psycho-social factors is therefore only to undertake partial analysis and, yet again, to fail to contextualise the nature of tourism development.

The tourism policy and decision-making process is extremely complex. The student of tourism policy is a modern-day Theseus trying to follow the thread of the decision-making process through the policy labyrinth. In studying the politics of tourism, the analyst is forced to recognise the 'questions of political theory and political values' which 'underlie explicitly or implicitly, public policy decisions' (Stillman, 1974, pp.49–50). Different analytical frameworks contain different strengths and weaknesses, and the analyst chooses 'between theoretical approaches to attack the issues of policy' (Jenkins, 1978, p.20). In order to understand how tourism is involved in the accumulation process and orders relations between people and place:

> we need a theorisation that explicitly recognises, and unveils, tourism as a predominantly capitalistically organised activity driven by the inherent and defining social dynamics of that system, with its attendant production, social, and ideological relations. An analysis of how the tourism production system markets and packages people is a lesson in the political economy of the social construction of 'reality' and social construction of place, whether from the point of view of visitors and host communities, tourism capital (and the 'culture industry'), or the state—with its diverse involvement in the system. (Britton, 1991, p.475)

The above statement by Britton will probably make a number of readers rather uneasy. Why? Because it is outside the 'normal' parameters of discourse within the field of tourism studies. However, 'policy problems are not textbook quizzes; they carry no guarantee that there always exist correct solutions against which analytic conclusions may be checked' (Majone, 1989, p.65). A different conceptualisation of the problem, other tools and models, or a few different judgements made at crucial points of the analysis and argument can lead to quite different conclusions. As noted in

Chapter 1, such challenges, or oppositional approaches, are vital to the development of knowledge of the political dimensions of tourism and to our understanding of tourism policy. Therefore, 'the essential need today is an improvement in the methods and conditions of critical debate and their institutionalisation at all levels of policy-making' (Majone, 1989, p.6).

Several authors (e.g. Hollinshead, 1992; Roche, 1992) have argued that the adoption of a dialectical approach to the study of tourism can assist critical inquiry into the foundations and assumptions of social phenomena and enable critical discourse between students of tourism. Dialectic is a method of argument characterised not so much by the form of reasoning but by the nature of its premises and the social context of its applications. 'The starting point of a dialectic argument is not abstract assumptions but points of view already present in the community; its conclusion is not a formal proof, but a shared understanding of the issue under discussion' (Majone, 1989, p.6). Roche (1992, p.591) argued that dialectical forms of conceptualisation are needed:

> to appreciate the difference and interdependence between social facts and social values, between theory and description, and between theory and policy. But further it requires [students of tourism] to appreciate the unity-in-difference in social reality of such complex phenomena as action and structure, continuity and change, consciousness and material conditions, micro and macro levels and so on.

The above relationships are inherently dialectical in nature. However, the vast majority of tourism research is one-dimensional and fails to adequately account for *both* tourism as a complex social phenomenon and the theoretical frameworks that are being utilised. In particular, much socio-political analysis fails to contextualise analysis adequately with reference to a number of processes which clearly affect tourism's position within macro structural change and modernisation in contemporary society (Britton, 1991; Roche, 1992), including cultural changes associated with postmodernism (cultural fragmentation, aesthetic and moral relativism, consumerism and hedonism); postindustrialism (the shift from industrialism to a high technology and services based formation in the contemporary capitalist economy); and post-nationalism (economic globalisation: the emergence of a distinctive and predominating transnational level in the contemporary capitalist economy, political transnationalism, and transnational social and environmental problems) (Roche, 1993b).

The process of dialectical inquiry would appear to be essential to the study of the political dimensions of tourism. Indeed, as noted in Chapter 1 in a discussion of the idea of policy analysis as craft, dialectical inquiry and policy analysis are closely related:

> Like dialectic, policy analysis usually starts with plausible premises, with contestable and shifting viewpoints, not with indisputable principles or hard facts. Like dialectic, it does not produce formal proofs but only persuasive arguments . . . Finally, policy analysis, like dialectic, contributes to public deliberation through criticism, advocacy, and education. Good policy analysis is more than data analysis or a modelling exercise; it also provides standards of argument and an intellectual structure for public discourse. Even when its conclusions are not accepted, its categories and language, its criticism of traditional approaches, and its advocacy of new ideas affect—even condition—the policy debate. (Majone, 1989, p.7)

Carlyle's assertion that 'creation is great, and cannot be understood' should not deter the student of the politics of tourism. Knowledge of the formation of decisions and the interaction of elements within the policy environment is crucial if there is an intention to affect the tourism policy-making process, tourism development and the management of resources. Yet knowledge of the policy process is not enough, as the results of research are themselves subject to use and abuse within the policy arena (Grodsky, 1982). Students of the politics of tourism are not outside the political arena which they study. Through their research, consultancies, conclusions and recommendations they are part of the tourism policy and development process, albeit sometimes marginalised. If analysts want their research to impact the policy process then they may have to assume an advocacy role. Value-free tourism research does not exist. Students of tourism must therefore be aware that 'policy analysis can be neither performed competently nor used properly without an appreciation of its craft aspects' (Majone, 1989, p.68). There are no policy facts; there are only policy arguments. It is hoped that this book will contribute, if only in small part, to such an argument.

References

Airey, D., 1983, European government approaches to tourism, *Tourism Management*, 4 (4): 234–244

Airey, D., 1984, Tourism administration in the USA, *Tourism Management*, 5 (4): 269–279

Alasia, S., 1989, Politics, in H. Larcy (ed.), *Ples bulong iumi—Solomon Islands: the past four thousand years*, Institute of Pacific Studies, University of the South Pacific, Suva

Albers, P. and James, W., 1983, Tourism and the changing photographic image of the Great Lakes Indians, *Annals of Tourism Research*, 10: 123–148

Alebua, E., 1992, Eco-forestry in Solomon Islands, *The Courier*, 132: 38–39

Alford, R. and Friedland, R., 1985, *Powers of theory: capitalism, the state and democracy*, Cambridge University Press, Cambridge

Allcock, J.B., 1991, Poland, in D.R. Hall (ed.), *Tourism and economic development in Eastern Europe and the Soviet Union*, Belhaven Press, London, pp.236–258

Allison, G., 1971, *The essence of decision*, Little, Brown and Company, Boston

Anderson, J., 1975, *Public policy making*, Praeger, New York

Andronicou, A., 1979, Tourism in Cyprus, in E. de Kadt (ed.), *Tourism—passport to development?*, Oxford University Press, New York

Aristotle, 1976, *The ethics of Aristotle: the Nicomachean ethics*, J.A.K. Thompson trans., H. Tredennick rev. trans., Penguin, Harmondsworth

Armstrong, D., 1988, Tourism '88: challenges and opportunities, *Pacific Islands Monthly*, February: 41–44

Arnstein, S., 1969, A ladder of citizen participation, *Journal of American Institute of Planners*, 35: 216–224

Ascher, B., 1984, Obstacles to international travel and tourism, *Journal of Travel Research*, 22: 2–16

Ashworth, G.J. and Bergsma, J.R., 1987, New policies for tourism: opportunities or problems, *Tijdschrift voor Economische en Sociale Geografie*, 78 (2): 151–155

Asia Travel Trade, 1989, Inbound's full of woes, *Asia Travel Trade*, 21 (May): 41

Asia Travel Trade, 1992, AFTA the coup, *Asia Travel Trade*, September: 8–9

Auburn, F.M., 1982, *Antarctic law and politics*, C. Hurst, London

Aucion, P., 1971, Theory and research in the study of policy-making, in G.B. Doren an P. Aucion (eds.) *The structures of policy-making in Canada*, Macmillan, Toronto, pp.10–38

Australian Government Committee of Inquiry into Tourism, 1987, *Report of the Australian government committee of inquiry into tourism*, vol.1, Australian Government Publishing Service, Canberra

Bachrach, P., 1969–70, A power analysis, *Public Policy*, 18: 155–186

Bachrach, P. and Baratz, M.S., 1970, *Power and poverty: theory and practice*, Oxford University Press, New York

Badie, B. and Birnbaum, P., 1983, *The sociology of the state*, University of Chicago Press, Chicago

Barber, D., 1992, Of tourism and tradition, *Pacific Islands Monthly*, August: 19

Barr, H., 1992, Worries over Maori bid to control parks, *The Dominion*, 21 July: 6

Barrett, S. and Fudge, C., 1981, Examining the policy–action relationship, in S. Barrett and C. Fudge (eds.) *Policy and action*, Methuen, London, pp.3–32

Bastin, R., 1984, Small island tourism: development or dependency, *Development Policy Review*, 2 (1): 79–90

Becker, H.S., 1978, Arts and crafts, *American Journal of Sociology*, 83 (4): 862–889

Benedict, B., 1983, The anthropology of World Fairs, in B. Benedict (ed.), *The anthropology of world fairs*, Scolar Press, London, pp.1–65

Bergin, A., 1985, Recent developments in Australia's Antarctic policy, *Marine Policy*, 9: 180–191

Bernstein, R., 1978, *The restructuring of social and political theory*, Harcourt and Brace, New York

Best, L., 1968, A model of pure plantation economy, *Social and Economic Studies*, 17 (3): 283–326

Bianchini, F. and Parkinson, M., 1993, *Cultural policy and urban development: the experience of West European cities*, Manchester University Press, Manchester

Blank, U., 1989, *The community tourism industry imperative: the necessity, the opportunities, its potential*, Venture Publishing, State College

Bodlender, J.A. and Davies, E.J.G., 1985, *A profile of government financial aid to tourism*, World Tourist Organization/Horwarth and Horwath International, Madrid

Boniface, P. and Fowler, P.J., 1993, *Heritage and tourism in 'the global village'*, Routledge, London and New York

Bouquet, M. and Winter, M., 1987, Introduction: tourism politics and practice, in M. Bouquet and M. Winter (eds.), *Who from their Labours Rest? Conflict and Practice in Rural Tourism*, Avebury, Aldershot, pp.1–8

Bragg, L., 1990, Ecotourism: a working definition, *Institute for Tropical Rainforest Studies Newsletter*, 2 (2): 7

Bramham, P., Henry, I., Mommaas, H. and van der Poel, H. (eds.), 1989a, *Leisure and urban processes: critical studies of leisure policy in Western European cities*, Routledge, London and New York

Bramham, P., Henry, I., Mommaas, H. and van der Poel, H., 1989b, Introduction, in P. Bramham, I. Henry, H. Mommaas and H. van der Poel (eds.), *Leisure and urban processes: critical studies of leisure policy in Western European cities*, Routledge, London and New York, pp.1–13

Bramwell, B. and Lane, B., 1993, Sustainable tourism: an evolving global approach, *Journal of Sustainable Tourism*, 1 (1): 6–16

Britton, S.G, 1982a, International tourism and multinational corporations in the Pacific: the case of Fiji, in M.J. Taylor and N. Thrift (eds.), *The Geography of Multinationals*, Croom Helm, Sydney, pp.252–274

Britton, S.G., 1982b, The political economy of tourism in the Third World, *Annals of Tourism Research*, 9 (3): 331–358

Britton, S.G., 1983, *Tourism and underdevelopment in Fiji*, Monograph No.13, Australian National University Development Studies Centre, Australian National University, Canberra

Britton, S.G., 1987, Tourism in Pacific island states, constraints and opportunities, in S. Britton and W.C. Clarke (eds.), *Ambiguous alternative: tourism in small developing countries*, University of the South Pacific, Suva, pp.113–139

Britton, S.G., 1989, Tourism, capital, and places: a contribution to the geography of tourism, paper prepared for the New Zealand Geographic Society Conference, 20–24 August, University of Otago, Dunedin

Britton, S.G., 1991, Tourism, capital and place: towards a critical geography of tourism, *Environment and Planning D: Society and Space*, 9 (4): 451–478

Britton S.G. and Clarke, W.C. (eds.), 1987, *Ambiguous alternative: tourism in small developing countries*, University of the South Pacific, Suva

Brookfield, H., 1991, Environmental sustainability with development: what prospects for a research agenda?, in O. Stokke (ed.), *Sustainable development*, Frank Cass, London, pp.42–46

Brown, G., 1985, The tourism industry in Australia, in J. Dean and B. Judd (eds.), *Tourist developments in Australia*, Royal Australian Institute of Architects Education Division, Canberra, pp.8–11

Brown, L.B., 1973, *Ideology*, Penguin, Harmondsworth

Buckley, P.J. and Klemm, M., 1993, The decline of tourism in Northern Ireland, *Tourism Management*, June: 185–194

Budowski, G., 1976, Tourism and conservation: conflict, coexistence or symbiosis, *Environmental Conservation*, 3 (1): 27–31

Burkart, A.J. and Medlik, S., 1981, *Tourism Past, Present and Future*, 2nd. edn., Heinemann, London

Burton, T.L., 1982, A framework for leisure policy research, *Leisure Studies*, 1: 323–335

Butler, R.W., 1974, The social implications of tourist developments, *Annals of Tourism Research*, 2 (2): 100–111

204 References

Butler, R.W., 1980, The concept of a tourist area cycle of evolution: implications for management of resources, *Canadian Geographer*, 24: 5–12

Cameron, C., 1989, Cultural tourism and urban revitalization, *Tourism Recreation Research*, 14 (1): 23–32

Carter, F.W., 1991a, Czechoslovakia, in D.R. Hall (ed.), *Tourism and economic development in Eastern Europe and the Soviet Union*, Belhaven Press, London, pp.155–172

Carter, F.W., 1991b, Bulgaria, in D.R. Hall (ed.), *Tourism and economic development in Eastern Europe and the Soviet Union*, Belhaven Press, London, pp.220–235

Castells, M., 1983, Crisis, planning, and the quality of life: managing the new historical relationships between space and society, *Environment and Planning D, Society and Space*, 1: 3–21

Cater, E.A., 1987, Tourism in the least developed countries, *Annals of Tourism Research*, 14: 202–226

Choy, D.J.L., 1984, Comment on Richter's political implications of Chinese tourism policy, *Annals of Tourism Research*, 11: 618–621

Clarke, J., 1981, Subcultures, cultures and class, in T. Bennett, G. Martin, C. Mercer and J. Woollacott (ed.), *Culture, ideology and social process*, Batsford, London, pp.53–79

Clarke, J. and Critcher, C., 1985, *The devil makes work: leisure in capitalist Britain*, University of Illinois Press, Urbana

Cohen, E., 1977, Toward a sociology of international tourism, *Social Research*, 39 (1): 164–182

Commission Consultative Fédérale pour le Tourisme, 1979, *Conception Suisse du tourisme*, Office Central Fédéral des Imprimes, Berne

Commonwealth Department of Tourism, 1992, *Tourism Australia's passport to growth: a national tourism strategy*, Commonwealth Department of Tourism, Canberra

Commonwealth of Australia and Government of New Zealand, 1991, *Costs and Benefits of a Single Australasian Aviation Market*, Australian Government Publishing Service, Canberra

Compton, P.A., 1991, Hungary, in D.R. Hall (ed.), *Tourism and economic development in Eastern Europe and the Soviet Union*, Belhaven Press, London, pp.173–189

Conant, J.S., Clarke, T., Burnett, J.J. and Zank, G., 1988, Terrorism and travel: managing the unmanageable, *Journal of Travel Research*, Spring: 16–20

Connell, J., 1988, *Sovereignty & survival: island microstates in the Third World*, Research Monograph No.3, Department of Geography, University of Sydney

Cook, D., 1989, China's hotels: still playing catch up, *Cornell Hotel Restaurant and Administration Quarterly*, 30 (3): 64–67

Cook, K., 1982, Guidelines for socially appropriate tourism development in British Columbia, *Journal of Travel Research*, 21 (1): 22–28

Coppock, J.T., 1977, Tourism as a tool for regional development, in B.S. Duffield (ed.), *Tourism: a tool for regional development*, Tourism and Recreation Research Unit, University of Edinburgh for the Leisure Studies Association, Edinburgh, pp.1.1–1.15

Cossons, N., 1989, Heritage tourism—trends and tribulations, *Tourism Management*, 10 (3): 192–194

Council of Europe, 1988, *Rural tourism in Europe*, Publications and Documents Division, Council of Europe, Strasbourg

Coventry, N., 1988, Japanese lead reawakening in Fijian tourism, *New Zealand Financial Review*, November: 89–91

Coventry, N., 1990, NZ/Australia tourism members press for one-entry concept, *Asia Travel Trade*, 22 (October): 6–8

Craik, J., 1989, The Expo experience: the politics of expositions, *Australian-Canadian Studies*, 7 (1–2): 95–112

Craik, J., 1990, A classic case of clientelism: the Industries Assistance Commission Inquiry into Travel and Tourism, *Culture and Policy*, 1 (3)

Craik, J., 1991, *Resorting to tourism: cultural policies for tourist development in Australia*, Allen & Unwin, St. Leonards

Crawford, J., 1979, *The creation of states in international law*, Clarendon Press, Oxford

Crean, J., 1988, Lifting the lid on outbound travel, *Asia Travel Trade*, July: 30–31

Crenson, M.A., 1971, *The un politics of air pollution: a study of non-decisionmaking in the cities*, The Johns Hopkins Press, Baltimore and London

Crick, M., 1989, Representations of international tourism in the social sciences: sun, sex, sights, savings, and servility, *Annual Review of Anthropology*, 18: 307–344

Crocombe, R., 1992, The future of democracy in the Pacific Islands, in R. Crocombe and E. Tuza (eds.), *Independence, dependence, interdependence: the first 10 years of Solomon Islands independence*, published jointly by the Institute of Pacific Studies, the University of the South Pacific Honiara Centre and the Solomon Islands College of Higher Education, Honiara, pp.9–27

Crozier, M., 1964, *The bureaucratic phenomenon*, University of Chicago Press, Chicago

Crush, J. and Wellings, P., 1983, The Southern African pleasure periphery, 1966–83, *Journal of Modern African Studies*, 21: 673–698

Crush, J. and Wellings, P., 1987, Forbidden fruit and the export of vice: tourism in Swaziland and Lesotho, in S. Britton and W.C. Clarke (eds.), *Ambiguous alternative: Tourism in developing countries*, University of the South Pacific, Suva, pp.91–112

Culler, J., 1981, Semiotics of tourism, *American Journal of Semiotics*, 1: 127–140

D'Amore, L., 1983, Guidelines to planning harmony with the host community, in P.E. Murphy (ed.), *Tourism in Canada: selected issues and options*, Western Geographical Series 21, University of Victoria, Victoria, pp.135–159

Damette, F., 1980, The regional framework of monopoly exploitation: new problems and trends, in J. Carney, R. Hudson and J.R. Lewis (eds.), *Regions in crisis*, Croom Helm, London

Darling Harbour, n.d., *Face to face, Tumbalong Park Darling Harbour* (brochure), Darling Harbour Authority, Sydney

Davis, G., Wanna, J., Warhurst, J. and Weller, P., 1993, *Public policy in Australia*, 2nd. edn., Allen & Unwin, St Leonards

Dawson, D., 1991, *Panem et circenses?* A critical analysis of ethnic and multicultural festivals, *Journal of Applied Recreation Research*, 16 (1): 35–52

De Burlo, C., 1989, Islanders, soldiers, and tourists: the war and the shaping of tourism in Melanesia, in G.M. White and L. Lindstrom (eds.), *The Pacific theater—island representations in World War II*, University of Hawaii Press, Honolulu

de Hanni, H., 1984, Controlling the development of tourism: possibilities and hindrances, in E.A. Brugger, G. Furrer, B. Messerli and P. Messerli (eds.), *The transformation of Swiss mountain regions*, Haupt, Berne

de Kadt, E. (ed.), 1979, *Tourism Passport to Development*, Oxford University Press, New York

Dear, M., 1977, Spatial externalities and locational conflict, in D.B. Massey and P.W.J. Batey (eds.), *Alternative frameworks for analysis*, London Papers in Regional Science 7, Pion Ltd., London

Demek, J. and Strida, M. (eds.), 1971, *Geography of Czechoslovakia*, Academia, Prague

Department of the Arts, Sport, the Environment, Tourism and Territories, 1988, *Directions for tourism—a discussion paper*, Department of the Arts, Sport, the Environment, Tourism and Territories, Canberra

Deutsch, K.W., 1986, State functions and the future of the state, *International Political Science Review*, 7 (2): 209–222

Dichen, G. and Guangrui, Z., 1983, China's tourism: policy and practice, *Tourism Management*, 4: 75–84

Dieke, P.U.C., 1989, Fundamentals of tourism development: a Third World perspective, *Hospitality Education and Research Journal*, 13 (2): 7–22

Do-sun, C., 1992, In the balance, *Asia Travel Trade*, April: 58–61

Dorfmann, M., 1983, Régions de montagne: de la dépendance à l'autodéveloppement, *Revue de Géographie Alpine*, 71 (1): 5–34

Dovey, K., 1989, Old Scabs/new scars: the hallmark event and the everyday environment, in G.J. Syme, B.J. Shaw, D.M. Fenton and W.S. Mueller (eds.), *The planning and evaluation of hallmark events*, Avebury, Aldershot, pp.73–80

Easton, D., 1957, An approach to the analysis of political systems, *World Politics*, 9: 383–400

Easton, D., 1965, *A systems analysis of political life*, University of Chicago Press, Chicago

Economist Intelligence Unit, 1989, The Pacific Islands, *EIU International Tourism Reports*, 4: 70–99

Edgell, D., 1978, International tourism and travel, in H.F. Van Zandt (ed.), *International business prospects, 1977–1999*, Bobbs-Merrill, Indianapolis, pp.171–173

Edgell, D.L., 1983, United States international tourism policy, *Annals of Tourism Research*, 10: 427–433

Edgell, D.L., 1984, US government policy on international tourism, *Tourism Management*, 5 (1): 67–70

Edgell, D.L., 1990, *International tourism policy*, Van Nostrand Reinhold, New York

Elliot, J., 1983, Politics, power and tourism in Thailand, *Annals of Tourism Research*, 10: 377–393

Elliot, J., 1987, Government management of tourism—a Thai case study, *Tourism Management*, 8 (3): 223–232

Erisman, H.M., 1983, Tourism and cultural dependency in the West Indies, *Annals of Tourism Research*, 10: 337–361

European Economic Community (EEC), 1984, Council Regulation (EEC) No.1787/84 of 19 June 1984 on the European Regional Development Fund, *Official Journal of the European Communities*, 28 June

European Economic Community, 1985, *The European Community and the regions: 10 years of Community regional policy and of the European Regional Development Fund (ERDF)*, Office for Official Publications of the European Communities, Luxembourg

Fagence, M., 1979, *The political nature of community decision-making*, Department of Regional and Town Planning, University of Queensland, St. Lucia

Farmer, W.J., 1987, The Antarctic treaty system and global interests in the Antarctic, *Australian Foreign Affairs Record*, 58 (3): 135–141

Farrell, B.H., 1974, The tourist ghettos of Hawaii, in M.C.R. Edgell and B.H. Farrell (eds.), *Themes on Pacific lands*, Western Geographical Series No. 10, University of Victoria, Victoria, pp.181–221

Field, A., 1992, Aviation update, *Ministry of Tourism Newsletter*, 4 (2)

Fiji Ministry of Tourism, 1992, *General information on tourism in Fiji: its past and future and impact on the economy and society*, Ministry of Tourism, Suva

Fiji Visitors Bureau, 1988, *Statistical report on visitor arrivals to Fiji*, Fiji Visitors Bureau, Suva

Fiji Visitors Bureau, 1992, *A statistical Report on visitor arrivals into Fiji calendar year 1991*, Fiji Visitors Bureau, Suva

Finney, B.R. and Watson, K.A. (eds.), 1977, *A new kind of sugar: tourism in the Pacific*, Center for South Pacific Studies, University of California Santa Cruz, Santa Cruz

Foley, P., 1991, The impact of major events: a case study of the World Student Games and Sheffield, *Environmental and Planning C: Government and Policy*, 9 (1): 65–79

Fondersmith, J., 1988, Downtown 2040: making cities fun, *The Futurist*, March/April: 9–17

Forster, J., 1964, The sociological consequences of tourism, *International Journal of Comparative Sociology*, 5 (2): 217–227

Francisco, R.A., 1983, The political impact of tourism dependence in Latin America, *Annals of Tourism Research*, 10: 363–376

Freedman, L., 1976, Logic, politics and foreign policy processes, *International Affairs*, 52: 434–449

Frieden, B. and Sagalyn, L., 1989, *Downtown, inc.: how America rebuilds cities*, MIT Press, Cambridge

Friedmann, J., 1980, An alternative development?, in J. Friedmann, T. Wheelwright and J. Connell (eds.), *Development strategies in the eighties*, Monograph No.1, Development Studies Colloquium, Department of Town and Country Planning, University of Sydney, Sydney, pp.4–11

Gallie, W.B., 1955–56, Essentially contested concepts, *Proceedings of the Aristotelian Society*, 56: 167–198

Gartner, W.C. and Shen, J., 1992, The impact of Tiananmen Square on China's tourism image, *Journal of Travel Research*, 30 (4): 47–52

Gay, J., 1985, The patriotic prostitute, *The Progressive*, 49 (3): 34–36

Getz, D., 1977, The impact of tourism on host communities: a research approach, in B.S. Duffield (ed.), *Tourism: a tool for regional development*, Tourism and Recreation Research Unit, University of Edinburgh, Edinburgh, pp.9.1–9.13

Getz, D., 1983, Capacity to absorb tourism: concepts and implications for strategic planning, *Annals of Tourism Research*, 10: 239–263

Getz, D., 1986, Models in tourism planning towards integration of theory and practice, *Tourism Management*, 7 (1): 21–32

Getz, D., 1987, Tourism planning and research: traditions, models and futures, paper presented at the Australian Travel Research Workshop, Bunbury, Western Australia, November 5–6

Getz, D., 1991, *Festivals, special events and tourism*, Van Nostrand Reinhold, New York

Giddens, A., 1989, *Sociology*, Polity Press, Cambridge

Gilg, A.W., 1988, Switzerland: structural change within stability, in A.M. Williams and G. Shaw (eds.), *Tourism and economic development: Western European experiences*, Belhaven Press, London, pp.123–144

Girvan, N., 1973, The development of dependency economics in the Caribbean and Latin America: review and comparison, *Social and Economic Studies*, 22: 1–33

Goodall, B., 1987, Tourism and regional development, *Built Environment*, 13 (2): 69–72

Gottdeiner, E., 1987, *The decline of urban politics: political theory and the crisis of the local state*, Sage Publications, Newbury Park

Government of the Solomons, 1993, *Tourism statistics—third quarter 1992, Statistical bulletin No.4/93*, Government of the Solomons, Honiara

Graham, M., 1990, Culture shock, *Asia Travel Trade*, 22 (February): 24–26

Gramsci, A., 1975, *Quaderni del carcere*, Einaudi, Turin

Gray, H.P., 1984, Tourism theory and practice: a reply to Alberto Sessa, *Annals of Tourism Research*, 11: 286–290

Greenberg, G.D., Miller, J.A., Mohr, L.B. and Vladeck, B.C., 1977, Developing public policy theory—perspectives from empirical research, *American Political Science Review*, 71 (4): 1532–1543

Greenwood, D.J., 1972, Tourism as an agent of change: a Spanish Basque case, *Ethnology*, 2: 80–91

Greenwood, D.J., 1976, Tourism as an agent of change: a Spanish Basque case, *Annals of Tourism Research*, 3 (3): 128–142

Greenwood, D.J., 1989, Culture by the pound: an anthropological perspective on tourism as cultural commoditization, in V. Smith (ed.), *Hosts and guests: the anthropology of tourism*, 2nd. edn., University of Pennsylvania Press, Philadelphia, pp.171–185

Greenwood, J., Willams, A.M. and Shaw, G., 1990, Policy implementation and tourism in the UK: implications from recent tourism research in Cornwall, *Tourism Management*, 11 (1): 53–62

Grodsky, P.B., 1982, Some limitations of social scientists in affecting public policy decisions, in F.S. Sterrett and B.L. Rosenberg (eds.), *Science and Public Policy II*, New York Academy of Sciences, New York, pp.47–55

Guangrui, Z., 1989, Ten years of Chinese tourism: profile and assessment, *Tourism Management*, 10 (1): 51–62

Gunn, C.A., 1977, Industry pragmatism vs tourism planning, *Leisure Sciences*, 1 (1): 85–94

Gunn, C.A., 1979, *Tourism planning*, Crane Russak, New York

Gunn, C.A., 1988, *Tourism planning*, 2nd edn., Taylor and Francis, New York.

Hail, J., 1992, Blow to Thai tourism, *Asia Travel Trade*, 23 (7): 6–8

Hall, C.M., 1989a, The politics of hallmark events, in G.J. Syme, B.J. Shaw, D.M. Fenton and W.S. Mueller (eds.), *The planning and evaluation of hallmark events*, Avebury, Aldershot, pp.219–241

Hall, C.M., 1989b, Hallmark events and the planning process, in G.J. Syme, B.J. Shaw, D.M. Fenton and W.S. Mueller (eds.), *The planning and evaluation of hallmark events*, Avebury, Aldershot, pp.20–39

Hall, C.M., 1991, *Introduction to tourism in Australia: impacts, planning and development*, Longman Cheshire, South Melbourne

Hall, C.M., 1992a, *Hallmark tourist events: impacts, management, and planning*, Belhaven Press, London

Hall, C.M., 1992b, Tourism in Antarctica: activities, impacts, and management, *Journal of Travel Research*, 30 (4): 2–9

Hall, C.M., 1992c, Sex tourism in South–east Asia, in D. Harrison (ed.), *Tourism and the less developed countries*, Belhaven Press, London, pp.64–74

Hall, C.M., 1992d, Issues in ecotourism: from susceptible to sustainable development, in *Heritage management: parks, heritage and tourism*, Royal Australian Institute of Parks and Recreation, Hobart, pp.152–158

Hall, C.M., 1994a, *Tourism in the Pacific Rim: development, impacts and markets*, Longman Cheshire, South Melbourne

Hall, C.M., 1994b, Tourism and the Maori of Aotearoa (New Zealand), in R. Butler and T. Hinch (eds.), *Tourism and native peoples*, Routledge, London, forthcoming

Hall, C.M., 1994c, *Introduction to tourism in Australia: impacts, planning and development*, 2nd. edn., Longman Cheshire, South Melbourne

Hall, C.M., 1994d, Ecotourism in Australia, New Zealand and the South Pacific: appropriate tourism or a new form of ecological imperialism?, in E.A. Cater and G.A. Bowman (eds.) *Ecotourism: A Sustainable Option?*, John Wiley & Sons/Royal Geographical Society, Chichester, pp.137–157

Hall, C.M. and Johnston, M. (eds.), 1995, *Tourism in polar regions*, John Wiley & Sons, Chichester

Hall, C.M., Keelan, N. and Mitchell, I., 1993, The implications of Maori perspectives on the interpretation, management and promotion of tourism in New Zealand, *Geojournal*, 29 (3): 315–322

Hall, C.M., Mitchell, I. and Keelan, N., 1992, Maori culture and heritage tourism in New Zealand, *Journal of Cultural Geography*, 12 (2): 115–128

Hall, C.M. and Rudkin, B., 1993, Ecotourism as appropriate tourism?: a case study from the Solomon Islands, paper presented at the *13th International Congress of Anthropological and Ethnological Sciences, symposium on tourism as a determinant of culture change*, Mexico City

Hall, C.M. and Selwood, H.J., 1989, America's Cup lost, paradise retained? The dynamics of a hallmark tourist event, in G.J. Syme, B.J. Shaw, D.M. Fenton and W.S. Mueller (eds.), *The planning and evaluation of hallmark events*, Avebury, Aldershot, pp.103–118

Hall, C.M. and Selwood, H.J., 1994, Event tourism and the creation of a post-industrial portscape: the case of Fremantle and the 1987 America's Cup, in S. Craig-Smith and M. Fagence (eds.), *Dockland redevelopment and tourism*, Springer-Verlag, New York, in press

Hall, C.M. and Zeppel, H., 1990, Cultural and heritage tourism: the new grand tour?, *Historic Environment*, 7 (3–4): 86–98

Hall, D.R., 1984, Foreign tourism under socialism: the Albanian 'Stalinist' model, *Annals of Tourism Research*, 11 (4): 539–55

Hall, D.R., 1990a, Eastern Europe opens its doors, *Geographical Magazine*, April: 10–15

Hall, D.R., 1990b, Stalinism and tourism: a study of Albania and North Korea, *Annals of Tourism Research*, 17 (1): 36–54

Hall, D.R. (ed.), 1991a, *Tourism and economic development in Eastern Europe and the Soviet Union*, Belhaven Press, London

Hall, D.R., 1991b, Introduction, in D.R. Hall (ed.), *Tourism and economic development in Eastern Europe and the Soviet Union*, Belhaven Press, London, pp.3–28

Hall, D.R., 1991c, Eastern Europe and the Soviet Union: overcoming tourism constraints, in D.R. Hall (ed.), *Tourism and economic development in Eastern Europe and the Soviet Union*, Belhaven Press, London, pp.49–78

Hall, D.R., 1991d, Evolutionary pattern of tourism development in Eastern Europe and the Soviet Union, in D.R. Hall (ed.), *Tourism and economic development in Eastern Europe and the Soviet Union*, Belhaven Press, London, pp.79–115

Hall, D.R. 1991e, Contemporary challenges, in D.R. Hall (ed.), *Tourism and economic development in Eastern Europe and the Soviet Union*, Belhaven Press, London, pp.282–289

Hall, D.R. 1991f, Albania, in D.R. Hall (ed.), *Tourism and economic development in Eastern Europe and the Soviet Union*, Belhaven Press, London, pp.259–277

Hall, J., 1974, The capacity to absorb tourists, *Built Environment*, 3: 392–397

Hamdi, H., 1991, Growing pains for South Korea market, *Asia Travel Trade*, February: 10–11

Harcombe, D., 1988, *Solomons Islands—a travel survival kit*, Lonely Planet Publications, South Yarra

Harrison, D. (ed.), 1992a, *Tourism and the less developed countries*, Belhaven Press, London

Harrison, D., 1992b, International tourism and the less developed countries: the background, in D. Harrison (ed.), *Tourism and the less developed countries*, Belhaven Press, London, pp.1–18

Harvey, D., 1987, Flexible accumulation through urbanization: reflections on 'post-modernism' in the American city, *Antipode*, 19: 260–286

Harvey, D., 1988, Voodoo cities, *New Statesman and Society*, 30 September: 33–35

Harvey, D., 1989a, *The condition of postmodernity: an enquiry into the origins of cultural change*, Basil Blackwell, Oxford

Harvey, D., 1989b, From managerialism to entrepreneurialism: the transformation in urban governance in late capitalism, *Geografiska Annaler B*, 71 (1): 3–17

Harvey, D., 1990, Between space and time: reflections on the geographical imagination, *Annals of the Association of American Geographers*, 80 (3): 418–434

Hau'ofa, E., 1987, The new Pacific society: integration and independence, in A. Hooper, *et al.* (eds)., *Class and culture in the South Pacific*, Institute of Pacific Studies, University of the South Pacific, Suva

Haulot, A., 1981, Social tourism: current dimensions and future developments, *Tourism Management*, 2: 207–212

Haveman, R.H., 1976, Evaluating the impact of public policies on regional welfare, *Regional Studies*, 10: 449–463

Hayes, B.J., 1981, The congressional travel and tourism caucus and US national tourism policy, *International Journal of Tourism Management*, June: 121–137

Haywood, K.M., 1988, Responsible and responsive tourism planning in the community, *Tourism Management*, 9 (2): 105–118

Heeley, J., 1981, Planning for tourism in Britain, *Town Planning Review*, 52: 61–79

Heenan, D., 1978, Tourism and the community, a drama in three acts, *Journal of Travel Research*, 16 (4): 30–32

Held, D., 1980, *Introduction to critical theory: Horkheimer to Habermas*, Hutchinson, London

Held, D., 1989, *Political theory and the modern state*, Polity Press, Oxford

Held, D. and Krieger, J., 1984, Theories of the state: some competing claims, in S. Bornstein, D. Held and J. Krieger (eds.), *The state in capitalist Europe*, Allen & Unwin, London, pp.1–20

Helu-Thaman, K., 1992, Ecocultural tourism: a personal view for maintaining cultural integrity in ecotourism development, in J.E. Hay (ed.), *Ecotourism business in the Pacific: promoting a sustainable experience*, conference proceedings, Environmental Science, University of Auckland, Auckland, pp.24–29

Henning, D.H., 1974, *Environmental policy and administration*, American Elsevier Publishing Company, New York

Henry, I. and Bramham, P., 1986, Leisure, the local state and social order, *Leisure Studies*, 5: 189–209

Hewison, R., 1987, *The heritage industry: Britain in a climate of decline*, Methuen, London

Hewison, R., 1988, Great expectations—hyping heritage, *Tourism Management*, 9 (3): 239–240

Hillman, S., 1986, Special events as a tool for tourism development, *Special Events Report*, 5 (16): 4–5

Hills, T.L. and Lundgren, J., 1977, The impact of tourism in the Caribbean: a methodological study, *Annals of Tourism Research*, 4 (5): 248–267

Hivik, T. and Heiberg, T., 1980, Centre–periphery tourism and self-reliance, *International Social Science Journal*, 32 (1): 69–98

Hollinshead, K., 1988, First-blush of the longtime: the market development of Australia's living Aboriginal heritage, in *Tourism research: expanding boundaries, the travel and tourism research association 19th annual conference proceedings*, Bureau of Economic and Business Research, Graduate School of Business, University of Utah, Salt Lake City, pp.183–198

Hollinshead, K., 1992, 'White' gaze, 'red' people—shadow visions: the disidentification of 'Indians' in cultural tourism, *Leisure Studies*, 11: 43–64

Holt, R.T. and Turner, J.E., 1974, The scholar as artisan, *Policy Sciences*, 5: 257–270

Hong, E., 1985, *See the Third World while it lasts*, Consumers Association of Penang, Penang

Horne, D., 1992, *The intelligent tourist*, Margaret Gee Publishing, McMahons Point

House of Representatives Standing Committee on Environment, Recreation and the Arts [HRSCERA], 1989, *Tourism in Antarctica*, Report of the House of Representatives Standing Committee on Environment, Recreation and the Arts, Australian Government Publishing Service, Canberra

Houston, L., 1986, *Strategy and opportunities for tourism development*, Planning Exchange, Glasgow

Hughes, H., 1984, Government support for tourism in the UK: a different perspective, *Tourism Management*, 5 (1): 13–19

Hughes, H.L., 1987, Culture as a tourist resource—a theoretical consideration, *Tourism Management*, 8 (3): 205–216

Hughes, H.L., 1989, Tourism and the arts: a potentially destructive relationship?, *Tourism Management*, 10 (2): 97–99

Hughes, R., 1987, *The fatal shore: a history of the transportation of convicts to Australia, 1787–1868*, Collins Harvill, London

Humphreys, J.S. and Walmsley, D.J., 1991, Locational conflict in metropolitan areas: Melbourne and Sydney, 1989, *Australian Geographical Studies*, 29 (2): 313–328

Huxley, M., 1991, Making cities fun: Darling Harbour and the immobilisation of the spectacle, in P. Carroll, K. Donohue, M. McGovern and J. McMillen (eds.), *Tourism in Australia*, Harcourt Brace Jovanovich, Sydney, pp.141–152

Industries Assistance Commission, 1989, *Travel and tourism*, Report No.423, Australian Government Publishing Service, Canberra

Isaccson, R., 1991, Big game parks . . . what future?, *Green Magazine*, June: 40–44

IUOTO, 1974, The role of the state in tourism, *Annals of Tourism Research*, 1 (3): 66–72

Jaensch, D., 1992, *The politics of Australian government*, Macmillan, South Melbourne

Jafari, J., 1974, The socio-economic costs of tourism to developing countries, *Annals of Tourism Research*, 1 (7): 227–262

Jafari, J. and Ritchie, J.R.B., 1981, Toward a framework for tourism education problems and prospects, *Annals of Tourism Research*, 8 (1): 13–34

Jameson, F., 1984, Postmodernism: or the cultural logic of capitalism, *New Left Review*, 146: 53–93

Jansen-Verbeke, M., 1989, Inner cities and urban tourism in the Netherlands: new challenges for local authorities, in P. Bramham, I. Henry, H. Mommaas and H. van der Poel (eds.), *Leisure and urban processes: critical studies of leisure policy in Western European cities*, Routledge, London and New York, pp.233–253

Japan Travel Bureau, 1991, *JTB report '91: all about Japanese overseas travellers*, Japan Travel Bureau, Tokyo

Jeffrey, L., 1991, Squeezed out, *Asia Travel Trade*, March: 34–40

Jeffries, D., 1989, Selling Britain—a case for privatisation?, *Travel and Tourism Analyst*, 1: 69–81

Jenkins, C.L., 1980, Tourism policies in developing countries: a critique, *International Journal of Tourism Management*, 1 (1): 22–29

Jenkins, C.L. and Henry, B.M., 1982, Government involvement in tourism in developing countries, *Annals of Tourism Research*, 9: 499–521

Jenkins, W.I., 1978, *Policy analysis: a political and organizational perspective*, St. Martin's Press, New York

Jeong, G.-H., 1988, Tourism expectations on the 1988 Seoul Olympics: a Korean perspective, in *Tourism research: expanding boundaries*, Travel and Tourism Research Association, Nineteenth Annual Conference, Montreal, Quebec, Canada, June 19–23, 1988, Bureau of Economic and Business Research, Graduate School of Business, University of Utah, Salt Lake City, pp.175–182

Jones, M.A., 1986, *A sunny place for shady people*, Allen and Unwin, Sydney

Jones, R. and Selwood, H.J., 1991, Fallout from a hallmark event: Fremantle after the departure of the America's Cup, paper presented at the World Leisure and Recreation Association Conference, July, Sydney

Judd, D. and Parkinson, M., 1990, *Leadership and urban regeneration: cities in North America and Europe*, Sage Publications, California

Kearney, E.P., 1992, Redrawing the political map of tourism: the European view, *Tourism Management*, March: 34–36

Keller, C.P., 1984, Centre–periphery tourism development and control, in J. Long and R. Hecock (eds.), *Leisure, tourism and social change: papers selected from a conference held at the University of Edinburgh in January 1983, and organised on behalf of International Geographical Union*

Commission on the Geography of Recreation and Leisure and Leisure Studies Association, Centre for Leisure Research, Dunfermline College of Physical Education, Dunfermline, pp.77–84

Kent, N., 1977, A new kind of sugar, in B.R. Finney and K.A. Watson (eds.), *A new kind of sugar: tourism in the Pacific*, Center for South Pacific Studies, University of California Santa Cruz, Santa Cruz, pp.169–198

King, R., 1988, Italy: multi-faceted tourism, in A.M. Williams and G. Shaw (eds.), *Tourism and economic development: Western European experiences*, Belhaven Press, London, pp.58–79

Kissling, C., 1993, Factors affecting trans-Tasman air services, *Geojournal*, 29 (3): 291–298

Klieger, P.C., 1992, Shangri-La and the politicization of tourism in Tibet, *Annals of Tourism Research*, 19 (1): 122–125

Korea Church Women United, 1983, *Kisaeng tourism, a nation-wide survey report on conditions in four areas Seoul, Pusan, Cheju, Kyongju*, Research Material Issue No.3, Korea Church Women United, Seoul

Kosters, M., 1984, The deficiences of tourism science without political science: comment on Richter, *Annals of Tourism Research*, 11: 610–612

Krippendorf, J., 1987, *The holiday makers: understanding the impact of leisure and travel*, Heinemann Professional Publishing, Oxford

Kroll, M., 1969, Policy and administration, in F.J. Lyden, G.A. Shipman and M. Kroll (eds.), *Policies, decisions and organisation*, Appleton-Century-Crofts, New York, pp.8–27

Kudu, D., 1992, The role and activities of the Tourism Council of the South Pacific, particularly in relation to ecotourism development, in J.E. Hay (ed.), *Ecotourism business in the Pacific: promoting a sustainable experience*, Environmental Science, University of Auckland, Auckland, pp.154–160

Lamb, A.N., 1988, Tourism development and planning in Australia—the need for a national strategy, *International Journal of Hospitality Management*, 7 (4): 353–361

Lanfant, M., 1980, Introduction: tourism in the process of internationalization, *International Social Science Journal*, 32 (1): 14–45

Lash, S., 1990, *Sociology of postmodernism*, Routledge, London

Lasswell, H.D., 1936, *Politics: who gets, what, when, how?*, McGraw-Hill, New York

Lavery, P., 1989, Tourism in China: the costs of collapse, *EIU Travel & Tourism Analyst*, 4: 77–97

Law, C., 1985, *Urban tourism: selected British case studies*, Working Paper, Department of Geography, University of Salford, Salford

Lea, J., 1988, *Tourism and development in the Third World*, Routledge, London

Lea, J., 1993, Tourism development ethics in the Third World, *Annals of Tourism Research*, 20 (4): 701–715

Lea, J. and Small, J., 1988, Cyclones, riots and coups: tourist industry responses in the South Pacific, paper presented at Frontiers in Australian tourism conference, Australian National University, Canberra, 30 June–1 July

Lee, G.P., 1987, Tourism as a factor in development cooperation, *Tourism Management*, 4 (4): 2–19

Lees, A., 1991, *A protected forests system for the Solomon Islands, report by the Maruia Society for the Australian National Parks and Wildlife Service*, Australian National Parks and Wildlife Service, Canberra

Lefebvre, H., 1976, *The survival of capitalism: reproduction and relations of production*, Allison and Busby, London

Leiper, N., 1990, The partial industrialization of tourism systems, *Annals of Tourism Research*, 17: 600–605

Leontidou, L., 1988, Greece: prospects and contradictions of tourism in the 1980s, in A.M. Williams and G. Shaw (eds.), *Tourism and economic development: Western European experiences*, Belhaven Press, London, pp.80–100

Lewis, J. and Williams, A.M., 1988, Portugal: market segmentation and regional specialisation, in A.M. Williams and G. Shaw (eds.), *Tourism and economic development: Western European experiences*, Belhaven Press, London, pp.101–122

Ley, D. and Olds, K., 1988, Landscape as spectacle: world's fairs and the culture of heroic consumption, *Environment and Planning D: Society and Space*, 6: 191–212

Lichtheim, G., 1974, *Imperialism*, Penguin Books, Harmondsworth

Lickorish, L.J., 1991, Developing a single European tourism policy, *Tourism Management*, 12 (3): 178–184

Lickorish, L.J., Jefferson, A., Bodlender, J. and Jenkins, C.L., 1991, *Developing tourism destinations: policies and perspectives*, Longman, Harlow

Lindblom, C.E., 1959, The science of muddling through, *Public Administration Review*, 19: 79–88

Lloyd, P., 1985, *CER—the implications for New Zealand*, Government Publishing Agencies, Wellington

Lord Young of Graffham, 1985, *Pleasure, leisure and jobs*, Cabinet Office, London

Lukes, S., 1974, *Power: a radical view*, Macmillan, London

Lundgren, J.O.J., 1973, The development of the tourist travel systems: a metropolitan economic hegemony par excellence, *Revue de Tourisme*, 1 (January/March): 2–14

Lyden, F.J., Shipman, G.A. and Kroll, M. (eds.), 1969, *Policies, decisions and organisations*, Appleton-Century-Crofts, New York

Mabogunje, A.L., 1980, *The development process: a spatial perspective*, Hutchinson, London

MacAloon, J.J., 1984, Olympic Games and the theory of spectacle in modern societies, in J.J. MacAloon (ed.), *Rite, drama, festival, spectacle: rehearsals toward a theory of cultural performance*, Institute for the Study of Human issues, Philadelphia, pp.241–280

MacCannell, D., 1984, Reconstructed ethnicity: tourism and cultural identity in Third World communities, *Annals of Tourism Research*, 11: 375–391

MacCannell, D., 1989, *The tourist: a new theory of the leisure class*, 2nd. edn., Schocken Books, New York

Majone, G., 1980a, The uses of policy analysis, in B.H. Raven (ed.), *Policy studies review annual*, vol.4, Sage, Beverly Hills, pp.161–180

Majone, G., 1980b, An anatomy of pitfalls, in G. Majone and E.S. Quade (eds.), *Pitfalls of analysis*, International Institute for Applied Systems Analysis/John Wiley and Sons, Chichester, pp.7–22

Majone, G., 1981, Policies as theories, in I.L. Horowitz (ed.) *Policy studies review annual*, vol.5, Sage, Beverly Hills, pp.15–26

Majone, G., 1989, *Evidence, argument and persuasion in the policy process*, Yale University Press, New Haven and London

Majone, G. and Quade, E.S. (eds.), 1980, *Pitfalls of analysis*, International Institute for Applied Systems Analysis/John Wiley and Sons, Chichester

Maori Tourism Task Force, 1986, *Maori tourism task force report*, Government Printing Office, Wellington

Martin, B. and Mason, S., 1988, Current trends in leisure, *Leisure Studies*, 7 (1): 75–80

Mathieson, A. and Wall, G., 1982, *Tourism: economic, physical and social impacts*, Longman, London

Matthews, H.G., 1975, International tourism and political science research, *Annals of Tourism Research*, 2 (4): 195–203

Matthews, H.G., 1978, *International tourism: a social and political analysis*, Schenkman, Cambridge

Matthews, H.G., 1983, Editor's page: on tourism and political science, *Annals of Tourism Research*, 10 (4): 303–306

Matthews, H.G. and Richter, L.K., 1991, Political science and tourism, *Annals of Tourism Research*, 18 (1): 120–135

McCoy, P., 1982, Barriers to trade belong on the bargaining table, *Business America*, 5 (22): 17–21

McDermott Miller Group, 1991, Destination South West Pacific, *Tourism FX: A Quarterly Analysis of New Zealand Tourism*, July

McDonald, G., 1986, Policy implications: comment on Var and Quayson, *Annals of Tourism Research*, 13: 645–648

McGahey, S., 1991, South Korea outbound, *EIU Travel & Tourism Analyst*, 6: 45–62

McIntosh, R.W. and Goeldner, C.R., 1986, *Tourism: principles, practices, philosophies*, 5th edn., John Wiley & Sons, New York

McKercher, B., 1993, Some fundamental truths about tourism: understanding tourism's social and environmental impacts, *Journal of Sustainable Tourism*, 1 (1): 6–16

McKinnon, J., 1990, *Solomon Islands world heritage site proposal, fact finding mission, 4–22 February 1990*, New Zealand Ministry of External Relations and Trade, Wellington

Meleghy, T., Preglau, M. and Tafertshofer, A., 1985, Tourism development and value change, *Annals of Tourism Research*, 12: 181–199

Mellor, R.E.H., 1991, Eastern Germany (the former German Democratic Republic), in D.R. Hall (ed.), *Tourism and economic development in Eastern Europe and the Soviet Union*, Belhaven Press, London, pp.142–153

Merelman, R.M., 1968, On the neo-elitist critique of community power, *American Political Science Review*, 62 (2): 451–460

Middleton, V.T.C., 1988, *Marketing in Travel and Tourism*, Heinemann Professional Publishing, Oxford

Mill, R.C. and Morrison, A.M., 1985, *The tourism system: an introductory text*, Prentice-Hall International, Englewood Cliffs

Mills, S., 1990, Disney and the promotion of synthetic worlds, *American Studies International*, 28 (2): 66–79

Mills, S., 1991, Spectacle in the city: from the Great Exhibition to the Glasgow Garden Festival, paper presented at the Institute of British Geographers Conference, Sheffield, January

Minerbi, L., 1992, *Impacts of tourism development in Pacific Islands*, Greenpeace Pacific Campaign, San Francisco

Mings, R.C., 1978, The importance of more research on the impacts of tourism, *Annals of Tourism Research*, 5: 340–344

Ministry of Transportation, Korea National Tourism Corporation, 1992, *Annual statistical report on tourism*, Ministry of Transportation, Korea National Tourism Corporation, Seoul

Mitchell, B., 1979, *Geography and resource analysis*, Longman, London

Mommaas, H. and van der Poel, H., 1989, Changes in economy, politics and lifestyles: an essay on the restructuring of urban leisure, in P. Bramham, I. Henry, H. Mommaas and H. van der Poel (eds.), *Leisure and urban processes: critical studies of leisure policy in Western European cities*, Routledge, London and New York, pp.254–276

Moon, J.D., 1991, Pluralism and progress in the study of politics, in W. Crotty (ed.), *The theory and practice of political science*, Northwestern University Press, Evanston, pp.45–56

Mowlana, H. and Smith, G., 1990, Tourism, telecommunications and transnational banking: a framework for policy analysis, *Tourism Management*, 11 (4): 315–324

Munns, J.W., 1975, The environment, politics, and policy literature: a critique and reformulation, *Western Political Quarterly*, 28 (4): 646–667

Murphy, D. and Reid, B., 1992, A Tasman marriage of convenience, *Time International*, 7 (37): 18–23

Murphy, P., 1985, *Tourism: a community approach*, Methuen, New York and London

Murphy, P.E., 1988, Community driven tourism planning, *Tourism Management*, 9 (2): 96–104

Nallbani, R., 1989, The Onufri Museum Berat, 8 Nëntori, Tirana

Narokobi, B., 1989, *Lo bilong yumi yet: law and custom in Melanesia*, The Melanesian Institute for Pastoral and Socio-Economic Service, Goroka, and the University of the South Pacific, Suva

Nash, D., 1977, Tourism as a form of imperialism, in V.L. Smith (ed.), *Hosts and guests: the anthropology of tourism*, University of Pennsylvania Press, Philadelphia, pp.33–47

Nash, D., 1989, Tourism as a form of imperialism, in V. Smith (ed.), *Hosts and guests: the anthropology of tourism*, 2nd edn., University of Pennsylvania Press, Philadelphia, pp.37–52

National Tourism Administration of the People's Republic of China, 1993, *The yearbook of China tourism statistics*, National Tourism Administration of the People's Republic of China, Beijing

218 References

National Tourism Office of Vanuatu, 1990, *A history of tourism in Vanuatu: a platform for future success*, National Tourism Office of Vanuatu, Port Vila

New Zealand Business Round Table and New Zealand Tourism Industry Federation, 1990, *Tourism: what incentives for growth—a study of labour issues affecting the outlook for tourism*, New Zealand Business Round Table and New Zealand Tourism Industry Federation, Wellington

New Zealand Herald, 1993, Air NZ seeks action on Korean links, *New Zealand Herald*, 15 May: 2

New Zealand Tourism Board, 1991, *Tourism in New Zealand: a strategy for growth*, New Zealand Tourism Board, Wellington

Nicholson, J., 1986, Antarctic tourism: the need for a legal regime?, *Maritime Studies*, 29 (May/June): 1–7

Nozick, R., 1972, Coercion, in P. Laslett, W.G. Runciman and Q. Skinner (eds.), *Philosophy, politics and society*, Blackwell, Oxford, pp.101–135

Nuñez, T., 1989, Touristic studies in anthropological perspective, in V. Smith (ed.), *Hosts and guests: the anthropology of tourism*, 2nd edn., University of Pennsylvania Press, Philadelphia, pp.265–279

O'Fallon, C., 1992, Government involvement in New Zealand tourism: a theoretical perspective, paper presented at the joint Institute of Australian Geographers/New Zealand Geographical Society Conference, University of Auckland, Auckland, January

O'Grady, R., 1981, *Third World stopover*, World Council of Churches, Geneva

Old Sydney Town, n.d., *Old Sydney Town re-creating the birth of a nation* (brochure), Old Sydney Town Heritage Park, Somersby

Olds, K., 1988, Planning for the housing impacts of a hallmark event: a case study of Expo 1986, unpublished MA thesis, School of Community and Regional Planning, University of British Columbia, Vancouver

Olds, K., 1989, Mass evictions in Vancouver: the human toll of Expo '86, *Canadian Housing*, 6 (1): 49–53

Ostrom, V., 1976, Language, theory, and empirical research in policy analysis, in P.M. Gregg (ed.) *Problems of theory in policy analysis*, Lexington Books, Lexington, pp.6–18

Ostrom, V., 1977, Some problems in doing political theory: a response to Golembiewski's 'Critique', *American Political Science Review*, 71 (4): 1508–1525

Ostrom, V., 1982, The theory and practice of public administration as a science of the artifactual, in J.A. Uveges, Jr. (ed.) *Public administration history and theory in contemporary perspective*, Marcel Dekker, New York, pp.39–53

Ostrowski, S., 1986, Poland's international tourism, *Tourism Management*, 6(4): 288–294

Ostrowski, S., 1987, Polish holiday villages: secular tradition and modern practice, *Tourism Management*, 8 (1): 41–48

Owen, C., 1992, Building a relationship between government and tourism, *Tourism Management*, 13 (4): 358–362

Page, S., 1993, The Wellington waterfront, in C.M. Hall and S. McArthur (eds.), *Heritage management in New Zealand and Australia: visitor management, interpretation and marketing*, Oxford University Press, Auckland, pp.218–230

Papson, S., 1981, Spuriousness and tourism: politics of two Canadian provincial governments, *Annals of Tourism Research*, 8 (2): 220–235

Parker, J.K., 1992, China syndrome, *Asia Travel Trade*, 23 (4): 46–48

Parker, R.S., 1978, *The government of New South Wales*, University of Queensland Press, St. Lucia

Paul, E.F. and Russo, P.A., Jr. (eds.), 1982, *Public policy: issues, analysis and ideology*, Chatham House Publishers, Chatham

Pearce, D.G., 1988, Tourism and regional development in the European Community, *Tourism Management*, 9 (1): 13–22

Pearce, D.G., 1989, *Tourism development*, 2nd edn., Longman Scientific and Technical, Harlow

Pearce, D.G., 1992, *Tourist organizations*, Longman Scientific and Technical, Harlow

Peck, J.G. and Lepie, A.S., 1989, Tourism and development in three North Carolina coastal towns, in V. Smith (ed.), *Hosts and guests: the anthropology of tourism*, 2nd edn., University of Pennsylvania Press, Philadelphia, pp.203–222

Pellicani, L., 1981, *Gramsci: an alternative Communism?*, trans. M. Manfrini-Watts, Hoover Institution Press, Stanford University, Stanford

Perez, L.A., Jr., 1975, *Underdevelopment and dependency: tourism in the West Indies*, Center for Inter-American Studies, University of El Paso

Pinder, D., 1988, The Netherlands: tourist development in a crowded society, in A.M. Williams and G. Shaw (eds.) *Tourism and economic development: Western European experiences*, Belhaven Press, London, pp.215–229

Polsby, N.W., 1963, *Community power and political theory*, Yale University Press, New Haven and London

Ravetz, J.R., 1973, *Scientific knowledge and its social problems*, Penguin, Harmondsworth

Reich, R.J., 1979, *Tourism in the Antarctic: its present impact and future development*, unpublished dissertation, Scott Polar Research Institute, Cambridge

Republic of China Tourist Bureau, 1992a, *1991 annual report*, Tourist Bureau, Ministry of Transport and Communications, Taipei

Republic of China Tourist Bureau, 1992b, *Report on tourism statistics, 1991*, Tourist Bureau, Ministry of Transport and Communications, Taipei

Reuter, 1993, Cairo bomb a mystery, *New Zealand Herald*, 1 March: 7

Reynolds, P., 1990, Tourism in China: is the honeymoon over?, in C.P. Cooper (ed.), *Progress in Tourism, Recreation and Hospitality Management*, vol. 2, Belhaven Press, London, pp.104–116

Richter, L.K., 1980, The political uses of tourism: a Philippine case study, *Journal of Developing Areas*, 14: 237–257

Richter, L.K., 1983a, Tourism politics and political science: a case of not so benign neglect, *Annals of Tourism Research*, 10: 313–335

220   References

Richter, L.K., 1983b, The political implications of Chinese tourism policy, *Annals of Tourism Research*, 10: 395–414

Richter, L.K., 1984, A search for missing answers to questions never asked: reply to Kosters, *Annals of Tourism Research*, 11: 613–615

Richter, L.K., 1989, *The politics of tourism in Asia*, University of Hawaii Press, Honolulu

Richter, L.K. and Richter, W.L., 1985, Policy choices in South Asian tourism development, *Annals of Tourism Research*, 12: 201–217

Richter, L.K. and Waugh, W.L., Jr., 1986, Terrorism and tourism as logical companions, *Tourism Management*, December: 230–238

Rijpma, S. and Meiburg, H., 1989, Sports policy initiatives in Rotterdam: targeting disadvantaged groups, in P. Bramham, I. Henry, H. Mommaas and H. van der Poel (eds.), 1989, *Leisure and urban processes: critical studies of leisure policy in Western European cities*, Routledge, London and New York, pp.141–155

Ritchie, J.R.B., 1984, Assessing the impact of hallmark events: conceptual and research issues, *Journal of Travel Research*, 23 (1): 2–11

Ritchie, J.R.B., 1988, Consensus policy formulation in tourism: measuring resident views via survey research, *Tourism Management*, 9 (3): 199–212

Ritchie, J.R.B. and Aitken, C.E., 1984, Assessing the impacts of the 1988 Olympic Winter Games: the research program and initial results, *Journal of Travel Research*, 22 (3): 17–25

Robinson, O. and Wallace, J., 1984, Earnings in hotel and catering industry in Great Britain, *Service Industries Journal*, 4: 143–160

Roche, M., 1990, *Mega-events and micro-modernization: on the sociology of the new urban tourism*, Policy Studies Centre, University of Sheffield, Sheffield

Roche, M., 1991, *Mega-events and urban policy: a study of Sheffield's World Student Games 1991*, Policy Studies Centre, University of Sheffield, Sheffield

Roche, M., 1992, Mega-events and micro-modernization: on the sociology of the new urban tourism, *British Journal of Sociology*, 43(4): 563–600

Roche, M., 1993a, Mega-event planning and citizenship: problems of rationality and democracy in Sheffield's Universiade 1991, *Vrijetijd en Samenleving*, in press

Roche, M., 1993b, Citizenship and social change: beyond the dominant paradigm, paper presented at 5th Conference of Association for Socio-Economics, New School for Social Research, New York

Roehl, W.S., 1990, Travel agent attitudes toward China after Tiananmen Square, *Journal of Travel Research*, 29 (2): 16–22

Roehl, W.S. and Fesenmaier, D.R., 1987, Tourism land use conflict in the United States, *Annals of Tourism Research*, 14: 471–485

Rogerson, C.M., 1990, Sun International: the making of a South African tourism multinational, *Geojournal*, 22 (3): 345–354

Rojek, C., 1985, *Capitalism and leisure theory*, Tavistock, London

Ronkainen, I.A., 1983, The conference on security and cooperation in Europe: its impact on tourism, *Annals of Tourism Research*, 10: 415–426

Rudkin, B., forthcoming, Ecotourism: passage to development?, unpublished masters thesis, Massey University, Palmerston North

Rudkin, B. and Hall, C.M., 1994a, Unable to see the forest for the trees: ecotourism development in the Solomon Islands, in R. Butler and T. Hinch (eds.), *Tourism and native peoples*, Routledge, London, forthcoming

Rudkin, B. and Hall, C.M., 1994b, Off the beaten track: the health implications of the development of special interest tourism activities in South-East Asia and the South Pacific, in S. Clift and S. Page (eds.), *Health and the International Tourist*, Routledge, London, forthcoming

Runyan, D. and Wu, C.-T., 1979, Assessing tourism's more complex consequences, *Annals of Tourism Research*, 6: 448–463

Sabatier, P.A., 1991, Public policy: toward better theories of the policy process, in W. Crotty (ed.), *Comparative politics, policy, and international relations*, Northwestern University Press, Evanston, pp.265–291

Santos, T. dos, 1968, *El nueve caracter de la dependencia*, Cuadernos de estudios socio-economicos, Santiago

Schattsneider, E., 1960, *Semi-sovereign people: a realist's view of democracy in America*, Holt, Rinehart and Wilson, New York

Schnell, P., 1988, The Federal Republic of Germany: a growing international deficit, in A.M. Williams and G. Shaw (eds.), *Tourism and economic development: Western European experiences*, Belhaven Press, London, pp.198–213

Senate Standing Committee on Environment, Recreation and the Arts, 1988, *The potential of the Kakadu National Park region*, Senate Standing Committee on Environment, Recreation and the Arts, The Parliament of the Commonwealth of Australia, Australian Government Publishing Service, Canberra

Sessa, A., 1976, The tourism policy, *Annals of Tourism Research*, 3 (5): 234–247

Sessa, A., 1984, Comments on Peter Gray's 'The Contributions of Economics to Tourism', *Annals of Tourism Research*, 11: 283–286

Seth, P., 1990, Adventurers wary of 'Paradise on Earth', *Asia Travel Trade*, 22 (November): 65–67, 69

Seymour, L., 1980, Tourism development in Newfoundland: the past revisited, *The Canadian Geographer*, 24: 32–39.

Sharrat, B., 1989, Communications and image studies: notes after Raymond Williams, *Comparative Criticism*, 11: 29–50

Shaw, G., Greenwood, J. and Williams, A.M., 1988, The United Kingdom: market responses and public policy, in A.M. Williams and G. Shaw (eds.), *Tourism and economic development: Western European experiences*, Belhaven Press, London, pp.162–179

Shaw, G. and Williams, A.M., 1990, Tourism and development, in Pinder, D., (ed.), *Western Europe: challenge and change*, Belhaven, London, pp.240–257

Simmons, R., Davis, B.W., Chapman, R.J.K. and Sager, D.D., 1974, Policy flow analysis: a conceptual model for comparative public policy research, *Western Political Quarterly*, 27 (3): 457–468

Simmons, R. and Dvorin, E.P., 1977, *Public administration: values, policy and change*, Alfred Publishing Co., Port Washington

Sinclair Knight, Buchanan, 1991, *Traffic calming: help us decide the future of your roads*, Sinclair Knight Buchanan, South Perth

Siwatibau, S., 1991, Some aspects of development in the South Pacific, in P. Bauer, S. Siwatibau and W. Kasper (eds.), *Aid and development in the South Pacific*, Centre for Independent Studies, Sydney

Smith, M.A. and Turner, L., 1973, Some aspects of the sociology of tourism, *Society and Leisure*, 3: 55–71

Smith, S.L.J., 1988, Defining tourism: a supply-side view, *Annals of Tourism Research*, 15 (2): 179–190

Smith, V., 1988, Geographical implications of 'drifter' tourism: Borocay, Philippines, paper presented at the International Geographical Union Commission on Leisure and Recreation Symposium, Christchurch, New Zealand, 13–20 August

Smith, V. (ed.), 1977, *Hosts and guests: the anthropology of tourism*, University of Pennsylvania Press, Philadelphia

Smith, V.L., 1989, Preface, in V. Smith (ed.), *Hosts and guests: the anthropology of tourism*, 2nd edn., University of Pennsylvania Press, Philadelphia, pp.ix–xi

Smyth, R., 1986, Public policy for tourism in Northern Ireland, *Tourism Management*, June: 120–126

Sofield, T., 1990, The impact of tourism development on traditional sociocultural values in the South Pacific: conflict, coexistence, and symbiosis, in M. Miller and J. Auyong (eds.), *Proceedings of the 1990 congress on coastal and marine tourism*, National Coastal Research and Development Institute, Honolulu, pp.49–66

Sofield, T., 1992, The Guadacanal track ecotourism project in the Solomon Islands, in J.E. Hay (ed.), *Ecotourism business in the Pacific: promoting a sustainable experience*, Environmental Science, University of Auckland, Auckland, pp.89–100

Solomon Islands Government, 1989, *National tourism policy*, Government Printer, Honiara

Spann, R.N., 1979, *Government administration in Australia*, George Allen and Unwin, Sydney

Stillman, P.G., 1974, Ecological problems, political theory, and public policy, in S. Nagel (ed.), *Environmental politics*, Praeger Publishers, New York, pp.49–60

Stock, R., 1977, Political and social contributions of international tourism to the development of Israel, *Annals of Tourism Research*, 5: 30–42

Susman, W.I., 1980, The people's fair: cultural contradictions of a consumer society, in H. Harrison (ed.), *Dawn of a new day: the New York World's Fair, 1939/40*, The Queens Museum/New York University Press, New York, pp.17–28

Symanski, R., 1981, *The immoral landscape: female prostitution in western societies*, Butterworths, Toronto

Teye, V.B., 1986, Liberation wars and tourism development in Africa: the case of Zambia, *Annals of Tourism Research*, 13: 589–608

Thomas, W.I., 1951, *Social behavior and personality*, Social Science Research Council, New York

Thorne, R. and Munro-Clark, M., 1989, Hallmark events as an excuse for autocracy in urban planning: a case history, in G.J. Syme, B.J. Shaw, D.M. Fenton and W.S. Mueller (eds.), *The planning and evaluation of hallmark events*, Avebury, Aldershot, pp.154–171

Thorne, R., Munro-Clark, M. and Boers, J., 1987, Hallmark events as an excuse for autocracy in urban planning: a case history, in *The effects of hallmark events on cities*, Centre for Urban Research, University of Western Australia, Nedlands

Thrift, N. and Forbes, D., 1983, A landscape with figures: political geography with human conflict, *Political Geography Quarterly*, 2: 247–263

Thurot, J.M. and Thurot, G., 1983, The ideology of class and tourism: confronting the discourse of advertising, *Annals of Tourism Research*, 10: 173–189

Time Australia, 1993, The Sheik from Jersey City, *Time Australia*, 15 February, 8 (7): 37

Tisdell, C. and Wen, J., 1991, Foreign tourism as an element in PR China's economic development strategy, *Tourism Management*, March: 55–68.

Tourism Council of the South Pacific, 1987, *Identification of nature sites and nature subjects of special interest*, Tourism Council of the South Pacific, Suva

Tourism Council of the South Pacific, 1988, *Nature legislation and nature conservation as part of tourism development in the island Pacific*, Tourism Council of the South Pacific, Suva

Tourism Council of the South Pacific, 1990, *Solomon Islands tourism development plan, 1991–2000*, Tourism Council of the South Pacific, Suva

Tourism Council of the South Pacific, 1991, *Solomon Islands nature sites development project: Lauvi Lagoon*, Tourism Council of the South Pacific, Suva

Trade and Industry Committee, 1985, *Tourism in the UK*, vol.1, HMSO, London

Trask, H., 1991, Lovely hula hands: corporate tourism and the prostitution of Hawaiian culture, *Contours*, 5 (1): 8–14

Triggs, G., 1986, *International law and Australian sovereignty in Antarctica*, Legal Books, Sydney

Tuppen, J., 1988, France: the changing character of a key industry, in A.M. Williams and G. Shaw (eds.), *Tourism and economic development: Western European experiences*, Belhaven Press, London, pp.180–195

Turner, L., 1974, Tourism and the social sciences: from Blackpool to Benidorm and Bali, *Annals of Tourism Research*, 1 (6): 180–205

Turnock, D., 1991, Romania, in D.R. Hall (ed.), *Tourism and economic development in Eastern Europe and the Soviet Union*, Belhaven Press, London, pp.203–219

UNESCO (United Nations Educational Scientific and Cultural Organization), 1976, The effects of tourism on socio-cultural values, *Annals of Tourism Research*, 4: 74–105

United Nations, Conference on International Travel and Tourism, 1963, *Recommendations on International Travel and Tourism*, United Nations, Rome

United States Travel and Tourism Administration, 1989, The national policy study on rural tourism and small businesses, study prepared for the United States Travel and Tourism Administration by Economics Research Associates in association with the University of Missouri and the United States Travel Data Center, Washington D.C., Economics Research Associates, Vienna, Virginia

Unsworth, B.J., 1984, New Darling Harbour Authority Bill, *NSW parliamentary debates*, Legislative Council, 26 November: 1485–1489

Urry, J., 1987, Some social and spatial aspects of services, *Environment and Planning D: Society and Space*, 5: 5–26

Urry, J., 1988, Cultural change and contemporary holiday-making, *Theory, Culture & Society*, 5 (1): 35–55

Urry, J., 1990a, *The tourist gaze: leisure and travel in contemporary societies*, Sage Publications, London

Urry, J., 1990b, The 'consumption' of tourism, *Sociology*, 24 (1): 23–35

Urry, J., 1992, The tourist gaze and the environment, *Theory, Culture & Society*, 9: 1–26

Uzzell, D., 1984, An alternative structuralist approach to the psychology of tourism marketing, *Annals of Tourism Research*, 11: 79–99.

Valentine, P.S., 1992, Ecotourism and nature conservation: a definition with some recent developments in Micronesia, in B. Weiler (ed.), *Ecotourism*, Bureau of Tourism Research, Canberra, pp.4–9

Valenzuela, M., 1988, Spain: the phenomenon of mass tourism, in A.M. Williams and G. Shaw (eds.) *Tourism and economic development: Western European experiences*, Belhaven Press, London, pp.39–57

Vuoristo, K.-V., 1981, Tourism in Eastern Europe: development and regional patterns, *Fennia*, 159 (1): 237–247

Waitangi Tribunal, 1991, *Ngai Tahu*, Government Printing Office, Wellington

Wanhill, S.R.C., 1987, UK—politics and tourism, *Tourism Management*, 8 (1): 54–58

Watson, S., 1991, Gilding the smokestacks: the new symbolic representation of deindustrialised regions, *Environment and Planning D: Society and Space*, 9: 59–70

Weber, M., 1968, *Economy and society*, Free Press, New York

Weiler, B. and Hall, C.M. (eds.), 1992, *Special interest tourism*, Belhaven Press, London

Wieman, E., 1989, Spectacular growth continues, *Asia Travel Trade*, 21 (May): 43–44

Wildavsky, A., 1979, *Speaking truth to power: the art and craft of policy analysis*, Little Brown, Boston

Williams, A.M. and Shaw, G. (eds.), 1988a, *Tourism and economic development: Western European experiences*, Belhaven Press, London

Williams, A.M. and Shaw, G., 1988b, Tourism policies in a changing economic environment, in A.M. Williams and G. Shaw (eds.), *Tourism and economic development: Western European experiences*, Belhaven Press, London, pp.230–239

Williams, A.M. and Shaw, G., 1988c, Tourism and development: introduction, in A.M. Williams and G. Shaw (eds.) *Tourism and economic development: Western European experiences,* Belhaven Press, London, pp.1–11

Williams, A.M. and Shaw, G., 1988d, Tourism: candyfloss industry or job generator, *Town Planning Review,* 59 (1): 81–103

Wilson, J., 1988, *Politics and leisure,* Unwin Hyman, Boston

Wilson, W., 1941, The study of administration, *Political Science Quarterly,* 55: 481–506

Witt, S. and Moore, S., 1992, Promoting tourism in the face of terrorism: the role of special events in Northern Island, *Journal of International Consumer Marketing,* 4 (3): 63–75

Wolfinger, R.E.C., 1971, Nondecisions and the study of local politics, *American Political Science Review,* 65: 1063–1080

World Tourism Organization, 1979, *Role and structure of national tourism administrations,* World Tourism Organization, Madrid

World Tourism Organization, 1980, *Physical planning and area development for tourism in the six WTO regions, 1980,* World Tourism Organization, Madrid

Wright, B., 1988, The co-ordinating, legislative and regulatory roles of government, in D. McSwan (ed.), *The roles of government in the development of tourism as an economic resource,* Seminar Series No.1, Centre for Studies in Travel and Tourism, James Cook University, Townsville, pp.29–33

Zeppel, H. and Hall, C.M., 1992, Review: arts and heritage tourism, in B. Weiler and C.M. Hall (eds.), *Special Interest Tourism,* Belhaven Press, London, pp.47–68

Zimmermann, F., 1988, Austria: contrasting tourist seasons and contrasting regions, in A.M. Williams and G. Shaw (eds.), *Tourism and economic development: Western European experiences,* Belhaven Press, London, pp.145–161

Zukin, S., 1990, Socio-spatial prototypes of a new organisation of consumption: the role of real cultural capital, *Sociology,* 24 (1): 37–56

Author Index

Place Name Index

Subject Index